AN EX~~~~~~~~~~~~~~~~

AIR SERVICE

BY

HIRAM BINGHAM

FORMERLY LIEUTENANT-COLONEL, AIR SERVICE, U. S. A.

MDCCCCXX

British Library Cataloguing-in-Publication Data
A catalogue record for this book is available from the
British Library

Introduction to the

World War One Centenary Series

The First World War was a global war centred in Europe that began on 28 July 1914 and lasted until 11 November 1918. More than nine million combatants were killed, a casualty rate exacerbated by the belligerents' technological and industrial sophistication – and tactical stalemate. It was one of the deadliest conflicts in history, paving the way for major political changes, including revolutions in many of the nations involved. The war drew in all the world's great economic powers, which were assembled in two opposing alliances: the Allies (based on the Triple Entente of the United Kingdom, France and the Russian Empire) and the Central Powers of Germany and Austria-Hungary. These alliances were both reorganised and expanded as more nations entered the war: Italy, Japan and the United States joined the Allies, and the Ottoman Empire and Bulgaria joined the Central Powers. Ultimately, more than 70 million military personnel were mobilised.

The war was triggered by the assassination of Archduke Franz Ferdinand of Austria, heir to the throne of Austria-Hungary, by a Yugoslav nationalist, Gavrilo Princip in Sarajevo, June 28th 1914. This set off a diplomatic crisis when Austria-Hungary delivered an ultimatum to Serbia, and international alliances were invoked. Within weeks, the major powers were at war and the conflict soon spread around the world. By the end of the war, four major imperial powers; the German, Russian, Austro-Hungarian and Ottoman empires— ceased to exist. The map of Europe was redrawn, with several independent nations restored or created. On peace, the League of Nations formed with the aim of preventing any repetition of such an appalling conflict, encouraging cooperation and communication between the newly autonomous nation states. This laudatory pursuit failed spectacularly with the advent of the Second World War however, with new European nationalism and the rise of fascism paving the way for the next global crisis.

This book is part of the World War One Centenary series; creating, collating and reprinting new and old works of poetry, fiction, autobiography and analysis. The series forms a commemorative tribute to mark the passing of one of the world's bloodiest wars, offering new perspectives on this tragic yet fascinating period of human history.

Amelia Carruthers

A Timeline of the Major Events of World War One in Europe

1914

28th June   Franz Ferdinand Assassinated
                   at Sarajevo.

29th June   Austro-Hungary send despatch to
                   Vienna accusing Serbian
                   complicity in the killing.

5th July   Kaiser Wilhelm promises
                   German support for Austria
                   against Serbia.

20th July   Austria-Hungary sends
                   troops to the Serbian frontier.

25th July   Serbia mobilises its troops,
                   Russia sends troops to the
                   Austrian frontier.

28th July   Austria-Hungary Declares war
                   on Serbia.

29th July	Austrians bombard Belgrade and German patrols cross the French border. Britain warns it cannot remain neutral.
1st August	Germany declares war on Russia. Italy and Belgium announce neutrality. French mobilisation ordered.
3rd August	Germany declares war on France and invades Belgium (Schlieffen plan). Great Britain mobilises.
4th August	Britain declares war on Germany and Austria-Hungary (after ultimatum to stand down). US declares neutrality. Germany declares war on Belgium.
6th August	First British casualties with the HMS Amphion sunk by German mines in the North sea. 150 men dead.
7th August	First members of the BEF (British Expeditionary Force) arrive in France.

11th August	Start of enlisting for Kitchener's New Army 'Your King and Country Need You'.
20th August	Brussels is evacuated as German troops occupy the city.
23rd August	The BEF started its retreat from Mons. Germany invades France.
26th August	Russian army defeated at Tannenburg and Masurian Lakes. BEF suffers over 7000 casualties at the Battle of Le Cateau –forced to retreat.
6th September	Battle of the Marne starts; checks German advance, but at the cost of 13,000 British, 250,000 French and 250,000 German casualties.
19th October	First Battle of Ypres.
29th October	Turkey enters the war (on Germany's side).
22nd November	Trenches are now established along the entire Western Front.
8th December	Battle of the Falkland Islands.

1915

19th January	First Zeppelin raid on Britain (Great Yarmouth and Kings Lynn – killing 5).

19th January — First Zeppelin raid on Britain (Great Yarmouth and Kings Lynn – killing 5).

18th February — Blockade of Great Britain by German U-boats begins. All vessels considered viable targets, including neutrals.

22nd April — Second Battle of Ypres begins. Widespread use of poison gas by Germany.

25th April — Allied troops land in Gallipoli.

2nd May — Austro-German offensive on Galicia begins.

7th May — The Lusitania is sunk by a German U-Boat – creating US/German diplomatic crisis.

23rd May — Italy declares war on Germany and Austria

31st May — First Zeppelin raid on London, killing 35 and shaking morale.

30th June	German troops use flamethrowers for the first time, against the British at Hooge, Ypres.
5th August	Germany captures Warsaw from the Russians.
21st August	Final British offensive in the Dardanelles (Scimitar Hill, Gallipoli). They lose, and suffer 5000 deaths.
25th September	Start of the Battle of Loos and Champagne. The British use gas for the first time, but the wind blows it over their own troops, resulting in 2632 casualties.
31st October	Steel helmets introduced on the British Front.
15th December	Sir Douglas Haig replaces Sir John French as Commander of the BEF.

1916

8th January

Allied evacuation of Helles marks the end of the Gallipoli campaign.

21st February

Start of the Battle of Verdun – German offensive against the Mort-Homme Ridge. The battle lasts 10 months and over a million men become casualties. (Finishes 18th December, the longest and costliest battle of the Western Front).

9th March

Germany declares war on Portugal. Six days later, Austria follows suit.

31st May

Battle of Jutland – lasts until 1st June. German High Seas Fleet is forced to retire despite having inflicted heavier losses on the Royal Navy (14 ships and 6,100 men). German fleet irreparably damaged.

4th June

Start of the Russian Brusilov Offensive on the Eastern front. Nearly cripples Austro-Hungary.

1st July	Start of the Battle of the Somme – 750,000 allied soldiers along a 25 mile front. Nearly 60,000 are dead or wounded on the first day.
14th July	Battle of Bazetin Ridge marks the end of the first Somme Offensive. The British break the German line but fail to deploy cavalry fast enough to take advantage. 9,000 men are lost.
23rd July	Battle of Pozières Ridge marks the second Somme Offensive, costs 17,000 allied casualties – the majority of whom are Australian. (ends 7th August).
10th August	End of the Brusilov Offensive.
9th September	The Battle of Ginchy. The British capture Ginchy – a post of vital strategic importance as it commands a view of the whole battlefield.
15th September	First use en masse of tanks at the Somme. The Battle of Flers-Courcelette signifies the start of the third stage of the Somme offensive.

13th November	Battle of Ancre. The fourth phase of the Somme Offensive is marked by the British capturing Beaumont Hamel and St. Pierre Division, taking nearly 4,000 prisoners.
12th December	Germany delivers Peace Note to Allies suggesting compromise.

1917

1st February

Germany's unrestricted submarine warfare campaign starts.

3rd February

US sever diplomatic relations with Germany as U-boats threaten US shipping. Intercepted messages reveal that Germany is provoking the Mexicans into war with the US.

21st February

The great German withdrawal begins. Serre, Miraumont, Petit Miraumont, Pys and Warlencourt are evacuated, falling back 25 miles to establish stronger positions on the Hindenburg Line.

15th March

Tsar Nicholas II abdicates as Moscow falls to Russian Revolutionaries. Demise of the Russian army frees German troops for the Western front.

6th April

USA declares war on Germany – troops mobilise immediately.

9th April	Battle of Arras. British successfully employ new tactics of creeping barrages, the 'graze fuse' and counter battery fire.
16th April	France launches an unsuccessful offensive on the Western Front. – Second Battle of Aisne begins as part of the 'Nivelle Offensive'. Losses are horrendous, triggering mutinies in the French Army.
7th June	The Battle of Messines Ridge. British succeed with few casualties, detonating 19 mines under German front lines – the explosions are reportedly heard from England.
13th June	Germans launch first major heavy bomber raid of London – kills and injures 594.
25th June	First US troops arrive in France.
31st July	Start of the Third Battle at Ypres – a 15 mile front in Flanders. Initial attacks are successful as the German forward trenches are lightly manned.

15th August — The Battle of Lens (Hill 70). – Canadians at the forefront , won a high vantage point, though loss of 9,200 men.

20th August — Third Battle of Verdun begins. French progress is marked by gaining lost territory in the earlier battles.

9th October — The third phase of the Ypres Offensive begins with British and French troops taking Poelcapelle. 25mm of rain falls in 48 hours and the battlefield turns into a quagmire.

12th October — British launch assault at Ypres Against the Passchendale Ridge. New Zealand and Australians take terrible casualties. Bogged down in mud and forced back to start lines.

24th October — Battle of Caporetto – Italian Army heavily defeated.

26th October — Second Battle of Passchendaele begins, 12,000 men lost and 300 yards gained (ends 10th November – 500,000 casualties,

140,000 deaths and 5 miles gained).

6th November	Britain launches major offensive on the Western Front.
20th November	Victory for British tanks at Cambrai - The Royal flying Corps drop bombs at the same time on German anti-tank guns and strong points. Early example of the 'Blitzkrieg' tactics later used by Germany in World War Two.
5th December	Armistice between Germany and Russia signed.

1918

16th January   Riots in Vienna and Budapest with dissatisfaction at the war.

3rd March   Treaty of Brest-Litovsk signed between (Soviet) Russia and Germany.

21st March   Second Battle of the Somme marked by the German spring offensive, the 'Kaiserschlacht'. Germans attack along a 50 mile front south of Arras.

22nd March   Victory for Germany with operation Michael - Use of new 'Storm trooper' assault to smash through British positions west of St. Quentin, taking 16,000 prisoners.

23rd March   Greatest air battle of the war takes place over the Somme, with 70 aircraft involved.

5th April   The German Spring Offensive halts outside Amiens as British and Australian forces hold the Line. The second 1917 battle of the Somme ends, as Germany calls off operation Michael.

9th April	Germany starts offensive in Flanders –Battle of the Lys (ends 29th April).
19th May	German air force launches largest raid on London, using 33 aircraft.
27th May	Operation Blucher – The Third German Spring Offensive attacks the French army along the Aisne River. French are forced back to the Marne, but hold the river with help from the Americans.
15th July	Second battle of the Marne started; final phase of German spring offensive. Start of the collapse of the German army with irreplaceable casualties.
8th August	Second Battle of Amiens – German resistance sporadic and thousands surrender.
27th September	British offensive on the Cambrai Front leads to the storming of the Hindenburg Line. Battle of St.

Quentin – British and U.S troops launch devastating offensives.

4th October	Germany asks the allies for an armistice (sent to Woodrow Wilson).
8th October	Allies advance along a 20 mile front from St. Quentin to Cambrai, driving the Germans back and capturing 10,000 troops.
29th October	Germany's navy mutinies (at Jade).
3rd November	Austria makes peace. German sailors mutiny at Kiel.
9th November	Kaiser Wilhelm abdicates and revolution breaks out in Berlin.
11th November	Germany signs the armistice with the allies – coming into effect at 11.00am (official end of WWI).

<u>1919</u>

10th January   Communist Revolt in Berlin (Battle of Berlin).

18th January   Paris Peace Conference Begins.

25th January   Principle of a League of Nations ratified.

6th May   Under conditions of the Peace conference, German colonies are annexed.

21st June   The surrendered German naval fleet at Scapa Flow was scuttled.

28th June   Treaty of Versailles signed.

19th July   Cenotaph unveiled in London.

By Amelia Carruthers

Air Warfare in the First World War

In 1903 the Wright brothers made the first recorded powered flight, achieving 12 seconds air time at Kittyhawk, Dare County, North Carolina, United States. In 1909, the first powered crossing of the English Channel was achieved by Louis Blèriot. Five years later, the First World War began.

Due to its still nascent technology, aviation was deemed of little use to the European armed services. One unknown British general commented that 'the airplane is useless for the purposes of war.' Likewise, the German General Ferdinand Foch is reported to have alleged that 'aviation is a good sport, but for the army it is useless.' These opinions reflected a widespread scepticism about aircraft, unsurprising given their delicate and undependable nature. Most aeroplanes in 1914 were constructed of hardwood or steel tubing, combined with linen fabric doped with flammable liquid to provide strength. They were incredibly fragile by later standards and frequently collapsed during flight, especially in combat situations.

As a result of these technical issues, when war erupted in July 1914, aircraft were used mainly for reconnaissance; feeding back information for artillery strikes, recording troop movements and taking detailed photographs of enemy positions. However, the diversity of uses, technological advances and sheer increase of numbers involved in air warfare during the period were astonishing. To illustrate, France had fewer than 140 aircraft at the outbreak of war, but by 1918 she had 4,500. However, France actually produced 68,000 aircraft during the war, with 52,000 destroyed in combat; a staggering loss rate of 77%. Aerial battles were extremely crude, but equally deadly – the pilots flew in tiny cockpits, making parachutes a rarity and death by fire commonplace. Many officers, especially the British, actually forbade the carrying of parachutes as it was feared they would lessen the fighting spirit of the men.

The typical British aircraft at the start of the war was the general purpose BE2X. It had a top speed of 72mph and was powered by a 90hp engine; it could fly for roughly three hours. By the end of the war, this had been replaced by planes such as the Sopwith Camel and the SE5a fighter, built for speed and manoeuvrability. The latter had a top speed of 138mph, now powered by a 200hp engine. The technological change which enabled these improvements was the 'pusher' layouts' replacement. Traditionally, propellers faced backwards, pushing the plane forwards – but the alternative design with a forward facing propeller (a 'tractor') provided far superior performance both in terms of speed and power. Another major advance was the replacement of the rotary engine. In this type of engine, where the crankshaft remained stationary whilst the pistons (attached to the propeller) rotated around it, there was an excellent power to weight ratio, but it lost out to the more powerful water cooled engines. By 1918, the Sopwith Camel remained the last major aircraft still using the older rotary technology.

Within the first months of the war, whilst still in the 'movement stage', the value of aerial reconnaissance was vindicated. On 22 August 1914, contradicting all other intelligence, one British Captain and his Lieutenant reported that General Alexander von Kluck's army was preparing to surround the BEF. This initiated a massive withdrawal towards Mons, saving about 100,000 lives. Similarly, at the First Battle of the Marne, General Joseph-Simon Gallieni was able to achieve a spectacular victory, using information provided by the French air force to attack the exposed flanks of the German army. But nowhere was the importance of aerial intelligence more forcibly asserted than at the Battle of Tannenberg on the Eastern Front. The Russian General, Alexander Samsonov ignored his own pilot's warnings, allowing almost all of his army to be captured or killed by the Germans. After the crushing defeat, Samsonov committed suicide whilst German Field Marshall Hindeburg stated 'without airmen, there would have been no Tannenburg.'

As aerial reconnaissance became more frequent and effective, new methods were developed to counter this threat. At first, infantry fired at planes from the ground, although this was largely ineffective due to ill-adapted guns. Yet quickly, airmen began directly attacking one another. Pilots and their observers attempted to shoot at the enemy using rifles and pistols; some threw bricks, grenades and ropes with grappling hooks attached. A more reliable solution was required. As early as 1912 the Vickers company had already produced an experimental airplane to be armed with a Maxim machine gun. Nicknamed the 'Destroyer', the EFB1 plane was powered via the old fashioned pusher layout, allowing the gunner to sit in front of the pilot, giving an uninterrupted field of vision. The nose was too heavy with the machine gun's weight though, and the plane crashed on its first flight. By 1914 many pilots took the initiative and experimented with machine guns themselves. The British pilot Louis Strange improvised a safety strap allowing the observer of his tractor driven Avro 504 to 'stand up and fire all round over top of plane and behind.' Similarly, on 5 October, 1914, a French pilot in a Voisin III pusher biplane became the first man of the war to shoot down another aircraft – his observer standing up to fire a Hotchkiss machine gun.

Only a few machine guns were small and reliable enough for use however, and the problem was not satisfactorily solved until Anton Fokker developed the 'interrupter gear' in 1915. This meant that a machine gun could be synchronised with the moving propeller blades – soon to produce the 'Fokker Scourge' for the allies. This development gave the Germans a strong advantage, not only strategically but in terms of morale. The Fokker, and its successor the *Eindecker* caused panic in the British parliament and press; also contributing to German successes at the Battle of Verdun as French reconnaissance failed to provide information on enemy positions. It took the allies an entire year to adapt the device to their own use.

These fighting aircraft were supported by the bombers; not directly involved in fights (if possible), but aimed at destroying the enemy's capacity to make war on the home front. Industrial units, power stations, shipyards and entire cities became targets; some of the most famous being Germany's Zeppelin raids on London – causing up to half a million pounds of damage with each vessel. At the start of the war, bomb aiming was crude in the extreme however. Bombs were simply dropped over the side of the aircraft when the pilot reached the vicinity of the target. Russia was the first to develop an airplane specifically for this purpose; the Murometz, a large four-engine airplane originally produced in 1913 as a passenger plane, was used successfully throughout the entire war. The Germans had the Gotha bomber plane, and the British had the Handley Page. Yet despite the strategic importance of these bomber planes, as the war continued it was the fighters who captured the public's imagination. Popular legends arose around the 'great aces' such as Manfred von Richthofen (the 'Red Baron'), Ernst Udet, and the French pilot Paul Rene Fonck. Governments were quick to trumpet the successes of their airmen for propaganda purposes, with the French and the Germans being the first countries to award the distinction of 'ace'.

This seemingly exotic and elegant war in the air was far removed from reality however. As noted, reconnaissance was the largest role of aircraft during the war, and the bravery of the pilots in fulfilling this dangerous and unglamorous work is seldom remarked. Newly recruited pilots were sent into the sky, often only with a few hours air training time (typically less than five), and as the war progressed it became unusual for new pilots to survive their first few weeks. The newer planes, often built more for manoeuvrability than stability were increasingly difficult to operate and if pilots were not shot down, bad weather, mechanical problems and simple pilot error could all intervene. Most died not in spectacular dogfights but after being shot from behind, unaware of their attackers.

Taken as a whole, air warfare did not play a fundamental strategic role in World War One, as it did in later conflicts – however bombers and fighters provided just as important a psychological weapon as they did a practical one. The main significance of World War One aviation was a rapid increase in technology and prestige, fostering a new found respect in the general public and military commanders for this hitherto unknown method of battle. The terrible capabilities of air warfare would be unleashed on a far greater scale in the next World War, with even more devastating consequences.

Amelia Carruthers

Memoirs, Diaries and Poems of World War One

In 1939, the writer Robert Graves was asked to write an article for the BBC's *Listener* magazine, explaining 'as a war poet of the last war, why so little poetry has so far been produced by this one.' From the very first weeks of fighting, the First World War inspired enormous amounts of poetry, factual analysis, autobiography and fiction - from all countries involved in the conflict. 2,225 English war poets have been counted, of whom 1808 were civilians. The 'total' nature of this war perhaps goes someway to explaining its enormous impact on the popular imagination. Even today, commemorations and the effects of a 'lost generation' are still being witnessed. It was a war fought for traditional, nationalistic values of the nineteenth century, propagated using twentieth century technological and industrial methods of killing. Memoirs, diaries and poems provide extraordinary insight into how the common soldier experienced everyday life in the trenches, and how the civilian population dealt with this loss.

Over two thousand published poets wrote about the war, yet only a small fraction are still known today. Many that were popular with contemporary readers are now obscure. The selection, which emerged as orthodox during the 1960s, tends to (understandably) emphasise the horror of war, suffering, tragedy and anger against those that wage war. This was not entirely the case however, as demonstrated in the early weeks of the war. British poets responded with an outpouring of patriotic literary production. Robert Bridges, Poet Laureate, contributed a poem *Wake Up England!* calling for 'Thou careless, awake! Thou peacemaker, fight! Stand, England, for honour, And God guard the Right!' He later wished the work to be suppressed though. Rudyard Kipling's *For All We Have and Are,* aroused the most comment however, with its references to the 'Hun at the gate... the crazed and driven foe.'

From Hemingway's *A Farewell to Arms*, to Remarque's *All Quiet on the Western Front*, to the poetry of Sassoon, Graves, and Brooke, there are numerous examples of acclaimed writing inspired by the Great War. One of the best known war poets is perhaps Wilfred Owen, killed in battle at the age of twenty-five. His poems written at the front achieved popular attention soon after the war's end, most famously including *Dulce Et Decorum Est, Anthem for Doomed Youth*, and *Strange Meeting*. In preparing for the publication of his collected poems, Owen explained 'This book is not about heroes. English poetry is not yet fit to speak of them. Nor is it about deeds, or lands, nor anything about glory, honour, might, majesty, dominion, or power, except War. Above all I am not concerned with Poetry. My subject is War, and the pity of War. The Poetry is in the pity.'

Dulce et Decorum Est, one of Owen's most famous poems, scathingly takes Horace's statement, 'Dulce et decorum est, pro patria mori', meaning 'It is sweet and proper to die for one's country' as its title. It chiefly describes the death of an anonymous soldier due to poison gas, vividly describing the suffering of the man, ending with a bitter attack on those who see glory in the death of others. Such themes were also widely utilised by authors unaccustomed with the literary canon - the common soldier noting down their experiences for their loved ones, and for posterity. Each unit in World War One was in fact required to keep a diary of its day-to-day activities, many portraying the anxiety and terror of the opening days of the war. Diaries from soldiers in the First Battalion South Wales Borderers (among others, recently released at the British National Archives) described the battles of the Marne and the Aisne, with one captain who said the scenes he witnesses were 'beyond description... poor fellows shot dead are lying in all directions... everywhere the same hard, grim pitiless sign of battle and war. I have had a belly full of it.'

Other, lighter aspects of everyday life including tugs of war, rugby matches and farewell dinners to mark the end of the fighting have also been documented, giving us a rare insight into what the First World War was like for the men on the front line. Letters were an incredibly important part of life as a soldier. Receiving and writing them helped keep them sane, and could take them away from the realities of trench life. Every week, an average of 12.5 million letters were sent to soldiers by family, friends, and partners. More formalised memoirs have also become a key way of understanding the conflict, from gas attacks, the fear of going over the top, methods of coping with death - as well as the jovial camaraderie which often grew up between the men. The first memoirs of combatants were published in 1922, not long after the armistice: *A Tank Driver's Experiences* by Arthur Jenkins and *Disenchantment* by Charles Edward Montague. These were shortly joined with *Good-Bye to All That* (1929) by Robert Graves, *A Subaltern's War* (1929) by Charles Edmund Carrington, and *Blasting and Bombardiering* (1937) byPercy Wyndham Lewis. Nurses also published memoirs of their wartime experiences, such as *A Diary without Dates* (1918) by Enid Bagnold, and *Forbidden Zone* (1929) by Mary Borden. Vera Brittain's *Testament of Youth* (first published 1933) has been acclaimed as a classic for its description of the impact of the war on the lives of women and the civilian population - extending into the post-war years.

Storm of Steel, written by Ernst Jünger, published in 1920 was one of the first personal accounts to be published - a graphic account of trench warfare, unusually glorifying the sacrifice encountered. The book has consequently been criticised for lionizing war, especially when compared with works such as Remarque's (albeit fictional) *All Quiet on the Western Front*. In the preface to the 1929 English edition, Jünger stated that; 'Time only strengthens my conviction that it was a good and strenuous life, and that the war, for all its destructiveness, was an incomparable schooling of the heart.' As is evident from this short introduction to the memoirs, diaries, letters and poems of the first world war

- it is an intensely complex field. Dependent on military rank, geographic position and placement, nationality and subjective experience and character, they take on a wide variety of forms and focuses. Such works give an amazing insight into the experiences of combatants and it is hoped the current reader is encouraged to find out more about this thoroughly worthwhile topic.

Amelia Carruthers

Field 9 of the Third Aviation Instruction Centre, Issoudun, France

CONTENTS

ILLUSTRATIONS

PREFACE

THE writer began to fly at Miami in March, 1917; was on duty at Aviation Headquarters in Washington from the first of May, 1917, until the first of April, 1918; was then on duty with the Chief of Air Service in the A. E. F. until the latter part of August, 1918; was in command of the Third Aviation Instruction Centre, Issoudun, until Christmas, 1918; and, on return to Washington, was again on duty at headquarters until March, 1919.

This book is a record of observations made during those two years, and is concerned chiefly with aviation training. It is hoped that it will be of interest to those who were in the Air Service and their friends, besides being of some assistance to future students of military aeronautics. To many of the pilots it may explain the reasons for some of the sufferings which they endured. It may serve also as a warning of the evil of unpreparedness. Nearly all of the errors, mistakes, and delays to which it refers might have been avoided, had the American people insisted on having their representatives in Congress make suitable preparation for an adequate army and a well-equipped Air Service in the event of our being thrown into the World War.

It may fairly be said that the Air Service was a genuine expression of the "American Idea," defined by Strunsky in one of his charming essays as "splendid courage accompanied by a high degree of disorder." We lacked men of experience; we lacked aviators of mature judgment; we lacked able executive officers with a sympathetic knowledge of aviation; we lacked airplanes fit to fly against the Huns; and we lacked facilities for building them. The airplane industry was still in the experimental stage. No one really manufactured airplanes in the generally accepted sense of that word. No one had even had any experience in the quantity production of airplane motors. Yet in July, 1917, Congress appropriated $640,000,000, in the fond expectation that before many months we could obtain 22,000 airplanes. In other words, America expected to win the war in the air and was utterly unprepared to do so. The American people laid an impossible task on the shoulders of the officers and citizens who obediently undertook to produce on a gigantic scale, and without adequate plans, one of the most difficult arms of modern warfare.

There is no question but that the Air Service suffered because of its newness and because it was

expected to grow in such an incredibly short time
from a relatively insignificant part of the regular
army to a force more than twice as large as that
army was before 1917.

When we entered the war, the Air Service had
2 small flying fields, 48 officers, 1330 men, and 225
planes, not one of which was fit to fly over the lines.
In the course of a year and a half, ▆ Air Service
grew to 50 flying fields, 20,500 officers, 175,000
men, and 17,000 planes. It was my good fortune to
witness this growth at close range, particularly as
regards the flying personnel.

Among the many officers and men whose devotion to the cause of their country led them to help me
with all their strength in the work in which we happened to be engaged together were: Major J. Robert
Moulthrop, whose long interest in military history
and whose natural tact and excellent judgment made
his assistance in conducting the Schools of Military
Aeronautics of inestimable value; Colonel W. E.
Gilmore, who bore the brunt of the attack when
I was Chief of Air Personnel in Washington, and
who, with large-hearted generosity, gave freely
from the wisdom acquired in his twenty years of service in the regular army; Colonel Walter G. Kilner,

whose ability as soldier, aviator, and executive were
excelled only by his loyalty to those who had the
good fortune to serve under him as I did; Lieutenant-
Colonel Phil. A. Carroll, a pioneer among Reserve
Military Aviators, whose friendly counsel on in-
numerable occasions helped me out of many difficulties; and Major Tom G. Lanphier, former star
full-back at West Point, veteran of the machine gun
defence at Château-Thierry and born flyer, whose
faithful coöperation as my executive officer at Issoudun was indispensable to success.

I only wish it were possible to mention by name
all of the officers and men with whom, at one time
or another, I had the honor to be associated. They
made me proud of being an American. In the face of
blind unpreparedness, stupendous obstacles, and the
necessity for utmost haste they strove valiantly and
unremittingly to make the Air Service worthy of
American traditions. Our chief regret was that we
were not sent earlier into the conflict.

HIRAM BINGHAM

Yale University, May, 1920

*Acknowledgments are gratefully made to their editors for permis-
sion to make use of articles that have appeared in " The U. S. Air
Service," " Historical Outlook," " The Outlook," " Aircraft Journal,"
and " Asia."*

AN EXPLORER IN THE AIR SERVICE

CHAPTER I

FIRST FLIGHTS

IN the latter part of 1916, I had the opportunity of hearing Mr. Herbert Bayard Swope of the *New York World* tell of conditions in Germany as he had seen them that summer. He convinced me of several things which had not been clear in the censored press despatches. One was that the British Navy had by no means solved the problem of the German submarines, although the small number of sinkings at that time was so interpreted in our newspapers. A corollary was that Germany was voluntarily restraining her piratical activities until such time as she could secure enough submarines to make an overwhelming drive on trans-oceanic commerce. And, finally, that such a drive was coming before very long. This information from such a well-posted source led me to the conclusion, about the first of December, that we should be at war with Germany within six months. My next thought naturally was the question: In what field would my training as an explorer offer the best opportunity for service? Personal experience with mules, Spanish Americans, pack oxen, Indians, ruined Inca cities, and Andean highlands would be of little use in France!

A few days later, a distinguished member of the Yale Mathematical Faculty brought back from a scientific meeting in Boston news regarding the remarkable progress that aviation was making on the western front. Major-General George O. Squier, then Lieutenant-Colonel in the Signal

Corps, had just returned from many months of service as
American Military Attaché with the British Army. Himself
a scientific investigator of the first rank—one of the few
army officers to have taken a Ph.D. "on the side," after graduating from West Point, and while serving as a Second
Lieutenant at an army post not far from Johns Hopkins
University—he had thrilled his hearers at the Boston meeting with a vivid account of the hundreds of airplanes
then in use, and which the censor had permitted us to learn
little or nothing about. General Squier's contagious enthusiasm and his remarkable vision had so infected my friend,
the mathematician, that I too caught the disease and became a crank on "Winning the War in the Air."

A fortunate circumstance took me to Baltimore about this
time, where Professor J. S. Ames of Johns Hopkins, a keen
student of aerodynamics, confirmed my belief that a rapid
development of the Allied Air Service was the best way to
defeat Germany quickly. Another bit of good fortune enabled
me to go to Miami, Florida, in February, 1917, and there to
talk with Glenn Curtiss, perhaps the most daring of all American inventors. His fondness for going faster than anybody
else—and his willingness to be content with doing it only
once—had led him to make a remarkable number of records,
both on land and sea, as well as in the air. With Orville
Wright, he represented America's leadership in the early
development of practical flying. His assurance that any one
who could ride horseback and sail a boat could learn to fly,
and the remarkable record for safety made by his flying

boats, led me to decide to attempt some flights. His statement that there were at that time less than twenty-five competent flying instructors in the United States seemed to open the door of opportunity.

Although then forty-one years old, it seemed to me that with the experience I had had in riding mules for months at a time in Venezuela, Colombia, and Peru, there was some hope that the new field of exploration might not prove too difficult, especially as I have also always been fond of sailing. My first flight was on March 3. The roar of the engine and the terrific wind pressure encountered in sitting out in front on the old F type flying boat spoiled the pleasure and nearly overcame the thrill of that first experience. For two weeks I took frequent flights with Harold Kantner over the beautiful waters of Biscayne Bay. Kantner's skill as pilot, and the experience which he had gained during the months that he had been employed in teaching flying in the Italian Navy, gave me great confidence in his ability. Nevertheless, I looked with envy on the more speedy army planes. On March 17, I had my first ride in a land machine, a JN-4, piloted by Roger Jannus. For a time I took lessons on both land and water, but after about ten hours' work in the flying boat, gave it up for "military tractors," as we called them then.

The report of the Executive Committee of the National Advisory Committee for Aeronautics, published about this time by Dr. Charles D. Walcott, gave me the information that larger plans were being made for aeronautics in the army than in the navy. The army had more room for be-

ginners, so my first idea of going in for sea-plane flying was
given up in order to learn all I could about military, as distinguished from naval, aeronautics.

Fortunately, the Curtiss Company had established a school
near Miami, where some forty or fifty Sergeants in the Aviation Section of the Signal Enlisted Reserve Corps were being
taught to fly at the expense of the Government. A few civilians were admitted, and, thanks to the courtesy of Mr. Curtiss, I was permitted to enjoy the privileges of the school.
In the light of what America afterwards did in the way
of flying schools, that school now seems ridiculously small
and inadequate, but considering the facilities which then
existed, we felt that we were fortunate indeed. There were
generally three or four planes in commission, but sometimes
only one. A severe hail-storm, which came at a time when
there were no hangars at the school, made more than two
hundred holes in the wings of the oldest, and put all "ships"
out of commission for a while.

Accidents were frequent. Connecting-rods broke in mid-
air and frightened new pilots by smashing holes in crank
cases. Roger Jannus went up one day to test out a newly
assembled plane, and while turning a loop had the novel
experience of having his propeller fly to pieces. His great
skill as a pilot, however, stood him in good stead, and he
made a perfect landing on the usual little bit of turf known
as the airdrome. Inspection of what was left of the hub of
the propeller showed that the fault was with some dishon-
est propeller manufacturer. The first series of holes bored

for the bolts which were to fasten it in place had been abandoned and plugged up. This naturally weakened the hub to such an extent that as soon as any strain was put upon it, the solid wood that was left gave way and the propeller disappeared.

We thought little of possible interior injury to planes. My first solo flight was made on an old ship that had been turned over on its back twice during the preceding forty-eight hours; in each case a new propeller had been put on, a cabane and a strut had been renewed, and that was all. We did n't worry about the longerons. We were glad enough to get a chance to fly at all.

One day the studt ■ whose turn preceded mine had engine failure after he had been up about seven minutes. As soon as his engine stopped he switched off the magneto and glided in, over-reaching the small field and landing in the long grass and shrubs. The mechanics at once went out to see what the matter was, made a successful attempt to start the engine, listened long enough to convince themselves there was nothing wrong, and then hauled the plane back to the landing field. The young pilot was reprimanded for having made an unnecessary landing and told to go up again, which he declined to do. So the machine was handed over to me. Two days before, I had made my first solo flight, and this was to be my third attempt without a teacher. The motor started off well and I had attained some little altitude after flying for about seven minutes, when the motor unaccountably stopped. I switched off and started to glide for the field, when it occurred to me that this trouble might not be anything serious and would only lead to my getting reprimanded as had my predecessor, so I switched on again, and to my delight the engine took hold and went very nicely for about a minute. Various switchings on and off succeeded in making the motor run occasionally, until I noticed that the wind was driving me some distance away from that little spot of dried everglade land that meant safety. Between me and the airdrome, however, was one of the dredged everglade drainage canals with twenty-five or thirty feet of limestone rock piled up on each bank. If I had to land this side of the canal, it would mean being tipped upside down, for the dried muck was too soft to allow the landing wheels to run on it. Consequently, the temptation to extend the glide and get over the canal to the hard ground beyond was irresistible. Then, too, the engine occasionally gave a burst or two which helped for a few seconds at a time. I got over the first bank of the canal all right, and by nosing down toward the water picked up just enough speed to clear the other bank and enable me to pancake in the sand on the edge of the airdrome. Fortunately, no damage was done. It certainly was wonderful what those old JN-4's could stand.

By the time the mechanics got out to the plane, they were able to start up the engine. It ran nicely for a few minutes—then stopped. After a while somebody found out what was the trouble. The night before, an enthusiastic

Miami: The next day after this accident happened I was sent up for my first solo flight in this same ship

Issoudun: Major Du Mesnil of the French Army decorating Captain R. S. Davis of Field 7 with the Croix de Guerre for bravery shown during his month at the Front

pilot, in his mad desire to get in a few moments' flying before dark, had hastily filled the gas tank and taken his flight without putting back the ventilated screw top. He went home with it in his pocket. The next morning the "sergeant" whose duty it was to fill the tank, not being able to locate the proper plug, hunted around in the little machine shop until he found one that fitted and thoughtlessly put it on, although it had no air vent in it. Consequently, after a little gasoline had run down out of the tank into the carburetor, a partial vacuum formed and prevented the engine from getting any gas until some air could leak in and release a little. Hence the strange behavior of what might have been a badly crashed engine.

One day a newly assembled plane, the wings of which were not exactly of the same pattern, was piloted by an inexperienced teacher who had with him a new pupil on his first or second flight. They got into a tail spin and fell over 1500 feet, making a complete crash. The engine was partially buried in the ground, and the plane was so flattened out that hardly any of it was more than a foot above the surface. It seemed like a miracle that neither one of the occupants was killed. Both of them were out of the hospital and hobbling around in about ten days. It gave us more confidence to see what might happen without a fatal ending.

There was plenty of opportunity to learn practical rigging and fitting. Tom Dee, who had been with the Curtiss Company for several years and who had forgotten more about airplanes than most of us would ever learn, was always willing to teach us how to repair damaged planes. But he had no use for loafers or gamblers.

One day Sergeant (later Captain) Blake arrived as the Government representative. He had been in the Signal Corps for many years and was an excellent type of the old regular army sergeant. He had rather a hard time with the noisy group of ambitious young pilots, who were impatient at delays in securing proper training equipment, and who saw little to be gained in doing "squads right" for an hour in the broiling tropical sun. Nevertheless, they stuck to it faithfully. In the course of the next year and a half several of them made enviable records in the Air Service. At least four were promoted to Captaincies. Most conscientious of all and most uniformly cheerful in the performance of his duty was Hamilton Coolidge of Groton and Harvard, who later earned the Distinguished Service Cross, and was one of the American Aces. He was killed by a direct hit from an anti-aircraft gun.

Others included John Mitchell, who also became a Captain in the Air Service and commanded a squadron at the Front; Fred Harvey, born flyer, who was so greatly appreciated that he was not permitted to go abroad until shortly before the Armistice was signed; and Arthur Richmond, who, like Harvey, was promoted to a Captaincy for distinguished service in American training schools, but, although he spoke French fluently, was denied the privilege of getting to France. Never in my life have I felt so old as I did during the two months of association with this brilliant group of young pilots, who had all been born while I was in college or since I had graduated, and whose youth and skill were to entitle them to render most meritorious and distinguished service in helping to win the war in the air.

As soon as war was declared, I telegraphed the Adjutant-General to ask that my former commission as Captain in the Tenth Field Artillery, Connecticut National Guard, the so-called "Yale Batteries," which I had resigned after the regiment was demobilized, be renewed, and that I be given flying duty. His reply was an application blank for the Aviation Section of the Signal Officers Reserve Corps. This I filled out and sent with a letter to General Squier telling him why it seemed to me that, even though well past the pilot's age limit of thirty years, I might be of use at least as an instructor in the Air Service. On April 30 I passed my final test for the Aero Club license and was brevetted as an "aviator pilot." The next day, greatly to my joy, I had a telegram from General Squier asking me to come to Washington immediately to assist in selecting and training aviators. Needless to say, I took the next train.

General Squier had recently been made Chief Signal Officer of the Army, and as such was in charge of all army Air Service activities. He explained that he had sent for me because he believed my experience in exploration and teaching, with the few months of intensive military training with the Yale Batteries and flying at Miami, had given me good preparation for the new undertaking. He said the first thing to do was to go to Toronto.

Just what I was to do in Toronto, apart from the fact that representatives of several universities were to meet me there, was not quite clear, but General Squier said that if I would simply announce my arrival in Washington to Dr. William F. Durand, the Executive Secretary of the National Advisory Committee for Aeronautics, he would explain the whole situation and tell me what to do. Dr. Durand's office was in the Munsey Building, that busy hive which contained so many of the activities of the National Council of Defense, and which at that time seemed to be the home of most of the dollar-a-year men. He greeted me with the disconcerting question, "What brings *you* to Washington?"

However, matters were soon explained and he very kindly gave me letters of introduction to the representatives of the Universities of California, Texas, Illinois, Ohio, Cornell, and the Massachusetts Institute of Technology, who had been invited to go to Toronto to see how the University of Toronto was coöperating with the Royal Flying Corps in giving ground school training to "would-be" military aviators. No one appeared to know exactly how the plan was to be worked out in this country.

The fact was, that our national policy of unpreparedness had brought us actually into the greatest of all wars without adequate plans for training aviators, although every one knew we would need them by the hundred.

It may not be out of place to state here that during the

first few months of my duty in Washington, the officer who, under General Squier, was in immediate charge of the Aviation Section of the Signal Corps, was not a pilot, had only been up once or twice, was frankly afraid to fly even as an observer, and went so far as to say to me that for the father of seven sons to take flying lessons showed that he did not love his children. I could not help wondering whether the Secretary of War would expect an officer who was afraid of riding horseback to direct the fortunes of the Mounted Service School or even command a cavalry regiment successfully.

CHAPTER II

TORONTO AND THE ROYAL FLYING CORPS

THE contrast between Washington and Toronto in the first week of May, 1917, was very striking. Both cities were at war, but one had scarcely begun to realize it as yet, while the other could not forget it for a minute. Washington was at that time scarcely any different from its ordinary self during the sessions of Congress. Our army officers were not in uniform, although we had been at war nearly a month. The orders came a week or two later. I never succeeded in discovering whether the delay was caused by the disinclination of the Secretary of War to change from a peace to a war basis, or whether some of the higher staff officers, who had been putting on weight at Washington for a number of years without the necessity of wearing service uniforms, caused the delay in order that they might have time to get proper sizes made before the order was published!

Toronto was full of men in uniform — officers driving madly about in Government cars; crippled soldiers sunning themselves on warm corners near great hospitals; gigantic posters urging further enlistments; recruits training in quiet streets. Toronto did more than her share toward providing those splendid troops that Canada so early sent to the western front. The clubs and hotels of Washington were filled with eager men in the prime of life anxious to find some way of serving their country. The hotels and clubs in Toronto, if you overlooked the presence of officers who had been in-

valided home, were sad and deserted, most of the men bearing
marks of anxiety or signs of mourning.

Among the soldiers in Toronto, none carried themselves
with quite such a swagger and none saluted their officers
so smartly as those who wore in white letters across their
sleeves the words "Royal Flying Corps ; " and incidentally,
none seemed to have so many admirers on the street. Many
of them had recently come over from England to aid in
carrying out the new project whereby Canadian aviators
and their more venturesome friends from across the border might receive preliminary and advanced training before
being sent abroad.

Our conference at Toronto was most interesting. Three
professors from each of the selected universities, chosen in
the main from the technical faculties, came prepared to
spend several days in visiting the flying schools, attending
classes at the School of Military Aeronautics at the University of Toronto, and listening to veterans of the World War.

We were most courteously received by General (then
Lieutenant-Colonel) Hoare and Major Allen at the headquarters of the Royal Flying Corps and given every facility
for studying their methods of administration and the course
of study which they had laid down. We were furnished
with typewritten copies of all the lectures used at their
School of Military Aeronautics, and were given sets of text-
books and service regulations. Everything was done to make
us feel that although we had been unaccountably long in
joining the common cause against the Hun, now that we

had come in, we were to be on a basis of perfect equality
with those who had been sacrificing everything for two
years and a half.

On the day following our arrival, it was arranged that
we should go out to Camp Borden, some seventy-five miles
from Toronto. At that time this was by far the largest and
most important flying field outside of Europe. We were
proud to find it commanded by an American, once the captain of a victorious Harvard crew, Major Oliver D. Filley.
He had been one of the first Americans to join the British
forces in the war, and had been for many months on the
western front. Seriously injured in an airplane accident,
he had recovered sufficiently to be placed in charge of this
great school. Afterwards he accepted General Squier's in-
vitation to come into our service, was commissioned Lieutenant-Colonel, placed in charge of the Observers' School
at Fort Sill, and later had charge of training American Handley Page squadrons in England.

Colonel Filley gave us a most instructive day, the best
part of which was the opportunity to converse with the
most experienced officers of the Royal Flying Corps who
were on his staff. He knew what sort of boys we would
have to train and emphasized the kind of personnel needed.
He impressed it upon the university representatives that
the pilot was far from being a "flying chauffeur," as some
seemed to think. True, his power came from a gasoline
motor and the wheels beneath him were protected by pneumatic tires, but here the simile ended. "As a matter of fact,"

IN EVENT OF MOTOR FAILING
DON'T TURN BACK. "PEAK" AND
MAKE LANDING AHEAD. IT IS BET-
TER TO "PANNE" EVEN, ON A FOR-
EST THAN VRILLE INTO A FIELD.

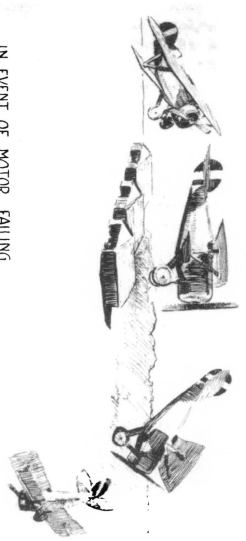

said the Colonel, "the pilot is more like the knight of old, or the modern cavalry officer ; he must first of all be (to quote the hackneyed phrase) an officer and a gentleman." He must be the kind of man whose honor is never left out of consideration. He must be as highly educated as possible in order that he may the more readily learn to adapt himself to rapidly changing tactics of the land army as well as the air forces. He must be resourceful, keen, quick, and determined. The Colonel said that polo players and football quarterbacks made excellent pilots. He did not recommend crew men !

A never-to-be-forgotten impression was made on the delegation by Captain Bell-Irving, the officer in charge of the repair shop, a member of a British Columbia family which greatly distinguished itself in the war. Captain Bell-Irving had been in the first Canadian force to be sent over, and after having been on the western front for some time, and wounded once or twice, had joined the Flying Corps and become a pilot in an observation squadron. One day his observer had succeeded in securing some very important photographs, when a shrapnel ball from a German anti-aircraft battery struck him in the temple, passed above his eye, and lodged itself above the brain. At first he was unconscious, then as the machine fell out of control he regained consciousness, and instinctively realized the precarious condition of his observer and the importance of getting his photographs back within the British lines. Wiping the blood from his face with his sleeve, he successfully piloted the machine back for nine miles and landed in safety not far from his own airdrome before again becoming unconscious. The bullet was still in his head, since the surgeons had not dared to attempt to extract it, and at times it gave him frightful pain so that he could scarcely see. But he was doing splendid work in his new job and was full of courageous optimism. His few words of assurance that it was most important to select the pilots with great care sank deeply into the hearts of the men who were to be the guiding spirits in the new United States Schools of Military Aeronautics and left a profound impression.

It was borne in on us by all those with whom we talked that the first necessity in the Air Service was to get the right type of personnel: fellows of quick, clear intelligence, mentally acute and physically fit; that the next thing was to make soldiers of them and teach them the value of military discipline; finally, that we should eliminate the unfit as fast as possible and avoid giving them flying instruction unless they proved themselves to be morally, physically, and mentally worthy of receiving the most expensive education in the world.

The next few days were spent attending as many classes as possible in the buildings of the university, where the Royal Flying Corps had established its local School of Military Aeronautics.

The adjutant of the school, a keen, young, wounded veteran of the war, was the son of one of the professors at the university whose name is well known in our historical circles. I mention this relationship because it enables me to illustrate how much better our Allies kept their military secrets than we did. The day after seeing the great flying school at Camp Borden, I had the honor of lunching with this officer's mother and father. The president of the university was one of the guests. The conversation naturally travelled around to aviation, and the wonder was expressed as to where the Royal Flying Corps would put its new big flying school. It had been on the tip of my tongue to speak about our amazement at what we had seen the day before at Camp Borden, when I suddenly realized that the secret of what was being done out there was so well kept that neither the president of the university which was housing the ground school, nor the father and mother of the young veteran aviator, who was its adjutant, was aware of what was going on. In the course of time, the work at Camp Borden came to be well known, but this incident and the caution of our Allies gave us American delegates a new sense of the importance of keeping our mouths shut concerning the things that were so generously laid open to us. It made us appreciate all the more the hearty coöperation of our new allies, and we marvelled at their willingness to offer us so freely all the secrets that they had learned at the cost of so much blood and treasure.

We found that the University of Toronto was supplying the Royal Flying Corps with buildings and grounds, but that most of the instructors were veterans of the western front, either pilots who had been injured or become stale, or non-commissioned officers of long experience as sergeant-instructors. While we could not hope to secure similar teaching personnel for our own Schools of Military Aeronautics, it was believed that by using trained instructors and giving them the very latest information as a basis for their lectures, we might not fall so very far behind our model.

Conferences with various instructors at the ground school developed the fact—which we had occasion later to notice repeatedly —that the veterans of the western front differed radically on the importance of the various subjects of study and the necessity for their being taught more or less thoroughly. All were agreed, however, that undisciplined, unmilitary pilots were extremely undesirable, and that any youth who followed individualistic tendencies to such a degree as to make him appear to be a poor soldier should not be trained as a pilot. They said he would soon come to grief over the lines where team play was so essential, and where the carrying out of missions exactly as ordered was so easy to avoid if the pilot were so inclined, or preferred to "go after a Hun."

We learned that the principle was adopted of admitting a new class of students each week and graduating them as they were needed in the flying school. The idea was to furnish a steady stream of pupils to the teachers of preliminary flying and to eliminate the undesirables at the relatively inexpensive ground school before they should have any opportunity of wasting the valuable time of flying instructors and the very expensive facilities offered on an airdrome. We felt that we could not do better than to copy as nearly as

possible the curriculum adopted by the Royal Flying Corps
after more than two years of war. On the advice of several
of the chief instructors, we enlarged the course in various
particulars so as to make it cover eight weeks instead of
six. Later, this was still further extended. Great stress was
laid on the importance of developing ability to observe artillery fire and to coöperate with both artillery and infantry.
The importance of a thorough knowledge of the machine
gun, the internal combustion motor, and wireless telegraphy
was emphasized. We decided to adopt the British method
of dividing the course into two parts: the first, of three
weeks, chiefly military studies and infantry drill; the second, of five weeks, technical aeronautics, with particular
emphasis on guns and motors.

These preliminaries having been decided, and a tenta-
tive programme of studies adopted, the delegates hastened
back to their respective universities to rush the preparation
for students who had already passed their entrance examinations as given by the Aviation Examining Boards in various
cities, and who were anxious to commence their training,
even though it meant first going to a ground school instead
of being immediately put in an airplane, as so many of them
hoped would be the case.

Our meetings in Toronto were concluded on May 11.
Ten days later the six new Schools of Military Aeronautics were ready to receive, and were actually receiving, their
first students. Of course special faculty meetings had to be
held, trustees had to vote credits, laboratories and classrooms

had to be hastily adjusted to meet new demands, lectures on new subjects had to be prepared from the material obtained in Toronto, and plans made to receive a small army post under the command of a recent graduate of West Point and San Diego. In one case, at the University of California, ground was immediately broken on the campus for a new building whose plans had been drawn on the train by the Toronto delegates, a building designed to accommodate exactly the needs of the new school. In every case, serious dislocations had to be quickly performed. It seemed incredible that they could be ready in ten days. Small wonder that General Squier endorsed my letter of May 13, informing him that the universities would be able to commence instruction in the cadet schools not later than Monday, May 21: "Splendid. Am much pleased. Go ahead full steam." And the universities made good!

If one did not know the tremendous loyalty and self-sacrifice that pervades American universities, their immediate response to the new demands of the Army Air Service would have been incredible. Had it only been as easy to build training planes and to obtain well-equipped flying schools as it was to secure the full coöperation of enthusiastic, high grade universities and use their equipment, the problem of sending American aviators to the Front would have been very much simpler.

CHAPTER III

WAR FEVER IN WASHINGTON

ON my return to Washington on May 13, the city looked more warlike, for in the mean time orders had been issued that all officers on active duty should wear service uniforms. At the same time this brought out an amusing feature of our unpreparedness which was particularly striking to one who had just been associating with the appropriately uniformed officers of the Royal Flying Corps. They wore wings, but none of them wore spurs, while at Washington the officers in the Aviation Section of the Signal Corps wore spurs, but did not wear wings. About six months later, our military aviators were authorized by the General Staff to wear wings, but when wearing boots were still obliged to wear spurs. Six months later, the War College, after we had been at war for a year, woke up to the ridiculous side of forcing aviators to wear spurs, when obviously from their wings they used airplanes and not horses, and issued a new regulation that aviators when wearing boots would *not* wear spurs. This was permitted, however, only as long as we were actively engaged in war, and in the following December the rule was changed back again, so that when I returned from France in January, 1919, I received a similar shock to this one after my first visit to Toronto, and found the unfortunate aviator once more compelled to wear spurs when wearing boots.

It would be interesting to delve into the inner conscious-

ness of the dear old boys down in the *sancta sanctorum* of the
War College. It is a queer sense of humor that requires
a field officer, who in the course of his duties suddenly is
called upon to mount his winged steed, to divest himself of
his spurs and put them in his pocket for safety. I speak the
more feelingly on this matter because of one Sunday afternoon at Potomac Park, when I was invited unexpectedly to
fly with Colonel Lee of the Royal Flying Corps and had to
listen to the laughter of the crowd while I took off my spurs.
It would not have been so bad had I not been wearing wings
at the same time. However, we were not the only branch or
the only army to suffer from archaic uniform regulations. A
post-bellum issue of *Punch* portrays the embarrassment of
a natty young railroad transportation officer, smartly clad
in very "horsey" regalia, roughly accosted by an infantry
colonel just returned at the head of a victorious regiment,
who inquired whether the "engines were feeling *frisky* this
morning."

On the other hand, the courtesy of the regular officers of
the permanent establishment to the newly appointed reserve
officers during the early months of the war, when we were
all so green, made so many mistakes, and had so much to
learn of army procedure, was particularly noticeable. It was
very pleasant and gave one a feeling of being part of a cordial family organization to have the older regular officers
meet a stranger on the street with their hearty "Good morning" when one appeared in uniform. This gracious recogni-
tion of the old army, however, soon died out as Washington

LANDINGS SHOULD BE MADE
AGAINST WIND. CROSS-WIND
LANDINGS SHOULD NOT BE AT-
TEMPTED BY THE INEXPERIENCED
FLIER.

Information Department
3rd. Aik. A.E.F. France

became swamped by the inrush of several thousand reserve officers who had not been accustomed to bowing to a stranger merely because he wore the uniform of the United States Army.

As we look back from this distance and have in mind the enormous structures which were built in Washington in 1918 to meet the requirements of the War Department, it is amazing to note the inadequate preparations and the small vision of the requirements that prevailed in May and June, 1917. Previous to our entry into the war, the War Department apparently had made no plans as to what it would do in case we were suddenly called upon to become one of the great military nations in the world. When the war, that is, our part in it, began, the Adjutant-General's office, as I was told by one of the best informed members of the General Staff, was receiving about three thousand communications a day, and these were being handled by six or eight officers and an adequate force of trained clerks. Foreseeing in some degree that an additional force would be required, the number of officers and clerks was merely doubled after we entered the war. On the particular day on which I made my inquiries as to why a certain communication had received no attention for nearly two weeks, I was informed that the incoming mail that morning at the Adjutant-General's office consisted of over forty thousand pieces, or about thirteen times as much as at the beginning of the war, while the office force was still only twice as large. Of course this was altered later, but it seemed to me at the time an adequate explanation of the reason why my own communication had not been answered more promptly.

During the month of May and part of June, my office, as Director of the United States Schools of Military Aeronautics, consisted of a desk in a small room where, besides myself and two assistants, there was also located the desk of Captain (later Colonel) Aubrey Lippincott, who was in charge of the personnel division of the Air Service; two other officers, who were in charge of the personnel of the Signal Corps proper, and Mr. W. M. Redding, whose sixteen years of service as one of the principal clerks in the office of the Chief Signal Officer made him an indispensable source of information as regards procedure and many other details. From this small room, then, for several weeks went out practically all of the correspondence covering the personnel of the Signal Corps as well as that of the Air Service, in addition to that concerned with the ground schools. But that was not all, for here between the hours of ten in the morning and four in the afternoon, we were subjected to a stream of callers, who wanted important information on every conceivable subject. In June we moved over to the Mills Building, where the "Schools Division" had at least one room, but this was speedily filled up with the desks of assistants, clerks, and stenographers until there was scarcely a chair for our importunate callers.

It may be interesting to know that within six months of the time when we were all huddled together in that little room on the fourth floor of the State, War, and Navy Building, the Air Personnel Division had begun to use the services of fifty officers and two hundred and fifty clerks, while the Schools of Military Aeronautics Division required the services of a dozen officers and forty clerks. Our growth was attended by many difficulties and numerous moves. Each move caused loss of time, misplacement of papers, and delays which were disappointing, and were often misunderstood by our friends and correspondents. As a matter of fact, the Schools Division moved five times in about as many months. These were feverish days of living from hand to mouth. One never knew from week to week what new conditions would have to be met either physically or mentally.

One of my first tasks was to have copies made of the lectures used by the Royal Flying Corps at Toronto and send these copies out to our new schools as fast as possible. There were practically no stenographers available for this purpose, but fortunately I was able to have the original lectures photostated and sent out in this form.

While in the throes of trying to do a dozen things at once, so as to give the greatest possible amount of assistance to the universities that were struggling with their new problems, I was suddenly presented with a highly trained and most enthusiastic assistant, Frank C. Page. General Squier had known him at the Embassy in London and gave him a commission as Captain, which was later increased to that of Major. What I should have done without Major Page during the next few months is diffi-

cult to imagine. His knowledge of aeronautics as well as
his editorial ability and his acquaintance with the ways of
the War Department enabled him to start right in, on the
day the General asked him to become my assistant, and without a moment's hesitation to become immensely helpful.

General Squier, while wisely avoiding the tyranny of
details and refusing to become discouraged by, or interested in, the difficulties which he believed should be solved
by his subordinates, had a most remarkable way of gath-
ering in useful people to help the Air programme. He was
quick to realize that, notwithstanding a lamentable lack of
former military training, editors, college professors, secre-
taries of learned societies, former national tennis champions,
managers of large business enterprises, distinguished engineers, and former police commissioners, all had something
of value in their make-up, as attested by their past history,
which would justify the Air Service in giving them commissions and securing their services. He knew they would make
mistakes. His year and a half on the Western Front had
taught him, however, what, unfortunately, many of the older
staff officers found it difficult to learn before the Armistice
was signed, that this war, unlike any which had preceded
it, could use to the fullest extent men who had succeeded in
the civilian world's occupations, even though they knew nothing of Army Regulations, or of infantry drill. He did not expect them to develop into active commanders on the Western Front. He repeatedly said that in the course of a few
months all the regular officers of the permanent establish-

ment would be needed on the firing line in France. But he did expect that the important positions in the War Department at home would be filled by near-civilians, and to give them the rank necessary for the places they were to fill did not worry him in the least, even though they had never served an eight years' apprenticeship as Second Lieutenants in the Line, and could not do "Squads right."

Furthermore, General Squier saw clearly the tremendous possibilities of the Air Service. His prophetic vision, rising above the practical difficulties and annoying details connected with such mushroom growth, soared away into space like a veritable comet. Every time I had the opportunity of a long conversation with my Chief, I came away filled with a new inspiration and a clearer idea of the gigantic task that lay ahead of us. Even in little things he saw more distinctly than any of us the requirements of our coming expansion. At a time when it seemed to me that two or three office assistants and half a dozen stenographers would be all that I should need, he waved the idea aside with the remark, "You must get ready to have at least a dozen officers and fifty clerks." And his vision was correct. It needed just about that many to handle the correspondence and the details of running the Schools of Military Aeronautics after they finally got going under full steam.

I think General Squier expected more of us than we could possibly perform. He had seen what miracles were being done in England and France, and he had the greatest optimism regarding American youth. Our Chief followed the

principle of giving his subordinates the widest possible
authority and permitting them to make decisions of the
greatest importance. Seldom did he deny our requests. Our
opportunity was tremendous and our responsibilities increased from day to day, but we always felt that we had General Squier behind us. His optimism was contagious, and
his belief in the great future of the American pilot spurred
us on to work at high speed early and late. Holidays were
welcome because they meant a freedom from callers and the
opportunity to accomplish more constructive work than on
ordinary week-days.

The universities coöperated to the utmost of their ability,
and showed unusual patience with the frequent changes of
plan and curriculum that were necessitated by military ex-
igency. Just as we would get comfortably settled in one course
of study, word would come by cable from General Pershing,
urging that more stress be laid on something else. The truth
was, that the General Staff knew practically nothing about
Military Aeronautics. Neither then, nor for many months
afterwards, was there a single General Staff officer in Washington who had attended a flying school, or who understood
through practical experience the needs of a School of Military Aeronautics. We had to work out our own salvation—
and keep going at the same time. Fortunately we had the
constant aid and assistance, during these difficult first six
months, of Colonel L. W. B. Rees, of the Royal Flying Corps,
who had been decorated for his extraordinary courage in
attacking single-handed ten German planes.

Colonel Rees had been used in England as an instructor, so his advice was particularly valuable. We learned to turn to him on all doubtful questions. That we did not make more mistakes was due chiefly to his long experience and good judgment. On my first tour of inspection of the cadets in the ground schools I had the good fortune to be accompanied by Colonel Rees, and to witness the enthusiasm which his presence aroused among the cadets and the eagerness with which the members of the various faculties plied him with questions both before and after his lecture. Merely to get a glimpse of him as he limped across the campus and to realize what he had done was enough to increase appreciably the zeal of the cadets.

He was in charge of a squadron at the Front just before the Somme offensive. Annoyed, as he whimsically relates, by the continual ringing of the telephone and the repeated asking of unnecessary questions by junior officers at Headquarters, he decided to take a patrol himself. At that time it appears to have been the custom for single machines to make patrols. Later, patrols were taken by flights or entire squadrons. While on his solitary patrol he saw a squadron of ten German machines headed for France. As I remember the story, they were two-seaters, and probably constituted a day-bombing squadron. With almost unparalleled daring, he attacked the squadron, broke it up, sent down at least three, if not four, of the enemy aircraft in flames, and had the satisfaction of seeing the others hurry homeward in a demoralized state. During the latter part of the engagement, he was suffering from the effects of a machine gun bullet, which entered his thigh and lodged near his right knee. This did not prevent him, however, from completing his victory by demolishing his last opponent and flying safely home to his own airdrome. He spent the next six months in the hospital, but eventually had the satisfaction of having the "V. C." pinned on his coat by the King himself.

It was only with the very greatest difficulty that one could get Colonel Rees to speak of his great fight, even in private. His lectures were confined to a discussion of recent developments in aerial tactics and amusing stories of mistakes that had been made by British pilots, due in some cases to inability to read maps, and in others to disobedience of specific instructions. His readiness to help us on the minutest details was particularly appreciated by Lieutenant John C. Farrar, whose duty it was to collect for the use of the schools all the latest information regarding military aeronautics. Lieutenant Farrar's keen enthusiasm for his work enabled him to unearth much that was of the greatest value both in Washington and Toronto, and later in France. We continually received the very latest confidential information prepared by the Royal Flying Corps. Its use in the courses at the ground schools was of great psychological value. It raised the morale of the cadets and made them take pride and interest in the course of instruction. Unfortunately, it could not help them to get to the Front any sooner.

THE IMPORTANCE OF KEEPING FORMATION CANNOT BE TOO
STRONGLY IMPRESSED UPON THE PILOT. LOSS OF POSITION IS
LIKELY TO LEAD TO AN ADVENTURE WITH THE JAGDELS.

"THE JAC

CHAPTER IV

ORGANIZING THE SCHOOLS OF MILITARY AERONAUTICS

THE United States Schools of Military Aeronautics were organized on a basis which permitted the Commandant, a regular officer of the permanent establishment and responsible directly to the Chief Signal Officer of the Army, to have complete control over the whole institution. As assistants to the Commandant there were an adjutant, a supply officer, and an officer in charge of military instruction. The Commandant's right-hand man, however, on whom more than on any other one person depended the success of the school, was the civilian President of the Academic Board, to whom the faculty were directly responsible, and who appeared to the students as a kind of Dean.

The commandants were drawn from the ranks of the junior officers in the Signal Corps. The newness of army aviation, and the unwillingness of older officers to take the risks associated with aviation training, had one unfortunate effect. The handful of regular army officers who had had practical experience in military aeronautics was for the most part composed of recent graduates of West Point, very young men, who had failed to secure that six or eight years' experience in handling men which was the ordinary lot of lieutenants in the infantry before being called upon to assume positions of responsibility. Most of them had had six months with troops, but neither their experience at West Point nor their training at San Diego had made them super-men. Due to the rapid expansion of the regular army at the beginning of the war, these second lieutenants almost immediately became captains, or rather majors, for the operation of the law regarding Junior Military Aviators gave them additional rank.

The fact that an officer was a major in the regular army and a graduate of West Point and San Diego made him liable to have great responsibilities thrust upon him, which few men of twenty-five (and most of our new J. M. A. Majors were not over twenty-five years of age) had either the experience or the judgment to assume successfully. Consequently, it was not surprising that some of them encountered difficulties in their new work, and that the Inspector-General of the Army very severely criticised the manner in which some of the ground schools, and also some of the flying schools, were conducted.

The ground schools had an easier time than the flying schools because the work was, after all, not so very different from the ordinary work of the long-established universities where they were located. Furthermore, they were under the sympathetic supervision of college presidents and conscientious deans, whose long experience with college students and university faculties enabled them to keep the new schools running smoothly, even when the young majors in charge were dismayed at the extent and variety of their new responsibilities. At the flying fields most of the professional instructors at that time were civilian flyers, whose training was for the most part not of the kind to lead to results that would please an Inspector-General.

Owing to the shortage of flying field officers, it became necessary to replace the Junior Military Aviator Majors in many cases with older officers, whose experience in the regular army enabled them to put the ground schools on a sounder basis. They were carefully selected with particular reference to their having had previous experience in instructional work. Their arrival was welcomed by the Presidents of the Academic Boards. The more mature years of the new commandants, their experience in dealing with civilians and soldiers, and longer years of service in various parts of the army enabled them to overcome the drawbacks that arose at first from their lack of knowledge of aeronautics.

One of the things which had to be worked out was the proper division of authority between the Commandant and the President of the Academic Board. After several months of experiment, the following system was adopted : The Commandant had general supervision over the entire school, and in particular was the commanding officer of the troops on duty at that school. It was his duty to make frequent inspection of the tuition furnished by the university in accordance with the terms of its contract with the War Department. It was also his duty to report to the President of the Academic Board any discrepancies in instruction or the work of the instructors. The President of the Academic Board was expected to discharge such instructors as in the opinion of the Commandant were not competent.

The President of the Academic Board was in charge of all technical instructors, and instructions to them were issued by him rather than by the Commandant, but the Commandant was in direct charge of all students, since they were enlisted men, and orders to them were issued by him or by officers authorized by him. It was found to be impracticable for the President of the Academic Board to have direct connection with the military side of the school. At the same time, there was a strong desire on the part of many of the students to "take their troubles to the Dean" rather than to the C. O. The rule was established that students should obtain permission from the officer in charge of their barracks before conferring with the President of the Academic Board. In this way, the general practice in the service of reaching higher authority through proper military channels was emphasized. One of the most difficult things for the average officer and man in our great new army to learn was that the rule concerning "military channels" was not designed to prevent him from reaching the highest authority, but was only intended to facilitate his doing so.

The Commandant was urged to establish cordial relations with the students and to make himself easy of access. He was held responsible for the character of the instruction, both military and technical. While it was necessary that the President of the Academic Board and the officer in charge of the Department of Military Studies should be independent of one another, it was equally important for the Commandant to coördinate and unite the efforts of these separate branches.

Under our contract with the universities, they furnished all equipment except Government publications, quartermaster supplies, and special aeronautical equipment, such as motors, airplanes, and spare parts. Machine guns, ammunition, and confidential material were also furnished by the War Department. The universities furnished the necessary instructors and other facilities needed for the proper operation of the school. In return, the Government agreed to pay a specified tuition fee for each man receiving instruction ($10 per week for the first four weeks and $5 per week thereafter), to furnish equipment of a special nature not procurable by the university, the curriculum of instruction to be followed, and such special information of instructional character as could be secured by the War Department from time to time. At first cadets received $33 per month; later, $100 per month, plus allowances for rations. July 1, 1918, the pay of cadets was again reduced to $33, a procedure that did not raise the morale of a volunteer corps where actual danger to life and limb in the flying schools was very great.

The course of study consisted of eight weeks, later increased to twelve. The Junior Wing of three weeks was given over to intensive military training, instruction in military topics, and practical work on the machine gun and the radio buzzer. The Senior Wing consisted of five weeks of lectures and laboratory instruction, and included signalling with buzzer, lamp, and panelled shutter, and a few lectures on the care of the radio apparatus; care of machine guns,

and practice in clearing jams; lectures on bombs, theory of
flight, cross-country flying, meteorology, and night flying;
explanation of instruments and compasses; practical work
in map reading; lectures on types of airplanes; classroom
work in aerodynamics; practical work in rigging and repairing; lectures on the principles of internal combustion
motors and on the care of motors and tools; practical work
with various types of engines; a little practice in trouble
shooting; lectures on the theory of aerial observation, with
special reference to observing artillery fire; practical work
with the buzzer on a miniature artillery range; and a few
lectures on liaison with infantry, and the latest tactics of
fighting in the air.

In order to standardize the instruction in the British
Schools of Military Aeronautics, the Royal Flying Corps
had found it necessary to have all examinations set and
read by a central office. This scheme was practical in England because the schools at Oxford and Reading were so
near to London. It was entirely impractical in America, on
account of the great distances separating our schools from
Washington. So we met the necessity of keeping the schools
at uniform grade by sending out frequent inspectors and by
having all examination papers sent to Washington after they
had been read and marked. Questions were set by the teachers who taught the courses. The marks which they gave
were accepted by us as final. Our ability to hold "post mor-
tems" on their work, however, enabled us to check up on instructors who showed lack of imagination in inventing new

questions or whose fatigue had interfered with their using good judgment in grading the papers.

We secured the services of trained college readers like Captain S. Merrill Clement and Lieutenant Stanley T. Williams of Yale and Captain Cobb of Amherst and Lieutenant Clarence G. Andrews of Ohio State University to examine the examination papers. While it was not necessary for them to read every one of the thousands of papers that were sent in, they were able to make cross-sections through the mass. When weak spots were discovered, these could then be further investigated. For instance, one week all the papers in the "Theory of Flight" examinations in all eight schools were read and the type of instruction in this subject as given in each school was thereby brought out. If it proved on investigation that the papers from one of the eight schools were noticeably much better than the others, investigation of all the papers in that subject from that school was made, and the result sometimes showed that the excellence of these papers was due not to the excellence of instruction, but to the fact that the majority of the questions had been used repeatedly in recent examinations, so that it had been very easy for the careful student to prepare beforehand to meet just those questions. On the other hand, if one of the sets of papers was distinctly inferior, the attention of the President of the Academic Board of that school was invited to the specific details wherein this particular instructor was not maintaining the desired standard.

We kept a very careful record of the percentages of

failures at each school, and whenever this made a marked departure from the general average, our examining officers would read all the papers from that school on all subjects for the past month. A full report of this investigation was then forwarded to the school. It was a new experience for most of our instructors to be checked up in this manner. Some of the schools liked it and immediately took advantage of the reports to improve and strengthen their methods of instruction. Others resented it as being an unwarrantable attack on that kind of academic freedom which does not like to be criticised or too closely inspected.

It has always seemed to me that there was no more reason for a college instructor to feel hurt at frequent inspection of his work on the part of his superiors than the captain of a military organization at the weekly inspection carried on by his superior officer. I know there is a tradition in many colleges that the classroom or lecture-room of a Professor is sacred to him and his class. During some fifteen years of college teaching at four American universities, I do not remember ever to have had the president of a university, the dean of a college, the head of my department, or a member of the corporation or board of trustees, enter my lecture-room or sit through a class exercise. As in the case of the great majority of instructors, my work, instead of being carefully inspected at regular intervals as it was in the army by representatives of the Inspector-General's Office, was judged partly by the character of my published books and articles, partly by the high marks or number of failures given in my classes

Nieuport 28, Monosoupape motor

Nieuport 27, 120 H.P. Le Rhone motor

in the course of a year, and partly by such undergraduate gossip as came to the ears of my superiors. In the army, an officer is never judged on barrack-room gossip.

Frequent inspections were made by various officers from our own office in Washington. In this way the schools were kept in touch with one another and with the latest developments in the air programme, difficulties which could not easily be put in writing were informally discussed, and it is believed that much good was accomplished. The following extracts from the report of one of our inspectors concerning methods of teaching at the Cornell school may prove of interest, particularly since he had had many years of experience as a college professor.

The theories of the gas engine, of carburetion, of ignition, etc., are given in lectures. After each period a man is given a chance to see and work on the subject of that lecture in the laboratory and to settle any question that may be troubling him. The laboratory classes are conducted on less military lines than others, giving men a chance to gather around the engines, ask questions of the instructors, and figure things out for themselves. The head instructor is in the laboratory constantly, going from group to group, explaining, watching, and criticizing. I have never seen in any laboratory so much interest in work and coöperation between instructor and student. The attitude of the men is one of careful interest, which cannot help but follow them on to hangars both in this country and abroad. The engines are left at a certain point of assemblage at the end of each period. Every squad finds one engine in exactly the same condition when it comes again. A log book is kept of both men and engines and checked off so that every man will get exactly the same amount of work and the engines will be kept at the proper stages.

Laboratory work at present is observation and explanation of the engines with some work on them, and one three-hour period devoted to the sketching of parts. Small clear sketches of various parts have been prepared and mounted on wood. These are given to the students to copy. Instructors are present during the entire period for consultation, and when a man has finished his sketches he must submit them for approval with his own explanation of the part drawn. This serves a double purpose—it gives an understanding of the part and furnishes the student with a good drawing for his notebook. Fourteen lectures are given in all, the last one being a lantern-slide lecture of various engines and their parts. The head instructor in this department has been much interested in the development of what he calls an entirely new method of teaching. When he first started he says that he had no idea that men could be taught so much in eight weeks. His lectures are very carefully prepared and mapped out, with a quiz each week. He and his assistants have been very progressive in the preparation of large colored charts, and they have also made two wooden models showing skillfully the action of a rotary motor and the principle of the four-cycle engine.

Whenever helpful accounts of methods were received, or when significant paragraphs came in the weekly reports from the Commandant of any school, they were immediately sent out to all the schools as suggestions. Instructors were encouraged to visit flying schools and other ground schools on their short vacations. Sometimes this led to their coming back with increased pride and satisfaction with their own institution, while at other times new methods of teaching proved worthy of adoption and caused changes at home.

The cadets all felt that too much stress was laid on military discipline, but the following cablegram from General Pershing was responsible for the rigorous manner in which military discipline was enforced at the ground schools. It read as follows:

I cannot too strongly impress upon the War Department the absolute necessity of rigid insistence that all men be thoroughly grounded in the school of the *soldier*. Salutes should be rendered by both officers and men in most military manner with especial emphasis on right position of soldiers in saluting and when at attention. A prompt military salute is often misunderstood by our people but it simply emphasizes an aggressive attitude of mind and body that marks the true soldier. The loyalty, readiness, and alertness indicated by strictest adherence to this principle will immensely increase the pride and fighting spirit of our troops. The slovenly, unmilitary, careless habits that have grown up in peace times in our army are seriously detrimental to the aggressive attitude that must prevail from highest to lowest in our forces. Strict methods used at West Point, in training new cadets in these elementary principles, have given the Academy its superior excellence. These methods should be applied rigorously and completely in the forces we are now organizing.

PERSHING

This was sent us, by order of the Secretary of War, for our "information and careful guidance," and we made every effort to carry out General Pershing's request.

It was conceded by British officers who visited our schools in the summer and fall of 1917 that some of them were quite as good as the similar schools of the Royal Flying Corps. Perhaps they were trying to flatter us, but remembering that British officers have very poor reputations as flatterers, we felt greatly encouraged. The school which particularly aroused the praise and admiration of our visitors was that maintained under the auspices of the University of Texas at Austin. The credit for this was due in part to Major Ralph E. Cousins, J. M. A., who organized the school and was its efficient Commandant for the first five months of its existence. His success was due largely to his faith in the academic members of the faculty, and in particular in the President of the Academic Board, Professor J. M. Bryant.

Professor Bryant had been one of the delegates to Toronto, and had shown great enthusiasm for the courses there and the possibility of adapting them to the needs of American students. His weekly reports forwarded to Washington by the Commandant showed a remarkable power of grasping new problems as they arose and dealing with them in a spirit of most cordial coöperation with the army. It was chiefly owing to his skill as an administrator, and his remarkable devotion to securing the best possible results with the students that were sent him, that this school achieved such success in securing the highest praise not only from the British officers who inspected it, but also from General Squier and his subordinates. General Squier said the cadets here reminded him more of West Pointers than any he had ever inspected. The success of this school was due also to President Robert E. Vinson of the University of Texas, whose wholehearted patriotism made him grant immediately every request which we made of him at a time when local difficulties and the animosity of the Governor of Texas might easily have justified him in hesitating.

In a similar manner, Professor B. M. Woods, President of the Academic Board in the school at the University of

California, by his enthusiastic and whole-hearted coöperation built up a plant that won General Squier's warmest
praise. Excellent work was done at Berkeley. The Regents
of the University of California deserve to be particularly remembered for their prompt action. At a time when all parts
of the country were willing to do their utmost to coöperate
in winning the war, no Board of Trustees showed greater
speed in voting credits and erecting temporary structures to
meet the needs of a new school.

The Trustees of Princeton University gave us the use of
their newest dormitories, and her officials determined to do
everything in their power to make their school the best of
the eight. President Hibben's long devotion to the cause of
Preparedness had led us to expect that Princeton would not
be behindhand in offering special facilities for carrying on
the work of her ground school, and we were not disappointed.
In November this school was visited by the late Colonel
Theodore Roosevelt, who wrote me that he was "immensely
pleased" with it and with the character of the men in it.

Cornell was fortunate in being able to devote her magnificent new armory entirely to our needs. President Schur-
man strained every nerve to meet our requirements and to
make the school successful. Its location near the Thomas-
Morse airplane factory gave the Cornell students an opportunity of coming into closer touch with the progress of
American flying than the students at the other schools. Cornell's excellent course in motors has already been described.

The success attained by the school at the University of

Illinois was due chiefly to the untiring efforts of Dean David Kinley, and the determination of his faculty to put their school first in point of advanced methods of teaching. Under the zealous supervision of President Thompson and later of Professor Blake, the school at Ohio State University was also fortunate in securing special buildings for its use. It was most encouraging during moments of depression at Washington to receive visits from earnest patriots like President Thompson and President Hibben, and to realize the extent to which they were willing to go to enable the air programme to succeed.

The Georgia Institute of Technology at Atlanta and the Massachusetts Institute of Technology at Cambridge also had engineering laboratories well adapted to the needs of the new schools. At Atlanta two student dormitories were assigned to our use, while at Cambridge barracks were established in available quarters of that splendid new group of buildings. The Massachusetts Institute of Technology was the only one of the eight schools that had for several years past been developing special courses in aerodynamics. Consequently, it was particularly well situated for training Aeronautical Engineers, when the need arose for having a special school for that purpose. The Georgia School developed a good course in Military Studies under Captain Blake—formerly Sergeant on duty at Miami—and was selected to train Aviation Supply Officers. Adjutants were trained at Ohio State University. Thus three of the ground schools came to be used largely for the training of non-flying officers.

Morane-Saulnier Monoplane, type 30, Monosoupape motor

Spad, 225 H.P. Hispano-Suiza motor

CHAPTER V
SELECTING THE FITTEST

CANDIDATES for commissions in the Air Service were secured from civil life, Reserve Officers Training Corps, colleges, and the Regular Army. The objects of the schools of military aeronautics were: first, to teach the candidates their military duties and to develop in them soldierly qualities and prompt obedience; second, to give a certain limited amount of training in such things as could properly be taught at a ground school, namely, aerodynamics, gunnery, radio, internal combustion motors, aerial tactics, and coöperation with other arms of the service; and third, to weed out those who were mentally, morally, or physically unfitted to become flying officers.

In view of the large number of applicants, the tens of thousands of young men who were anxious to fly, the enormous expense of flying instruction (our allies estimated that it was costing them about $25,000 for every military aviator sent to the Front), the shortage of training equipment, the scarcity of flying schools (our flying schools were not all completed even by the time the Armistice was signed), and the necessity of getting the best men trained as rapidly as possible, it was felt that the most important function of the ground school was the elimination of those who did not give immediate promise of becoming good flying officers. About twenty-five per cent of those who passed the physical examining board and the preliminary "once over"

given by the aviation examiner, were dropped from the
ground schools and given an opportunity to enlist in some
other branch of the service, or to join an air squadron as
enlisted men and take their chance of later being recommended by squadron commanders as worthy of being given
a second opportunity to train as candidates for commission.

The plan was adopted, and during the six months of my
occupancy of the directorship of the Schools of Military Aeronautics rigidly adhered to, of permitting the commanding
officers of the schools to discharge a man for cause, or to
grant those students who failed in any subject the opportunity of being placed on probation. One more failure, and
the student was automatically dropped and his place filled
by a new aspirant. This system undoubtedly worked hardship in many cases and deprived us of the services of many
men who would have made excellent pilots. On the other
hand, it justified itself in the results on the flying fields,
where it was seldom necessary to interfere with the expensive flying training of a pilot because of his stupidity or the
inferiority of his mental or moral calibre.

While it seemed doubtful to some military aviators at
first whether the professional, but non-flying, instructors of a
university would be able to pass the right kind of pilot personnel, the results soon convinced them that the system was
right. Two of the first cadets to go from the School of Military
Aeronautics at the Massachusetts Institute of Technology
disappointed the officers at the Mineola Flying School. One
of them was rapidly eliminated and the other had been or-

dered before the board for elimination, when word was received that both of these students had in reality failed to graduate, but due to the ramifications of red tape had not received their discharge papers before being sent to Mineola. This circumstance naturally increased the confidence of the flying officers in the work of the ground school instructors.

While at that time there was no suitable physical means of determining whether a man lacked the proper sense of balance to become an acrobatic flyer, the severe requirements of the ground schools, the necessity for learning a large number of new things in a very short time, the need of working under high pressure for several weeks without breaking down, and the skill, enthusiasm, and good judgment displayed by the self-sacrificing instructors, who were willing to give up the opportunity for more brilliant service abroad, combined to produce a splendid body of graduates.

There were undoubtedly a number of cases where we lost some excellent personnel owing to mistakes in judgment on the part of officers charged with determining the standards and setting the tests. It was General Squier's feeling, however, that where so many thousands of the best youth of America were striving to get into what we believed, and what they believed, to be the most attractive branch of the service, we were justified in declining to continue as candidates any about whom there should arise the slightest doubt. To the individuals concerned, the adverse decisions seemed unaccountably severe and often unfair. From an intimate knowledge of how these decisions were reached during the first

ten months of our participation in the war, I can say without
fear of contradiction that our sole motive in making these
decisions was the desire to see the American Air Service
contain only the most efficient, mentally alert, physically
perfect, and soldierly body of young men to be found in the
American Army. Over and over again senators, representatives, distinguished citizens, and depressed parents came
to beg special consideration for sons, nephews, cousins,
friends, and acquaintances. Their calls used up a lot of time,
but their importunity deserved the most sympathetic treatment. Due to the remarkable efficiency of Miss F. Pol, who
was in charge of our files, we were able to answer questions
quickly and locate the cause of the trouble, even though
this seldom completely satisfied our callers.

The average American citizen took the attitude that any
young fellow who was willing to enter the hazardous game
of aviation was thereby exhibiting such tremendous patriotism and extraordinary courage that he ought to be lightly
wafted on his way into the air, notwithstanding any mental deficiency which the ground school examinations had
disclosed. One congressman even wanted imperfect eyesight to be waived!

The fact that there were at least 50,000 young Americans all eager to become pilots, and that the War Department could not afford to give "the most expensive education
in the world" to any except those who were best qualified to
use it, did not appeal to the caller who had been so deeply
impressed by the willingness of the one young man in whom

he was interested to take the "fearful risks" of military aviation. Some callers were more insistent than others. In the ten months that I was on duty in Washington, I do not remember receiving a single communication from a New England senator asking for special consideration for one of his constituents, although the rate of failure was very high in the School of Aeronautics at the Massachusetts Institute of Technology, and the New England Examining Boards declined to pass more than half of their applicants. In striking contrast was the extraordinary amount of correspondence that poured in over the signatures of some of the southern senators. I suppose some one will be able to offer a convincing reason for this extraordinary disparity.

We tried to see that each one got a square deal, but we insistently refused to make exceptions and grant favors even to senators who happened to be members of the Military Affairs Committee, or owners of powerful newspapers who felt that because they had supported the Administration they deserved special consideration. Some of their young friends went to Canada. It was quite obvious that, by placing attractive flying schools so near our large centres of population, the Royal Flying Corps had reasonable expectations of securing many very capable volunteers from the United States who could quietly travel across the line and pass themselves off as Canadians if they so chose. As a matter of fact, a large number did so elect, and some of the most brilliant pilots of that splendid corps were young Americans who either could not wait for our slow grinding machinery to reach them or else had not been able to measure up to the physical or mental requirements which we were able to maintain by reason of the enormous supply of first class material that was offered to us. The British had been fighting for so long, and both they and the Canadians had been so lavish of their finest youth, that it was obvious they were unable, in 1917, to maintain as high a mental or physical standard as we were.

On July 14, 1917, when the first class of 132 graduated from the ground schools, 1570 cadets had been accepted for training, and 1370 had been sent to the ground schools. Four months later, when I left the Schools Division to take up my new duties in the Personnel Division, 6670 cadets had been sent to the ground schools, 3140 had been graduated, and of these, more than 500 had already been graduated from American flying schools as Reserve Military Aviators.

A great many of those who successfully passed the ground schools and became pilots, in looking back on their courses, were grateful for the excellent teaching they had received in the fundamentals of machine gun care and operation, motor construction, and radio sending and receiving. On the other hand, many became pursuit pilots in France and, therefore, had no occasion to send or receive radio, nor opportunity to use the Lewis machine gun (which had been the only one available in the early days of the ground schools), and no occasion to use the Curtiss or Hall-Scott motor (again the only ones available for early instructional purposes). They felt that their eight weeks in the ground schools had been a total loss of time. No one can blame them for feeling so. Very few of them appreciated the fact that the elimination of those not so mentally alert as themselves was greatly to their advantage and aided materially in speeding up the work at the flying schools. The first graduates were less inclined to feel any gratitude to the ground schools because of what happened in France—but that is another story.

From the date of establishment of these ground schools, May 21, 1917, up to their discontinuance, the following number of flying cadets were handled:

Total number of cadets entered	22,689
Total number graduated	17,540
Total number discharged	5,149

The distribution of cadets was as follows:

	Opened	Closed	Entered	Discharged	Graduated
UNIVERSITY OF CAL., Berkeley, Cal.	May 21, 1917	Feb. 1, 1918	3,737	705	3,032
CORNELL UNIVERSITY, Ithaca, N. Y.	May 21, 1917	Nov. 23, 1918	3,645	833	2,812
GA. SCH. OF TECH., Atlanta, Ga.	July 2, 1917	May 11, 1918	406	79	327
UNIVERSITY OF ILL., Urbana, Ill.	May 21, 1917	Nov. 23, 1918	3,453	809	2,644
MASS. INST. OF TECH., Cambridge, Mass.	May 21, 1917	Sept. 7, 1918	797	175	622
OHIO STATE UNIV., Columbus, Ohio	May 21, 1917	Aug. 31, 1918	1,291	199	1,092
PRINCETON UNIVERSITY, Princeton, N. J.	July 2, 1917	Nov. 23, 1918	3,586	1,088	2,498
UNIVERSITY OF TEXAS, Austin, Texas	May 21, 1917	Feb. 1, 1919	5,774	1,261	4,513

In addition to the above mentioned cadets, there were also entered and trained during this period the following:

	Entered	Discharged	Graduated
Supply Officers	963	111	852
Engineer Officers	964	238	726
Adjutants	887	98	789

In the spring of 1918 an Aviation Concentration Camp was established at Camp Dick, Dallas, Texas, for preliminary training of ground school candidates awaiting assignment to ground schools, and graduates of ground schools awaiting assignment to flying schools.

The last curriculum under which the schools operated provided a course for bombers and observers, but owing to the signing of the Armistice, these courses were never actually put into effect.

Such text-books as the following were used in connection with our courses: Sherrill's *Military Map Reading*, Audel's *Gasoline Engines*, Von Verkatz's *New Methods of Machine Gun Fire*, Barber's *The Aeroplane Speaks*, Loening's *Military Aeroplanes*, Grieve's *Map Reading*, Ellis & Carey's *Plattsburg Manual*, Rees' *Fighting in the Air*, Moss' *Officers' Manual*, Milham's *Meteorology*, Carlson's *Notes on Radio Telegraphy*, Dyke's *Working Models of Engines and Magnetoes*, Burl's *Aero Engines*, Keene's *Aero Engines*, Page's *Aero Engines*, Mathew's *Aviation Pocket Book*, Zahm's *Aerial Navigation*, Savage Arms Co. *Machine Gun Catalog*, together with the following Government publications: *Equipment for an Aero Squadron*, *Manual of Physical Training*,

REDRESSING TOO HIGH
AND STALLING CAUSES
"PANCAKING"

Information Department,
3rd A.I.C. A.E.F. France.

Room 11, 24 Bureau, 4th Floor

Infantry Drill Regulations, Army Regulations, Field Service Regulations, Manual of Courts Martial, Silhouettes of Airplanes, Small Arms Firing Manual, Interior Guard Duty, Signal Corps Manual, Unit Equipment Manual.

My right-hand man during the summer and fall was Major J. Robert Moulthrop. He was an invaluable assistant. He later took entire charge of the schools. He was in turn succeeded by Captain George A. Washington, whose legal training and long interest in militia activities made him particularly well qualified for his duties.

CHAPTER VI

THE PERSONNEL OFFICE IN WASHINGTON

O N November 20, 1917, General Squier asked me to take charge of "Air Personnel." Lieutenant-Colonel Lippincott, who had been in charge, was promoted to a full Colonelcy, placed in command of the second regiment of Air Service Mechanics, and sent overseas. At that time the Personnel Section of the Air Division was occupying part of one floor in the old Southern Railway building at 119 D Street. Most of the clerks had but recently entered the War Department. Many of them were school teachers, who had never used a filing cabinet or acted in any clerical capacity whatsoever. Few had had any training in a business office. Although they all worked with goodwill and patriotic devotion, they greatly needed careful instruction and practical experience.

The congestion and confusion were appalling. Desks were placed as closely together as they could possibly be jammed and still leave a narrow space whereby the occupant could come and go. Thus those that occupied interior desks were unable to move without asking two or three others to move also. No effort was made to keep out callers, and every one of the twenty-five or thirty officers then in charge of the one hundred and fifty clerks was subject to continual interruption on the part of both candidates and officers in the Air Service, as well as their friends and congressmen. Fifty filing clerks, most of them entirely without training, were huddled together at long tables where their elbows touched, and where the conditions under which they labored were such as to produce the greatest possible confusion in the files. It usually took over an hour to find a desired paper, and frequently two or three hours would be spent in a vain search for a valuable document. Too often papers could not be found at all, as many unfortunate candidates will remember only too well.

Our incoming mail consisted of about three thousand pieces daily, or as many as in that of the Adjutant-General of the Army at the beginning of the war. We were much worse off than he was, however, for the officers on his staff were men of long experience in the regular army dealing with familiar problems on a well-established basis, while with one or two exceptions the officers then on duty in Air Personnel were near-civilians with very slight knowledge of army paper work. They were dealing with entirely new problems and constantly changing regulations. Furthermore, many of the clerks in the Adjutant-General's office had been in the War Department for years and were thoroughly familiar with the ramifications of red tape. Our clerks, on the other hand, were nearly all entirely new to War Department requirements.

There was no adequate system of distributing the mail. The girls at the distribution desk did the best they knew how, and when in doubt put the letters into the basket of Captain Dunham, whose remarkable memory enabled him to carry on his desk an enormous amount of detail. Distribution baskets were labelled with the names of officers instead of with the titles of subdivisions of the office. In other words, the division was suffering from growing pains.

Fortunately, there was in the division an officer who had had experience in reorganizing partly defunct factories — a graduate of the Harvard School of Business Administration, Captain Willard P. Fuller. He understood thoroughly the means for securing a scientific distribution of the incoming mail. He arranged a chart which showed the distributors exactly to which section any kind of inquiries should be sent. In each one of the sub-sections separate distributing desks were established, so that all mail could promptly reach its proper destination. It seems like a simple thing now, but as a matter of fact there had been little time to develop a proper organization for the office during the period of its phenomenally rapid growth.

When I first saw the division, in May, 1917, its work was being performed by one officer and half a dozen clerks. It seems incredible that Captain Lippincott should have been able to receive callers as well as run the office and dictate letters. He worked nights and Sundays. The rapid growth of the office and the tremendous increase in the amount of mail soon snowed him under. Greatly handicapped by lack of space and lack of trained assistants, it soon became almost impossible to handle the volume of business that was coming in. To add to these difficulties, there were constantly increasing demands on the part of congressmen and other government officials that their friends receive special and speedy attention.

My first month at his old desk was like a nightmare. It will be remembered that it was in the middle of December that the new draft law went into effect, so as to prevent any further voluntary enlistment of those within the draft age. As the date approached, our callers became more numerous, until they reached more than 500 per day. Had it not been for the yeoman's service rendered by Lieutenant Walter Tufts, we should have been completely overwhelmed. Applications for non-flying commissions rapidly increased. During the week ending December 6 there were only 80; during the week ending December 13 they rose to 1500; and the following week there were almost as many.

During the first week in December we received 2700 applications from would-be pilots who had made up their minds to take their chances as aviators rather than as soldiers in the draft army. In the week ending December 19 we received 2900 applications for flying commissions, but the following week, after the day of voluntary enlistment was passed, applications, although still permissible, fell to 1100; and to 700 in the week after that. Many of these last applications, however, came from soldiers already in uniform.

The growth of the Air Service, during the four months in which I was familiar with the details of the Air Personnel Division, went from a total of about 30,000 enlisted men on the 20th of November, 1917, to 126,000 on the 21st of March, 1918. About the first of December, General Squier had said to me that it looked as though the difficulties of securing enough planes and motors had been solved, but

that we were not going to have enough personnel to take
care of them. Consequently we made a strenuous drive during the first two weeks of December so as to attract into
the enlisted ranks of the Air Service as many skilled mechanics as possible before they should be caught in the draft
and assigned to some branch of the service that might not
appeal to them as strongly as ours. As a result of this drive,
we gained about 50,000 recruits. Captain Clayton Dubosque
was largely responsible for this. His training in publicity
work was of great value.

In the mean time I had made every possible effort to secure more space for our hard-working staff. This resulted
in our being transferred to a large loft in the building occupied by the Union Garage. Here we had space enough,
to be sure, but the fumes and poisonous gases that came up
from the garage caused severe headaches and greatly reduced the efficiency of the staff. Meantime, the other sections of the Air Division had moved to the Barrister Building,
which further increased the difficulty of operation. About
this time, in order to enable quicker action to be taken, the
Personnel Section of the Air Division was made a separate
division under the title of Air Personnel Division, in the office of the Chief Signal Officer of the Army.

Notwithstanding the fact that every time we moved we
lost at least two days, due to confusion and the necessity
of getting settled in new quarters, it was determined shortly
before Christmas to move again, this time into the old
post-office building on K Street near the railroad station.

This proved to be most satisfactory. Here we had three entire floors—plenty of room and light, comparative quiet, and freedom from the noises and odors of the garage. Offices were established on the ground floor for giving special attention to visitors. It was found necessary, also, to establish under the very able direction of Captain (later Lieutenant-Colonel) John B. Reynolds a branch to handle the constantly increasing correspondence and inquiries made by members of Congress and other government officials. It was believed, however, that the resulting freedom from interruption that was thus granted to the heads of all other branches in the office enabled our work to be carried on much more expeditiously and efficiently. Colonel W. E. Gilmore as Executive Officer of the Division was a tower of strength in meeting and solving difficult points. Colonel Harry Bull kept an eagle eye on the candidates and accomplished wonders in eliminating undesirables.

A few more highly paid, thoroughly experienced clerks were obtained under special dispensation, and the work of training our clerical personnel for their particular tasks and seeing to it that misfits were avoided wherever possible was given special consideration. The files, which were increasing at an astounding rate, were still far from satisfactory. Accordingly, an expert and twelve assistants were put on a night shift with orders to make a thorough and comprehensive examination of all the files. As a result, hundreds of errors that had occurred during the days of confusion and congestion were discovered and corrected. It became possible to reduce the number of filing clerks and at the same time secure greater rapidity of service, so that by the first of March one could secure the papers of any individual in less than two minutes.

In order to reduce the causes of friction with the Adjutant-General's office and other divisions of the War Department, including the various branches of the Air Service itself, a number of officers were designated as Liaison Officers, whose duty it was to make daily visits to the various officers with whom we had dealings, listen to their complaints, and work out methods of improving the service.

A weekly meeting was held of the chiefs of all sections. Reports were presented and results were shown on graphic charts prepared by Captain Fuller and hung on the walls of my office. Competition between the different sections was keen. Due to the lack of familiarity with army regulations and also to the constant changes brought about by new decisions, it was found expedient to establish an Authorities Section, to which copies of all letters containing decisions and new policies were sent. Thanks to the skill and devotion of Captain Hamilton Hadley, it soon became possible for the officers and clerks of the division to submit here all doubtful points and learn the established rules and procedure.

When I became Chief of the Air Personnel Division, about 7500 candidates for flying commissions had passed the aviation examining boards and been accepted for training. Under the able direction of Major John B. Watson and Captain C. C. Little, we established aviation examining boards at most of the great concentration camps and in thirty-two of the principal cities of the country. They were able to examine about 2500 candidates a week. The work of the examining boards was found to be very uneven. For instance, the board in Omaha would be rejecting, say, twenty-five per cent of all applicants, while that in Boston would be rejecting sixty per cent. It was found necessary to give the Examining Boards Section of the office a sufficient staff to enable the boards to be inspected and their work constantly correlated and compared, so as to approach a uniform standard as far as possible.

The board which had the most pressing and difficult problems was the Washington board. Here Major William Larned, Major Robert Wren, and later Major William J. Malone toiled and strove with all possible tact and judgment to unravel knotty problems.

During the next four months the number accepted for training increased to 19,500; a large proportion of these had been sent to the ground schools, and 2000 had been taught to fly and been recommended for commission. These figures will give a little idea of the amount of work that had to be transacted in our office, where the orders were issued and records filed. As a matter of fact, it kept 50 officers and 250 clerks very busy six days in the week and quite a number of them on Sundays as well. Undoubtedly many mistakes occurred because of the amount of work that had to be placed in inexperienced hands. Every effort was made to expedite routine. "Passing the buck" was eliminated as far as possible.

Speaking of this ancient game in which a piece of work or any other disagreeable duty is passed from one person to another in such a manner "that the smallest possible portion of the work or duty is accomplished and the identity of the person whose duty it is to do it is hidden from the person interested in having it done," the following article which came to my desk in France from an anonymous source in the summer of 1918 may prove of interest to those who have suffered, and will certainly arouse sympathy among many who have endeavored to get something accomplished:

"PASSING THE BUCK"

The claim often advanced by American enthusiasts that the game originated in the United States is not founded on fact. The game is as old as history and as widespread as geography.

Wherever and whenever it originated, its development and perfection in the United States have made it to all intents and purposes an American game, as inseparably American as chewing-gum itself. Introduced into America in early Colonial times, the game won immediate and lasting popularity among all classes, but its greatest impetus came from its semi-official adoption in Government circles as the National Indoor Sport. Its growth has been as steady and as rapid as the increase in population, except in the District of Columbia where the population has n't been able to keep up. In no other country of the world is the game played by so many people, or with such great skill and daring.

Army Regulations and the Quartermaster's Manual are the two principal rule books of the game. A careful study of them will give the beginner a fairly good understanding of this fascinating sport. Besides these, there are many other rules, some of which will be found on the backs of the numerous forms used in the game, but most of which have never been printed. New rules are being made every day to cope with the new duties and labors that come with war. The official umpires are the Auditor for the War Department and the Comptroller of the Treasury. They are seldom appealed to except to umpire big league games, but their services are available to all players, from the newest beginner to the most skilled.

It is impossible to give in this short space anything like a complete description of the game, or even a comprehensive summary of the rules. There are, however, certain general principles and a few rules that must be observed in counting points, and which may profitably be mentioned here.

First of all, the new employee should bear well in mind that rendering service to the public, or trying in any way to please it, is not a part of the game. New employees entering the service from civil life often bring with them a fund of enthusiasm of this nature that is difficult to control. This enthusiasm takes the form of an insane desire on their part to make themselves useful and agreeable to the general public with which they come into contact, and to their fellow employees. This is a thing most studiously to be avoided. Its harmful effects are threefold. It counts against the player himself in the game; it spoils the game for other more experienced players; and it stores up trouble for the new player against the time when constant floundering in the meshes of red tape will have choked from him the last gasp of whatever splendid enthusiasm he may once have had.

When there are ten or more players in the game, and the buck is passed to each and by each, in turn, until it makes a complete circle, and then is thrown aside without any actual work having been accomplished, a perfect score is said to have been made, and everybody gets a hundred.

Although there are many notable cases of new players having been conspicuously successful from the start, the finished players are, for the most part, men who have been long in the service and grown up with the game. The present generation owes them a great deal. The skill of some of them is such that they count their perfect scores by dozens, and even by hundreds. It is said that the man who com-

piled the Quartermaster's Manual was voted a life championship
certificate, and then permanently disqualified from further competition in amateur games on the ground that he had become professional. It was feared that if he continued to compete in amateur
games his phenomenal success might discourage other players from
putting forth their best efforts. This would cause a lagging of interest that might bring about the death of the game and drag Government work down to the level of ordinary business procedure.

Every one who could do so was glad to escape from the
"meshes of red tape." At the beginning of the war our swords
were sharp and we could cut red tape freely, but as time
went on, the necessity for playing according to rule increased, and we had to make some ourselves!

Apart from the difficulties of organizing and operating an
office which utilized the services of so many officers and clerks
who had had no army experience, our greatest difficulty lay
in the fact that the General Staff had failed to prepare an
adequate programme or set down in advance suitable rules
for our guidance, and adequate tables of organization. About
the middle of February we received a memorandum from
the Air Division stating that fifty thousand more enlisted
mechanics would be required for air squadrons during the
next six or seven months. A determined effort to secure these
resulted in our exceeding the specific official authorizations
made by the General Staff. It was apparently understood by
the officers of the Air Division that the General Staff would
increase these authorizations as fast as necessary, but I believe it was ultimately found imperative to transfer a considerable number of our men to other branches of the service.

In order to get things done promptly, it was frequently necessary to go far beyond what had been authorized and approved. Oral indications of the desires of the Chief Signal Officer, and intelligent guesswork, had to be relied upon to a great extent. The work could not have been done had it not been for the splendid enthusiasm of officers like Lieutenant Geroid Robinson, Captain Julian Ripley, Major Fickel, Major Litchfield, and Major C. B. Cameron, who brought all the experience they had gained in their previous occupations as men of business or professional men, and with it a willingness to work early and late, Sundays and holidays, with the sole desire of getting everything possible done to promote the air programme.

While most of the work was a steady grind of routine, there came through the mail occasional flashes of humor that were passed around to cheer up every one in the office. Here is a sample reproduced verbatim except that the names are changed:

SA-VOY CAFE

New York, 1917

WAR DEPARTMENT,
    WASHINGTON, DC.

GENTLEMEN: —

receive your letter some time ago and papers which to sign but as i were going to sign i dropped a bottle of ink on it, and so i am asking you to forward me another one also gentlman i wishes to ask you by reading the letter you state that i have to have three years of recognized university and a theoretical knowledge of or practical experience with internal combustion engines so i wishes to say that

if any man that wanted to join the aviation section will have to learn
so i only asked senator —— to recommend me to you so which he
did and which i thank him for doing so. also if i can do any thing for
this govment i will be glad to do so but if i can not get in there i
wish you would be kind enough to please give me the best position
so please give me a position before they go to conscrip before i would
be conscriped i would go to the army so please do so at once.

yours

SAJED N. LOOMID

I am an american born syrion
i am five feet and six inc.
   i weight at about one hundred & fourtyfive
   i have went high as the sixthgreade but have
   a verry good education also i have a verry good
   and smart mind and am verry healthy young man in
   every reform so what else a man must have.

Here is another one that gave us courage and cheered us on
our way:

Richmond, Va.
October 11, 1917

GENTLEMEN:

   To who it may consern.

   I Sam Jones, *wishes* to know what chances you will give me in the
aviation corps. I wont something that will let me fly in France after
6 moths in school none of This America stuff. My teeth are not in
so bad condition that is my lower ones, But my uper ones are false
will you Please give spacial Permition my health is fine everything
except my teeth. I stand 5′ 8″ waight 143. Penn. Birth and nerve
enuff To fight a Bull dog with both hands tied behind me nerves fine,
eye sight splendid.

I remane

Your ever,

S. J.

The enthusiasm to get into the Air Service was general throughout the country. Woe betide the unfortunate Aviation Examining Board which declined the application of a youth whose father or whose uncle was locally of political importance. Some senators, like my classmate, "Jim" Wadsworth, regularly declined to interfere with the routine decisions of examiners; others were continually calling, writing, or telephoning in regard to the cases of "sons of our best families" who for some reason or other were being thwarted in their commendable desire to fly in France.

Here is part of a letter that objected strenuously to the action of the Indianapolis Examining Board. It illustrates some of the difficulties in the correspondence that we had to carry on:

I certainly regret that the Indianapolis Board gave an unfavorable report upon my examination for I believe that I really am eligible to the above service, for several reasons, and I certainly do wish that you would permit me to be reëxamined.

. . . .

At no time have I ever noticed any forces other than balanced ones at work upon my body or intuition in any activity.

. . . .

My fainting has always been due to a mental shock I receive when I allow my mind to ponder upon pain.

. . . .

Please do allow me another trial for I certainly do feel that I can make it.

Occasionally proposals of another sort got into our mailbag and had to be passed along to the technical experts.

There was, for example, this plan for disguising our submarines and enabling their work of discovering enemy submarines to proceed more successfully:

By using a hull, shaped exactly like a whale composed of inner steel lining, outside wood casing, and a rubber covering, with power furnished by a submarine that is *fastened underneath*, with jaws that open and close and which is an inlet for water that is later on forced out of the blow hole on the whales head, this being done with the aid of a force pump.

The eyes are fitted with strong lenses, while the nostrils are made on the pattern of conical shutters, and which can dialate instantly to allow the sending of a torpedo. Then by using a storage battery and motor of good strength and with a gyroscopic rudder, a torpedo could be given a definite course; and be able to travel a far greater distance.

As a rule, however, most of our callers were concerned with the disaster that had overtaken them or their friends in not being able to pass certain "unimportant" examinations.

Captain Reynolds, who received many of our callers, had many trying experiences, but his tact and courtesy were unfailing. He saw many people at their worst. He was sometimes roundly abused by influential visitors who failed to have the rules altered or overlooked in their favor. But there were no complaints of unfair treatment or favoritism. Captain Victor Henderson and Lieutenant Avery Tompkins also were of invaluable assistance in smoothing out difficulties.

DANGER OF LANDING WITH WIND — RESULTS OF OVERSHOOTING

Information Dept
30 AVE AveXX
France

CHAPTER VII

OVERSEAS

ON February 18, 1918, there came a cable from General Pershing which contained the following paragraph:

Urgently request that at least 12 experienced administrative and executive officers be sent to France within the next six weeks to assist in organization and training of air service personnel in France, England and Italy.

Feeling that the work of reorganizing the Air Personnel Division, which had been given me three months previously, had been virtually completed, so that my services could perfectly well be spared at this time without in the slightest degree interfering with the progress of that department, I wrote on February 25 to General Squier, asking to be selected as one of the twelve officers to be sent to France "within the next six weeks." My request was favorably considered, and after the twelve names had been chosen and sent to France for approval and a cable received directing that the twelve be sent immediately, I was given my orders in the last week in March and immediately left for Hoboken.

The trip across on the Aquitania was interesting as a study in psychology. She was at that time almost the largest ship on any ocean, and a fairly good target for a submarine. It was her first voyage with American troops, and there were rumors that the Germans were going to make a special effort to spoil it. When we got about half-way over, we began to follow an extremely irregular course, zigzagging at frequent intervals day and night, so as to make it difficult for a submarine to figure out where we would be at a given moment and lie in wait for us at that point. This zigzagging had an interesting result. One night when the sea was running rather high, we had frequently to proceed in the trough of the sea. This caused an amount of rolling which had not been at all anticipated when the Aquitania was constructed, and for which no provision had been made by securely screwing down all tables and chairs. As it was, we woke up to hear a terrific amount of noise. It was occasioned by tables, chairs, trunks, boxes, anything in fact that was not rigidly fastened down, rolling about on the decks and in the staterooms. The adjutant's office just over my cabin was nicely wrecked by tumbling typewriters!

As we approached the active submarine zone, we were warned to have our life-preservers always at hand, never to appear without them, and to sleep in our clothes. There was a certain amount of excitement visible on all faces that evening. The next morning, when a loud explosion occurred at dawn and the ship trembled violently and there was a sound of breaking glass, followed by several shots from the ship's guns, we all supposed that we had been struck by a torpedo. It appeared, however, that the unusual noise and concussion were caused by one of our own six-inch guns firing at a periscope, or what the gun crew and the guard watch believed to be a periscope, which suddenly appeared alongside the steamer and only a few feet away. The concussion from the shot, which passed very close to the port bulwarks, was sufficient to blow in sheets of plate-glass three-eighths of an inch thick in the cabins on that side.

Colonel Butts, of the 2d Division, who slept in one of these cabins and who supposed, as did every one that was aroused by the shot, that we had been attacked by a submarine, told me that his first thought was of wonder as to how his regiment (none of whom had ever been under fire) would take their first experience. Others said their first thought was of extreme anger. A distinguished civilian whose diplomatic duties had forced him to cross several times during the war, and who had become more hardened to submarine attacks than the rest of us, said his first thought was of the intense coldness of the water and the "very unpleasant" idea that he would soon be shivering in the icy waves!

We landed in Liverpool on April 11 after a fairly exciting passage in which we fired some fifty or sixty rounds at what were supposed to be periscopes. The chief result of our firing, so far as I could learn, was to irritate the captains of four or five destroyers which were convoying us during the last three days of our journey, and which had several narrow escapes from our shells.

In Liverpool the children on the streets looked fairly well fed. The dock laborer did not appear to take the war too seriously. A few days before, notwithstanding the extremely critical situation in France (the great German spring drives began in the latter part of March), he had insisted on tak-

ing his three days' Easter holiday as though nothing were
happening. The bill of fare at the hotels was very meagre,
however, and we were unable to get any meat, since we were
transients and had no meat cards.

In London it was the same way, only there the war was
felt much more keenly. Children showed the effects of the
shortage of butter and milk. Some of our friends were particularly hard hit. It made one's heart ache. Yet on the channel boats from Southampton to Havre there was abundance
of everything, including meat and bread.

I landed at Havre on April 14, and discovered that my
confidential order from the War Department to "Report
by wire to the Commanding General, etc.," was a joke
played on all casual officers who went overseas. One or two
had actually attempted to make their presence known to
General Pershing, with somewhat unsatisfactory results!
The great majority of us meekly consented to being ordered
by the very polite first lieutenant, who met us here, to proceed *via* Paris to Blois.

In Paris the daily bombardment by Big Bertha was going
on and causing great congestion in south-bound trains.
While there was neither butter nor sugar at the hotels, there
did not appear to be a shortage of anything else. Bread cards
were coming into use, but were not as rigidly demanded as
a few months later. It was an interesting commentary on
the food habits of the two nations that while meat tickets
were required in England, none were needed in France.
On the other hand, in Paris bread tickets were in use while

none were necessary in London. Travellers who remember
the delicious "roast beef of Old England" and the surpass-
ing delicacy of French rolls will need no further explanation.

The picturesque old town of Blois with its charming historical chateaux and its winding hilly streets on the banks
of the Loire was the scene of more heart-burning, so far as
the American Army was concerned, than any other spot in
France. In the first place, here were gathered hundreds of
casual officers of all ranks who had come over, many of
them by "request received in special cable from General
Pershing" to do definite and "very important" work, with
high hopes of being able immediately to take their share
in bringing this war to a triumphant close. Here they suddenly found themselves herded together with others equally
unfortunate in an unimportant town far from G. H. Q. —
still farther from the front line trenches, and at quite a considerable distance from any of the important posts to which
they were so anxious to be sent.

A few received welcome orders to proceed elsewhere and
report on a real job after they had been here only three or
four days. There were many others who could sympathize
with the young Lieutenant in the Sanitary Corps, an important specialist in some branch of Army Sanitation who
had been "specially cabled for," and who, when I saw him,
had been in Blois nearly six weeks doing nothing. He was
standing in the lovely old garden of the Bishop's palace
looking out toward the chateau of Chambord. In reply to
my question he murmured: "I was trying to discover if

there were any place within the radius of a day's walk that
I had not yet seen. You see I have to report at least once a
day for orders." It certainly gave one a helpless feeling to
be unexpectedly dumped into this reservoir. As a matter of
fact, General Pershing and his staff were drawing from it,
as fast as needed, officers required for different positions.

Blois also contained another and more serious group of
unfortunates, namely, those officers who had failed to make
good on the job to which they had been first assigned and
who had been sent back for reclassification. When one considers the fact that the United States was faced with the necessity of commissioning several thousand officers after
only three months' intensive training in camps like Plattsburg, and that many men were graduated from those camps
with the rank of Captain of Field Artillery who had never
seen at close range a modern gun until a few weeks previous, it is small wonder that there were a goodly number who
failed to please the critical staff officers in the advanced
training area, or who failed to measure up to the requirements of rapidly changing tactics at the Front. So far as
one could judge, there was no partiality. Efficiency was the
only watchword, and it made no difference whether an officer was a member of the regular permanent establishment,
a national guardsman, or a recently appointed reserve officer. If he failed to satisfy those who were held responsible
for his performances, he was quickly relegated to Blois.
Naturally his presence here did not conduce to the cheer-
fulness of the historic town, but—thanks to an enlightened

policy which has been described as "salvaging human material"—he was in most cases speedily fitted into another job which the Classification Board decided was better suited to his capacity. A few were sent home.

It is not a pleasant sight, however, to see forty or fifty "failures" gathered together to come before an "Efficiency Board," and this undoubtedly added to the anxiety of the recently arrived casual officers. To be sure, a few of the younger ones were kept busy drilling replacement troops and casuals just out of the hospital, but most of us, after having walked through the Chateau three or four times and having exhausted our ingenuity in attempting to get word to General Pershing that in accordance with his cabled request we had arrived, found the time hang rather heavily on our hands.

At last, however, the orders came for me to go to Tours, which was at that time the headquarters of the "S. O. S."— Services of Supply, known at various times by the names of Lines of Communication or Service of the Rear. Here we found that it was so many weeks or months since we had been cabled for that "they" had in the interim forgotten just what it was we were particularly wanted for. Furthermore, the plan of campaign had altered materially, due to the inability of the French airplane manufacturers to deliver the planes needed for service at the Front. Consequently it was necessary to "have patience for a few days more." Meanwhile I heard some sad stories and began to realize how low the morale of many of our aviators had fallen.

CHAPTER VIII

THE DISADVANTAGES OF BEING A PILOT

TWO or three weeks before the first class graduated from the ground schools, word had come by cable from Air Service representatives in France that they had been able to arrange with the French flying schools to take a considerable number of our graduates. A few weeks later we received the request to send across the ocean five hundred cadets a month for training in France, and were assured by cable that they would be able to take care of even more than this number. Acting on this information, and on other cables that reached us from time to time, we were able to offer to honor graduates of the ground schools the privilege of being immediately sent to France to receive training on the latest type of French planes. This offer, coupled with the natural desire of every young man to get to France as soon as possible, and the fact that the new American flying schools in the United States were slow in getting under way, and inadequately provided with airplanes, added tremendous zest to the work in the ground schools. Experienced teachers at Cornell and elsewhere assured me that the amount of work which these new students were able to do in a few weeks and the amount of knowledge and skill they were able to acquire was a perfect revelation. Never before had any attempt been made to teach so much in so short a time. Never before had it been assumed that the *average* student would work ten hours a day and would strive to his utmost to be included in the upper ten of the class. Never before

Issoudun: Field 8
Over the fields in the distance two thousand American pilots learned the tactics of aerial combat

had there been such powerful incentives to succeed in the classroom and the laboratory. On the other hand, never had there been such keen disappointment awaiting those who failed on a second attempt to pass a single examination. Every one worked with an intense devotion to the matter in hand. The fortunate ones who graduated with honors, as the result of almost unparalleled student industry, were sent rejoicing to the port of embarkation.

Later on, as the cables called for more cadets, entire graduating classes were despatched to France. In the latter part of October we were told that we must send at least six hundred a month overseas. By this time our own flying schools were getting into shape to receive more than we could send them, but it was insisted that the greatest need and the greatest opportunity lay in the flying schools of France. So our graduates were rushed to Garden City and Hoboken as fast as they could pass the final examinations. Here the rushing stopped.

Due to the ramifications of red tape, the necessity of securing satisfactory certificates of typhoid inoculation, cumbersome methods of shipping service records, and the general inability of the War Department to expand suddenly from the requirements of a generation of comparative peace to the demands of a World War, there were weeks of delay at the port of embarkation in sending over the first few hundred cadets. Hence there was lost some of the precious summer and fall which might have been used to great advantage on French flying fields. Added to this was an extraordinarily long period of bad weather in the fall of 1917, which prevented the usual amount of flying, and which interfered with the progress of our own new flying school at Issoudun. Meanwhile, General Squier was not kept well informed of the actual progress of the training programme in France and had to act on meagre cables.

About December first an entirely unexpected cable came like a bolt out of the blue, directing that no more cadets be sent to France until further notice. The sailing orders of perhaps two hundred and fifty cadets were immediately cancelled, and everybody was kept in suspense for several weeks, until it appeared that the plans for rapid training in France had completely broken down, and that no more cadets were to be sent abroad for many months to come. As a matter of fact, no more were ever sent until after they had passed their preliminary flying tests, and as Reserve Military Aviators earned the right to wear wings, and the bars of a Lieutenant.

Never did a bright, iridescent soap-bubble burst more disappointingly. Nothing that I know of in the war caused more mental suffering or greater loss of morale than the failure to provide properly for the honor graduates who went to France as cadets. As I remember it, about eighteen hundred cadets had been sent to France with the understanding that they were to receive immediate instruction in foreign flying schools. When they arrived there and found themselves confined for months at a time in concentration and mobilization camps far from sight or hearing of an airplane, forced to study over and over again the very subjects which they had mastered with so much enthusiasm at American ground schools, treated by despairing officers as though they were "draft dodgers" who needed military discipline and who deserved reprobation rather than sympathy, their souls were filled with bitterness and their minds with evil thoughts against the War Department in general, and those officers in particular who commanded them in France. Some of these cadets had no opportunity to receive flying instruction for *six months* after they reached France. It has been well said that the greatest tragedy of youth is being obliged to wait. When in addition to the necessity of waiting is added a burning sense of injustice due to lack of faith and failure to keep promises, the result is truly appalling.

There was worse to come, however, for in the spring of 1918 there began to arrive in France as First Lieutenants, wearing wings, and speedily to be placed in positions of authority, the very classmates of these unfortunate cadets, who had not been quite keen enough to graduate with honor from the ground schools, had accordingly been sent to American flying schools, received their preliminary training, passed their tests as Reserve Military Aviators, received their commissions, and been sent abroad in response to other cables asking for a certain number of flying officers. It was hard enough to have to wait weeks and months for one's flying training, but it was adding insult to injury when, as a cadet with the rank of Private, First Class, and the status of an enlisted candidate for commission, you had respectfully to salute and take orders from these young officers whom you had passed in the race, months before, thanks to your own diligence and hard work. And there was the added bitterness that when you finally received your commission, you would still be outranked, due to the priority of their commissions.

Feeling as keenly as I did about this terrific disappointment that had been the lot of the earliest and most brilliant graduates of the ground schools, I made every effort when I arrived in France in the spring of 1918 to try and discover who was responsible for the hideous mistake, and why we had received no warning before that cable of the first of December. But I never obtained any satisfaction on these points. So far as I could learn then, no one person, but rather a series of events, was at the bottom of the trouble.

To our first representatives who went abroad in the late spring and early summer of 1917, the French airplane manufacturers (naturally anxious to be as obliging as possible) had optimistically promised a large number of airplanes both for training and fighting purposes, to be delivered at the rate of about one thousand per month. Their hopes were vain, and their promises were not carried out. Some of the raw material which they had counted on was sunk by Hun submarines; some of it was diverted to our own programme of building in this country. Perhaps, also, our representatives had not properly discounted the natural optimism of manufacturers anxious to obtain huge American contracts. So far as I could learn unofficially, at a time when we should have been in receipt of seven thousand airplanes, we had received about one thousand. As a matter of fact, it was not until June, 1918, that the deliveries began to come anywhere near our demands and expectations. Then, of course, planes came through faster than we could use them, and caused another sudden dislocation of plans. But that is another story.

As so often happens, it takes "outsiders" to see what is the matter with a factory. The men who have been conscientiously trying to make it run become blinded to conditions which an outsider, called in to criticise, sees at first glance. Accordingly, it was not strange that when General Foulois and his large staff of Air Service officers arrived in France in November, 1917, they at once saw things in a new light. Before many days they came to the conclusion that no more cadets ought to be sent to France. Hence, the cable of December first.

In the mean time, enormous damage had been done to the morale of the cadets. The problem of caring for the eighteen hundred who were on hand demanding flying instruction was one that required earnest consideration for many months to come. As has been stated, the difficulties were intensified by an unusually bad winter. Furthermore, the French system of training, which we were forced to adopt, was not nearly as rapid as the English system or our own. The preliminary training plane in general use in France was the old-fashioned Caudron, which has no ailerons and no fuselage. In order to fly it you have to warp the wings, a process requiring a considerable amount of exertion and a very heavy hand. Rough landings can be made almost with impunity. The ship will not dive fast. It is in general a very safe old "bus," resting on long skids and having no wheels. It flies at low speed, can be landed almost anywhere without crashing, and is very amusing to one accustomed to modern planes. It was the type of plane used by Vedrines when he made his sensational landing on top of a department store in Paris in the spring of 1919.

All of these things mean that, in our opinion, it was not nearly so well adapted to teach preliminary flying as the Curtiss JN-4 or the English Avro. When one considers that the next step in advanced flying, after having mastered the Caudron, was to learn to fly a Nieuport, which is almost the exact opposite of a Caudron, it seems as though the French officers who designed this system had purposely made it as difficult as possible. Instead of being slow on the controls like the Caudron, the Nieuport is extremely sensitive to handle. It will dive with great rapidity. It is difficult to land, and bad landings cannot be made with impunity. For example, on Field No. 2 at Issoudun — where advanced students received their first instructions in flying a Nieuport, using the Nieuport 23-meter, dual control, with an experienced teacher in the front seat — eighty-three machines were put out of commission on the landing-field in two days of fine weather in May, 1918. As I remember it, the four remaining machines did not last long on the next day. To be sure, the cause for this amazing casualty list was an entire lack

Nieuport 80, 23-meter, 80 *H.P. Le Rhone motor*

Avro, 110 *H.P. Le Rhone motor*

of wind and the tendency of the Nieuport to make a *cheval-de-bois*, or spin around on the ground as in an old-fashioned square dance. When there is a little wind, it is fairly easy to keep the Nieuport rolling straight ahead, as it loses speed after landing, but when there is no wind to assist the beginner in maintaining steerage-way, a *cheval* is difficult to avoid. Since the Nieuport had no wing skids and since it was very difficult to adjust suitable skids to the bottom of the single "V"-shaped strut, this tendency to *cheval* was continually causing the breakage of lower wings.

Many of the pilots declared that it was like learning to fly all over again when one went from a slow-going, safe old bus like the Caudron to the fast, delicate, tricky Nieuport. Men who had been trained to fly on the Curtiss JN-4 made much better progress, and those who received their first instructions on an Avro went even faster. Our cadets in France in the winter of 1917–18, however, had to depend upon receiving their first instruction on Caudrons. Furthermore, some of the cadets who left New York in November, 1917, had no opportunity even to get into a Caudron before June, 1918.

In the mean time, the Secretary of War had been to France and become personally acquainted with the woes of these unfortunate candidates for commissions. As a result of his visit, those cadets who had not yet passed their flying tests were commissioned in May and June, these commissions being conditioned on their eventually being able to fly, and subject to cancellation in case they did not succeed. This relieved the situation so far as pay and rank were concerned, but it did not actually hasten their arrival at the Front. The goal for which they had worked so hard in those strenuous days in the ground schools in the summer of 1917, namely, the opportunity to get into squadrons and fly over the lines, was still far away.

Then there came another blow, which seemed directed at what little vanity remained, and intended to destroy whatever satisfaction they might feel in having at last become officers. In common with all other student officers in France, they were forbidden to wear the insignia of an officer while in a training camp. As most of them were faced with the necessity of spending several months longer in attending the courses in advanced and specialized flying, this seemed almost like taking all the pleasure out of life. To be given a commission and then told you could not wear the insignia connected with it was like giving candy to children and telling them they could not eat it.

There were several reasons for this decision on the part of G. H. Q. In the first place, it had been the custom in the Officers Training Camps at home for officers who held reserve commissions and had been sent to these camps to receive further instruction to remove their student insignia as long as they were student officers. In the second place, many of the cadets were very unmilitary, and it was believed that it would be easier to secure adequate military discipline if the students did not obviously outrank the instructor sergeants who were giving lessons. In the third place, there

was a story that what finally brought about the issuance of
the order was an occurrence in one of the advanced schools
of the staff or the line. It seems that a number of field officers arrived to take the course. An efficient young second
lieutenant who had been at the Front for several months
attempted to take them in charge and have them march in
an orderly manner to their barracks. To this the colonels and
majors made amused protest and decided to go along as they
pleased, feeling that it was not necessary to take orders in
this manner from a second lieutenant. Consequently, in order
to enable the efficient but youthful instructors to accomplish
their ends with greater facility and less embarrassment to
themselves and to their students, the general order was issued
that student officers would remove insignia while in school;
an order which our young pilots felt was directed particularly against them.

In the course of time this was changed, but in the mean
while, although it probably was of assistance in maintaining
discipline, it did not help to cheer up the student officers of
the Air Service. To be sure, in itself it was only a little thing,
but coming as it did on top of so many other indignities and
disappointments, it was felt very keenly.

The loss of morale that followed in the wake of cadet
delays and disappointments showed itself in a number of
ways, which in turn reacted on the fortunes of the un-
happy flying officers. The sentries at the gate of one of the
flying schools would stop young officers with the irritating
question: "Are you an officer or a flying lieut?"

Some of the pilots had been so badgered and tormented by their superior officers that they no longer desired to be good soldiers. Some instructors maintained that many of their students did not wish to learn to fly, were afraid of the air, and were anxious to avoid its dangers. It was said that the students seized every opportunity to offer excuses for not flying. It was claimed on the part of the students that their teachers were often unsympathetic and even brutal in their attitude, and that it was impossible to do good work under such methods of instruction. The truth was that officers in charge of flying, working under a great strain, sometimes failed to take into consideration the reasons for this loss of morale and attributed it most unfeelingly to other causes. Undoubtedly there were serious instances of harsh treatment by instructors, occasioned by misconduct on the part of students, but causing in their turn still further lowering of morale and loss of interest in the Air Service.

Another disappointed hope was that of becoming Junior Military Aviators. The boys used to refer to the printed statements that on completing the R. M. A. test, the pilots would be commissioned First Lieutenants, and that on completing the more difficult J. M. A. test, the pilots would secure an advance in grade and 50 per cent increase in pay. There were very few of the thousands of young men that came into the Air Service during the first few months of the war that did not expect to be Captains before very long, provided they could learn to fly at all. This was *one* of the

reasons why they volunteered to undergo the most dangerous training of any branch of the army. Having enlisted in
the Signal Enlisted Reserve Corps, and having started on
the aviation road, there was nothing for them to do but swal-
low their disappointment when, as the months went on, they
discovered that most of them were destined to be Second
Lieutenants, and that they were never to be allowed to take
the J. M. A. test and secure additional rank and pay as contemplated by Congress and set forth in the original official
bulletins.

This disappointment was a source of constant grumbling
and complaint and the cause of many accusations of breach
of faith and unfair dealing. No business organization which
failed so glaringly to keep faith with its employees could expect to have their loyalty. It was certainly most unfortunate
that the unwisdom of promising so much rank and pay to
youthful, high-spirited boys of nineteen and twenty could
not have been foreseen earlier.

An immense amount of complaint was caused by the
necessity of arbitrarily setting a date which affected thousands of cadets who had been accepted as candidates for a
First Lieutenant's commission and were then undergoing
or awaiting training, and stating that if they graduated
or took their R. M. A. test after this date, they would automatically become Second Lieutenants. In a majority of cases
it was entirely beyond the control of the cadet as to what
date he should graduate. In many cases injustice was unavoidable. The consequent lowering of morale due to in-

fection and contagion from the disappointed and disaffected aviators was very natural.

There were other causes of dissatisfaction: the amount of power, rank, and promotion given to non-flying officers; the slowness of promotion among flying officers; the unwillingness of the army to provide a comfortable blouse for the pilot; and the failure on the part of the army to realize that different standards of work and discipline should be expected of a highly technical and purely voluntary service like aviation, where individual initiative and high morale are so necessary. It would seem obvious that in no branch of the service should more attention be given to preparing carefully thought-out plans which it will not be necessary to change in such a way as to destroy confidence and hope. Changes that disappoint and hurt the feelings of those whose morale must be built up should be avoided at all costs. Everything should be done to make the young pilots glad they belong to such a keen corps instead of being sorry, as so many of them were, that they had ever been misled into joining the Army Air Service.

The story of the flying cadets is the worst page in the history of the Air Service. They were forced by a combination of circumstances, over which no one seemed to have any control, to suffer serious and exasperating delays, disappointments, and "raw deals," which tended to break their spirit and destroy their self-respect. Notwithstanding this, the great majority of them completed their training and performed such duties as were assigned to them to the best of their knowledge and ability. It should not be forgotten that their sufferings were due fundamentally to the blind unpreparedness with which we drifted into war.

CHAPTER IX

THE PERSONNEL OFFICE IN TOURS

ON the last day of April, 1918, I was designated as Chief of Personnel for the Air Service, A. E. F., in which position I continued until August 23 of the same year. Air Service Headquarters in Tours were located at Beaumont Barracks, which had only recently been completed for the use of French Cavalry, but had never been occupied until it was leased by the American Expeditionary Forces. It was by far the pleasantest of any of the barracks used in Tours by the Services of Supply.

At the time of my arrival a general reorganization in the Air Service in France was going on. In other words, they were doing what we had done so often at Washington — attempting to make the clothes fit the rapidly growing child. By the time the clothes were altered, the child had grown so much more that they were still too small. This particular reorganization was effected after several weeks of study on the part of a board composed of the most efficient Colonels on duty in the office of the Chief of Air Service. The general result was to give more responsibility and authority to the Section Chiefs, namely, the Chief of Training, Chief of Personnel, Chief of Supply, and Chief of Balloon. The Chief of Balloon also had under his jurisdiction the Information Section, the Photographic Section, and the Radio Section.

In general, the organization was well conceived and practicable. The feature of grouping Balloon, Radio, Photography, and Information under one head was satisfactory only because of the ability of Colonel Chandler, who filled this unique position. His long experience, even temperament, unfailing courtesy, and wide technical knowledge enabled him to give satisfaction in a position that probably would have brought disaster to any one else.

The chief stumbling-block to the success of the new plan lay in the fact that the sections could not all work in the same place. The Supply Section was obliged to be near the principal sources of supply, that is, the offices and factories of the French in Paris. The Personnel Section was obliged to be in Tours because all orders were issued by Headquarters S. O. S., located in Tours. The Training Section should have been at Chaumont, in close touch with the Training Section of the General Staff, in constant liaison with the activities at the Front, and able to reach all schools in the S. O. S. As a matter of fact, it was located so far away from the Front as to earn the adverse criticism of organizations at the Front and the distrust of the General Staff.

The Chief of Air Service, himself, found it necessary to spend a great deal of time on the road and to maintain three separate offices, one in Chaumont, one in Paris, and one in Tours. As a result, it was difficult to keep in touch with him, and many decisions had to be made either without consulting him or with inadequate information on his part. During the whole period of my stay in France, the necessity for the Chief of Air Service to be in three places at once militated very seriously against the success of our programme. The hopelessness of the situation would seem to emphasize the need of a different kind of organization. It was foolish to expect one man to fight for supply with the French and British Governments and manufacturers, to direct the movement and training of all personnel in such widely diverse activities as balloon, radio, photography, and flying, and at the same time be in charge of aerial activities at the Front, direct the movements and activities of the squadrons and companies in the zone of advance, and attend to the details of squadron organization.

The new scheme went into effect shortly before the first of May, but it did not last long. In the latter part of May, General Foulois was sent to take command of active operations at the Front and General Mason M. Patrick of the Engineer Corps, who had never been in the Air Service but had been in charge of the Division of Construction and Forestry, was made Chief of Air Service. There is a tradition in the army that any regular officer can take any army job, and General Patrick certainly justified this tradition. Notwithstanding his unfamiliarity with aviation and his belief that at his age he could give better service by travelling on the ground than in the air, he rapidly assimilated a thorough knowledge of the Air Service in the A. E. F. His remarkable memory and extraordinary capacity for the mastery of minute details enabled him in a very few weeks to secure a thorough grasp of the situation and to undertake a new reorganization.

His office memorandum No. 23 reorganized the duties of

the officer in charge of Air Personnel, and it explains better than anything else my duties as they were in the summer of 1918.

OFFICE OF THE CHIEF OF AIR SERVICE

Tours

OFFICE MEMORANDUM No. 23.

1. There will be an Officer in charge of Personnel, upon whom will rest the responsibility for providing the man power needed to carry out approved programs and estimates of needs furnished to him. The Chief of Personnel will have charge of the Personnel Section of the Office of the Chief of Air Service and of Air Service Replacement Concentration Barracks. He will be a member of the Strategic Section and will be furnished as far in advance as possible with copies of approved programs and estimates of personnel needs.

2. The Personnel Section has the following duties:—

(a) To procure and assign officers, cadets, candidates, enlisted men and civilian personnel, for the Air Service, and to coördinate and list requests for the same in their relative order of emergency.

(b) To keep track of all incoming personnel and to give destinations for it as long as possible in advance.

(c) To notify the Commanding Officer at the destination to which incoming troops are to be sent as far in advance as possible so that proper provision may be made for caring for such arrivals.

(d) To provide the requisite number of officers for all squadrons, particularly for those which are being sent to the front.

(e) To prepare plans for the distribution of these squadrons in accordance with the approved Air Service program.

(f) To request from proper authority orders for travel and change of station.

(g) To handle all correspondence relative to personnel and keep such records and files pertaining to Air Service personnel as may properly be kept in the Office of the Chief of Air Service.

(h) To keep a list of officers by rank, grade and occupation.

(*i*) To refer to properly constituted examining boards the names of approved candidates for flying training. To receive the reports of these examinations and review the action of the board before forwarding report to higher authority.

3. Air Service Replacement Concentration Barracks [St. Maxient] has the following duties:

(*a*) To classify all officers and men that may be sent there for duty.

(*b*) To complete the Quartermaster and Ordnance equipment of enlisted men passing through this station.

(*c*) To examine the organization of squadrons passing through the barracks, and see that these organizations conform as far as possible to that laid down in the approved tables of organization. To organize squadrons from available troops. To see that all squadrons passing through are provided with suitable ground officers, and in general act as the agent of the Personnel Section in organizing squadrons according to the plan of mobilization for squadrons as laid down by the Chief of Air Service.

(*d*) To maintain a ground school for aviation students in accordance with the program laid down by the Chief of Training, who will exercise direct supervision of the course of study, designate instructors, inspect the school, nominate a liaison officer who shall be a member of the staff of the Commanding Officer of the Barracks to represent the Chief of Training in all matters pertaining to the ground schools for aviation students.

(*e*) To maintain a ground officers' school for training adjutants, supply officers and engineering officers in accordance with program laid down by the Chief of Personnel who will exercise supervision of the course of study, nominate instructors and be responsible for the proper training of ground officers, and for providing such training for flying officers who have temporarily or permanently lost flying ability as will enable them to be useful for other than flying duty.

(*Signed*) MASON M. PATRICK,
Major General, N. A.
C. A. S.

To assist me in this undertaking there were in the Personnel Office in Tours some sixteen officers, and seventy-five enlisted men who acted as clerks; while at St. Maxient there was Colonel A. Lippincott, the commanding officer of the post, and his staff. All worked with unremitting energy to carry out the programme as laid down.

Of the difficulties that were due to lack of proper office equipment and scarcity of efficient stenographers, it is hardly necessary to speak, for they were not in any way confined to our office, but were well-nigh universal in the A. E. F. It was a pleasure to see how everybody strove to overcome all obstacles. Particular mention must be made of Captain Cleveland Cobb, whose careful attention to the details of the Officers' Section brought it to a high state of efficiency; Captain Hamilton Hadley, whose thorough familiarity with army regulations and the latest authorities oiled the wheels of our intercourse with other branches of the service; Lieutenant Walter Tufts, whose courtesy and tact in dealing with anxious visitors permitted the routine work of the office to proceed with a minimum number of interruptions; and Master Signal Electrician Walter Buchanan, whose long experience in the care of records and files made possible the smooth running of that machinery on which a personnel office depends so largely for its efficiency.

In my new position I had an opportunity to learn much about the kind of personnel in our squadrons. The enlisted personnel of the Air Service was remarkable for its high-grade technical ability and splendid devotion to duty. In the

face of many difficulties the enlisted men always showed a
willingness to accept disagreeable assignments as well as
to perform their regular duties at unusual hours that was
extremely praiseworthy. Many of them came from highly
paid trades, and a large number had enlisted expecting to
fly. The way they did their work and accepted the inevitable
was very fine. It was my observation that it would have been
difficult, if not impossible, to have secured better men. I believe that it was fortunate that enlistment in the Air Service was possible at a time when enlistments in most branches
of the army were forbidden. Consequently we had an opportunity to secure the more intelligent American mechanics.

I believe it would have been better had we earlier adopted
a plan whereby enlisted men above the grade of corporal
could have become candidates for non-flying commissions.
When an enlisted man had done extremely well, and was
anxious to fly, but was turned down by the doctor as being
physically unfit to be a pilot, there was no hope for him to
secure a commission in most cases, unless he left the service
in which he had received his training. Therefore it was
unfortunate that so many of the positions of Adjutant, Supply Officer, and Engineer Officer were given to men without
military experience. To have reserved a large number of
these places for enlisted candidates would have furnished an
additional incentive and stimulated competition. As would
be expected, however, our enlisted mechanics frequently
showed remarkable ingenuity and inventiveness. Some ef-

Two of our Best Squadrons

fort was made to procure from the enlisted personnel descriptions and drawings of their inventions and ideas.

In the Personnel Office we also saw and heard many things about the conduct of our cadets and even of our flying officers. It should be remembered that the cadets were, for the most part, drawn from among a class of young, irresponsible, venturesome, athletic boys, who were willing to take the risks of aviation training at a time when about four per cent of all advanced students were killed in training. They felt they were gambling with their lives whenever they went up. Had they had a greater sense of responsibility, it is doubtful whether many of them would have volunteered for flying duty. Consequently it is not to be wondered at that many of them committed indiscretions of conduct in public which brought upon them severe criticism. The fact that they wore wings or special white hatbands made them particularly conspicuous, and made it possible for the average person to identify them with the Air Service. Officers or candidates of other services could not be so readily identified by casual observers. The destruction of morale by the long period of disappointment and delay which most of the cadets encountered showed itself in an unsoldierly attitude toward military rules and discipline, which, while reprehensible, was not surprising. The noteworthy and remarkable thing is that so many of them did so well.

The same remarks apply to a large percentage of the flying officers. It was particularly hard for student flying officers to submit to the necessary discipline. I believe that

in the future it would be far better to postpone the actual commission of the pilot until his training is completed and he
is ready to take his place in a squadron.

Had the older flying officers of higher rank done more
flying, they could have raised the spirits and enthusiasm
of the younger men. It would be hard for a cavalry regiment to be commanded by a colonel who either did not
know how to ride horseback or who was afraid of a horse. It
is just as hard for a group of aviators to be commanded by
an officer who does not know how to fly or is afraid of the
air. It was most unfortunate that circumstances demanded
the presence in the Air Service of so many non-flying officers. I believe there should be no officers in the Air Service
who have not earned their wings, and are not willing and
ready to make frequent flights, either as pilots or observers.

It was also unfortunate that quite a proportion of the
non-flying officers sent to France had received little or no
military training, having been commissioned in the summer of 1917, before schools for non-flying officers with their
keen competition and stringent examinations were established. Some of these officers did well; while others, who
had no experience in handling men, were failures, as was
to be expected. I believe that in the future non-flying positions in the Air Service should be filled by former flyers or
by candidates from among the best enlisted men in the
squadrons, who, after being selected, should be required to
take thorough courses and pass strict and competitive examinations, both on the ground and in the air.

Feeling as I did about the necessity of having the older officers ready to assume at any time the risks of flying, I wanted to fly as much as possible myself. While on duty at Washington there had been no opportunity to fly after I passed my Reserve Military Aviator test. Some members of my family and many of my friends insisted that it was foolish for me to take the risks of flying when not required to do so by the nature of my work. After giving the matter considerable thought, I sent the following communication to the Chief of Air Service:

. . . .

. . . request to be allowed to use such time as can be spared from my duties as Chief of Personnel, without seriously interfering with the business of this office, in continuing my flying instruction which ended at Mineola last August with the passing of my R. M. A. test.

My principal reason for making this request is the belief that it is good policy for the older flying officers in the Air Service to keep up with their flying. It is believed that it is not beneficial for the morale of the Air Service that Field Officers, who are in charge of important parts of the Air Service program, should seldom ever fly themselves. It is believed to be just as important for the Field Officers in the Air Service to subject themselves to the ordinary risks of flying as it is for the Field Officers in the Infantry Regiments to subject themselves to the ordinary risks of trench warfare.

My request was approved, and whenever occasion offered I continued flying. I learned how to fly a Caudron and a 23-meter Nieuport, but it was difficult to fly regularly, and I had two crashes, one due to my own stupidity, and one due to engine failure.

The first thing that impressed me after my arrival at Air

Service Headquarters in Tours was that some of the older officers of the regular army who were in positions of authority in the Air Service appeared to be more interested in the progress of the Infantry in the trenches than in the problems of the Air Service. I may have been mistaken, but that is the way it seemed to me. Furthermore, it was evident from their conversation that several of them who had been in the Air Service in France for five or six months, and who had been given advanced commissions in the Air Service, had made little or no attempt to study Military Aeronautics. Some of them were unfamiliar with the ordinary terms used on a flying field. They had spent very little time with pilots or aeronautical engineers. They could not talk the same language. That such men should have the power to make important decisions and determine aviation policies was bound to lead to discontent and dissatisfaction on the part of the aviators.

The failure of a large proportion of the regular army officers who accepted commissions as Colonels and Majors in the newly expanded Air Service in the fall and winter of 1917, to make any effort to qualify either as pilots or observers and who did not even travel cross-country as passengers, made it hard for the young pilots to accept ungrudgingly some of their decisions. The situation was quite similar to what would happen if a Captain in the Navy were put in charge of a Cavalry Post and never was seen to mount a horse or attempt to learn to ride, or if a Captain in the Army was put in charge of a battleship and never went out of port.

At the flying schools it was most essential that the commanding officer be a flyer if he were to secure the respect of his staff, and be able to command his post with sympathetic understanding. A few incidents which were current gossip among the pilots will serve to show why some of the non-flying commanders of flying fields failed to make good, even though they had had long experience as infantry or cavalry officers in the regular army. At one of the largest fields, the commanding officer on his first tour of inspection was greatly astonished to see several relatively new airplanes badly smashed up and hopelessly out of commission. He inquired whether they had been properly made and properly inspected on their arrival, and when he was assured that this was the case, asked, "Why, then, are they out of commission now when they are only a few weeks old?" "Rough landings," was the laconic reply of the officer in charge of flying. "This new bunch of cadets will persist in making bad landings." "I will remedy that," said the new C. O. And the next day he issued a written order that there should be "no more rough landings."

To his mind, trained by a dozen years in the cavalry, it was like saying that horses went lame because they were not shod properly, and he proposed to insist that in the future this deficiency should be remedied as it could have been in the cavalry by issuing a military order. Thoughtlessness or perhaps utter lack of experience in learning to fly naturally made him suppose that rough landings were caused entirely by carelessness and disregard of the value of Government property.

Another excellent cavalry officer at another flying school signalized his arrival to take command by ordering a hitching-post erected in front of his headquarters. He had been accustomed for many years to performing his outdoor duties on horseback, and it was perfectly natural that he should wish to continue the practice. As soon as he got his hitching-post put in he ordered his orderly to bring his horse, and proceeded to attempt to inspect the flying field on horseback! His horse took exception to the noise caused by several machines whose engines were being warmed up "on the line" in front of the hangars. As his horse pranced around in front of the planes, he waved his hands, and as soon as he could make himself heard, shouted out the order, "Stop those fans! Don't you see they scare my horse?" It may be easily imagined how glad the young pilots of the flying school were to take orders from one who was so keenly interested in their work.

The ignorance of some of these old cavalry officers of the very A B C of aeronautics was quite extraordinary. One of them in command of one of our flying fields in France had apparently never even read that the Wright Brothers had solved the secret of practical flight by making the wings of their first airplanes capable of being warped. This warping of the wings, while no longer used in most planes, was still a feature of the Caudron biplane with which his school was largely provided. Soon after he took command of the school he learned that the Caudron was not popular with the young pilots, who gave as one of the reasons for their dissatisfaction with this old-fashioned bus, that instead of its being equipped with ailerons, the wings warped. To this he immediately replied that he would prevent that in the future, and ordered that all planes be immediately taken into the hangars and not left out in the sun "where their wings could warp." It was at this school, as I have been told by several pilots, that their morale reached its lowest point, and that many of them would have been glad to be able to get out of the Air Service and into the trenches.

No body of pilots ever had a keener sense of loyalty to their leaders or better morale than the Royal Flying Corps. There is a story told about General Brancker, one of the chief officers in the R. F. C., that illustrates how far the higher officers of the British Air Service carried the idea of the importance of using airplanes rather than motor cars for their tours of inspection. General Brancker was not a very good pilot and frequently made rather bad landings and crashed his running gear, but this never deterred him from the belief that it was better not to adopt any safer means of transportation than were used by his own pilots. One day in landing on an airdrome for the purpose of inspection, and before he had time to take off his helmet and goggles, the young Officer in Charge of Flying rushed up greatly excited, told him to get out of the machine and never to enter one again, and that he was a disgrace to the service.

"I do not think you know who I am," said the distinguished pilot, adjusting his monocle. "I am General Brancker." "Oh, I beg your pardon, sir," replied the horrified Lieutenant. "I thought you were that young 'Hun' who hopped off just three minutes ago to try and make one more landing and prove to me that the instructor was wrong who had given him up as hopeless." Nobody cared that General Brancker did not fly as well as the younger pilots. What they did care about was that he played the game and was not afraid.

It is true that in the summer of 1918 orders were issued in Washington encouraging all officers in the Air Service to learn to fly, but these orders could be carried out only partially in France, where facilities for preliminary instruction in flying were extremely limited, and where every training plane was needed to hasten the progress of cadets and flying officers on their way to the Front.

CHAPTER X

A FEW HOURS AT THE FRONT

WE watched the German advance toward Paris in the spring of 1918 with alarm. Most of the French factories were in the Paris area, and many of them were north of Paris. It was the location in that "north of Paris" district of such a very large percentage of French munition factories, as well as airplane works, that made the situation so serious.

It will be remembered that after the downfall of Russia, the Huns gathered themselves together for a series of crushing attacks in great force on the Western Front. The first came in March and resulted in a gain of about thirty miles. The second came in the early part of April and caused the dissolution of the British Fifth Army and netted another gain of about thirty miles for the Germans. The third came in the latter part of May and netted still another thirty miles. This time the Huns reached the River Marne at Chateau-Thierry, and were stopped only by the timely arrival of American troops, in particular by the remarkable work of the 7th, 8th, and 9th Machine Gun Battalions. Their performance was all the more noteworthy because they had arrived in France only six weeks before and had not completed their training.

The story of how they marched north to Chateau-Thierry in the face of thousands of war-weary retreating French troops, and of how they refused to be discouraged by the sight of French machine gun battalions, veteran troops, hurrying south by the same roads on which they were slowly working their way north, is one that will always make Americans proud. Our men had never been in action before, yet they displayed a courage and coolness which won unstinted praise from the French Generals who witnessed their performance. The French generously and frankly admitted that it was the Americans who had stopped the Germans at Chateau-Thierry.

It should not be forgotten, however, that in this third big push the Huns had practically reached their objective before our troops came into action. Each one of the three big drives had been successful in gaining about thirty miles advance ground. If they could manage to do it once more—and there was no apparent reason why a fourth attempt should not be as successful as the first three—it would bring them so near Paris that the great manufacturing area in the district north of Paris would either be captured or entirely destroyed by artillery fire. This would mean the loss of what was the source of more than eighty-five per cent of the munitions that were at that time supplying not only the French Army, but ours. We understood that this referred particularly to ordnance and aeronautical supplies.

Furthermore, such an advance on the part of the Germans would enable them to bring so large a number of guns to bear on Paris itself as to necessitate a move south on the part of the French Government. Plans for this move seem to have been perfected in the latter part of June and early part of July. For several weeks thousands of motor

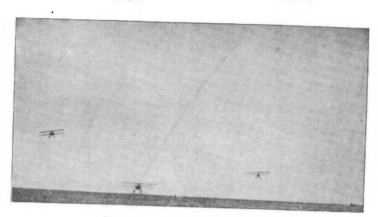

Formation Flying: Taking-off

Formation Flying: Group

trucks waited for a "hurry call" to take official Paris to Bordeaux.

Had this happened, it is doubtful whether Clemenceau could have retained his hold on the Government. His ministry would probably have fallen. The Socialists under Briand would have come in; and they *might* have been willing to accept favorable terms from the Germans. The situation was grave in the extreme. It looked as though there was an excellent probability that the Germans would offer such attractive terms to the new French Government as to force them to realize that the loss of the great manufacturing district north of Paris made it impractical and unwise for them to attempt to continue the conflict any longer.

Fortunately, the thousands of trucks never were needed. The rapid arrival of fresh American troops, brought over at the expense of adequate shipments of supplies, turned the scales. The distribution of these troops up and down the Western Front was one of the master strokes of Marshal Foch. The presence of American soldiers encouraged the weary troops of the Allies, and the fact of our being able to fight under the eyes of the war veterans encouraged our men to perform feats of valor practically unheard of in the annals of green, inexperienced armies.

One other thing seems to have been of paramount importance. That was the development under Marshal Foch of aerial night reconnaissance. The success of the great Hun drives of March, April, and May, 1918, had been due in a large measure to the old-fashioned element of surprise, an element which aerial photographers and the progress of photographic interpretation had almost eliminated in 1917. The German General Staff met this situation by moving their troops at night, and by doing it in such a manner as to leave no marks which the aerial photographers could secure the next day. The enemy troops were ordered to stick to the roads and carefully instructed to make no new paths. In the daytime they were entirely concealed in villages and woods. At night they moved on foot and not in trains, so that balloon observers and others accustomed to spotting the movement of trains would be baffled in their attempts to analyze the situation. Furthermore, no effort was made to prevent Allied aerial reconnaissance in the daytime as had usually been the case in regions where large bodies of troops were concentrating. Finally, the shock troops, whose movements it is to be presumed were kept under peculiar surveillance by Allied spies, and who were in villages fifty miles behind the lines the day before the attack, were put in motor trucks at the last possible moment and moved from their rest billets directly into the front line trenches on the night of the attack. In fact, it was said that they got out of the trucks and rushed immediately into action.

In the great drive which ended at the bridge of Chateau-Thierry we heard that the French General in command of that sector of the line had learned of the attack which was to demolish him, only two or three hours before it was upon him. He barely had time to bring up his reserves. His whole army was crushed by a single blow. The Huns

merely had to march along comfortably for the next two
or three days, capturing an enormous amount of material,
including several hundred hangars and a large number of
the latest French airplanes.

To prevent a repetition of this complete surprise, Marshal Foch developed aerial night reconnaissance. His planes,
equipped with lights and flares, were instructed to fly very
low over the roads — so low, in fact, that they could closely
observe the movement of troops and estimate the character
and extent of this movement. The German General Staff
was not able to devise any efficient means of stopping this
night reconnaissance. Accordingly, when the time came in
the middle of June for the next great Hun push which was
to have captured Paris and the munitions and airplane factories, Marshal Foch knew just exactly where, and when,
it was coming. He made his own plans accordingly, and
started a gigantic offensive on his own account at the very
same sector of the line, and a few minutes before the Germans were ready to begin theirs. As a result, on July 18
the tide turned and France was saved. All honor to those
brave French pilots who, in the face of extraordinary difficulties and unknown dangers, were the first to develop successfully aerial night reconnaissance.

My only experience at the Front was on a tour of inspection while Chief of Personnel in the latter part of July, when
it was my good fortune to be permitted to see our squadrons and balloon companies in operation in the Chateau-
Thierry sector on July 23 and 24. The Second Balloon

Company was only two or three miles from the retreating
Germans at that time, and had been severely shelled a few
hours before my visit. One of the shells, a six-inch projectile,
had passed through the peak of a shelter tent, exploded in
the rocky hillside immediately in front of the tent, and destroyed the tent and the tree behind it, without in the least
injuring the lanky sergeant who had been resting within,
his feet only a few inches from where the shell struck.

I had the opportunity of going with Captain Philip J.
Roosevelt over the battlefields of the preceding two or three
days near Belleau Wood and Vaux, where the dead were
still lying as they had fallen, and where one could not fail
to be impressed with the enormous waste of men and material which spells the modern battlefield. It was amazing
to see the thousands of hand grenades and hundreds of
thousands of rounds of small arms ammunition that had
been left on the field without being used.

The thing that surprised me most and which we in the
rear had heard least about was the large number of balloons that were being used for artillery observation. One
could judge very easily the approximate position of the lines
by the balloons. In the early days of the war the reconnaissance airplane, using a small radio set, rapidly developed
great efficiency in regulating artillery fire. The old type of
spherical balloons bobbed about in the air to such an extent
that the observer in the basket was frequently made most
uncomfortable. The new type of kite balloons, invented and
developed during the war, provided a far more suitable plat-

form for the observer than anything that had previously
gone up in the air. The harder the wind blew, the steadier
rode the balloon at the end of its cable. By perfecting the
hauling-down mechanism it was possible, when the balloon was attacked, to bring it safely to its nest faster than
the fastest passenger elevator descends.

In the mean time, the Germans had learned how to make
artillery observation from an airplane very difficult by means
of improved anti-aircraft fire, and very unsatisfactory by
using powerful radio to counteract the radio messages sent
out by the reconnaissance planes. Consequently, the balloon
observer was at a great advantage over the airplane observer.
The balloon observer could talk by means of a telephone
whose wire ran down through the cable that held the balloon, and could communicate most satisfactorily with the
artillery commander without any danger of having his line
cut by the Germans except when an attack by their airplanes caused his hydrogen-inflated balloon to burn up and
necessitated his seeking safety in a parachute descent. Notwithstanding the danger of being shot down and the unpleasant features of the parachute, only one man was killed
on the Western Front in a parachute descent, and this accident was caused by the parachute catching fire from the
burning balloon.

Had we been able to inflate our balloons with helium, a
quantity of which was already on the docks when the Armistice was signed, there would have been no danger from
fire, for helium is non-explosive and non-inflammable. Had

we been able to perfect helium-filled balloons with numerous compartments, it would have been extremely difficult
for the Germans to have shot our balloons down. In the
future, this should greatly change the whole process of
artillery observation. It will also affect warfare in another
way. The Zeppelin raids over London were given up because it was so easy for an airplane, by firing a few shots,
to bring down the expensive dirigible in flames. The use of
helium and of a gas container made up of many sections
will make the rigid dirigible a very potent factor in bombing
raids.

My few hours at the Front not only convinced me of the
great value of lighter-than-air ships for certain important
purposes; it also made me realize more than ever the necessity for close and constant coöperation between the Training
Schools and the Front. Hostility due to failure to understand conditions and inability to appreciate the point of
view of the hard-working pilot at the other end caused
mutual suspicion and unfriendliness. There should have
been more rotation of the flying personnel. Those at the
Front naturally are sure they know best what it is they
want. Those at the schools in the rear, conscious of their
own keen desire to go to the Front and to risk all that any
one is risking, but compelled by force of circumstances to
miss the thrill of actual combat, are obliged to take what
satisfaction they can in developing what they think is the best
system of training. Each mistrusts the other.

One of the most serious faults of our conduct of the war

— so far as the Air Service went — was the unwillingness
of those in command to allow highly efficient officers to be
transferred from front to rear and *vice versa;* from France
to America, and from America to France. We were gradually coming to this in the autumn of 1918. It is only a pity
we did not adopt that policy earlier. I saw men at schools
who were stale. I saw men at the Front who were stale. It
should be remembered that no matter how good or how important a man is, he is likely to get into a rut and become
stale if he is kept too long working at one job under the
high pressure of actual war conditions. His efficiency will be
increased and the whole service will be improved if he is not
kept too many months at a very interesting or highly important piece of work.

CHAPTER XI

THE THIRD AVIATION INSTRUCTION CENTRE

IN August another reorganization of the Air Service took place. More activities were centred in Paris, and the organization of squadrons was taken out of the hands of the Chief of Personnel. General Patrick at the same time had pity on the woes of an explorer who had been tied for many months to office work and sent him to Issoudun to take command of his largest flying school.

All the American flying schools in France were at that time (August 23, 1918) under the immediate direction of Colonel Walter G. Kilner, Chief of Training for the Chief of Air Service. Colonel Kilner was the best Chief that any one in the Air Service could ask to have. A graduate of West Point and of the aviation school at San Diego, he had served on the Punitive Expedition into Mexico, had had interesting experiences with Mexican bandits and old-fashioned "ships," was in command at Mineola when I took my tests as a Reserve Military Aviator, and had gone overseas with General Foulois. He had shown extraordinary ability at Issoudun in bringing order out of chaos during the winter of 1917–18. He had taken the school at a time when it is said that General Pershing had called it "the worst mudhole in France," and in five months had made it "the most comfortable camp in the A. E. F." His military education, his technical training, his ability as a pilot, and his skill as an administrator made him an ideal Chief of Training. He was later decorated with the Distinguished Service Medal.

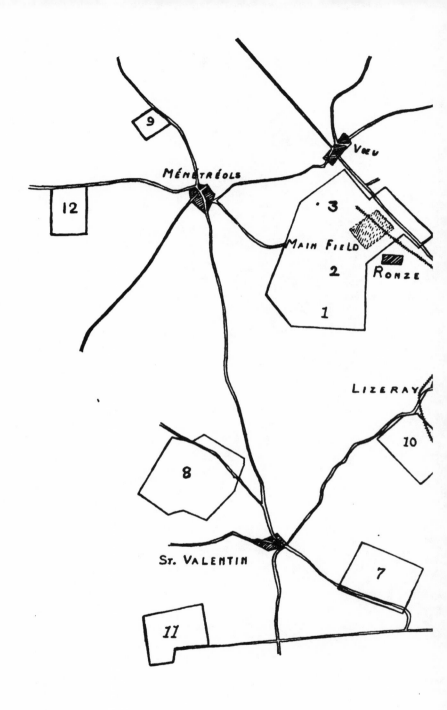

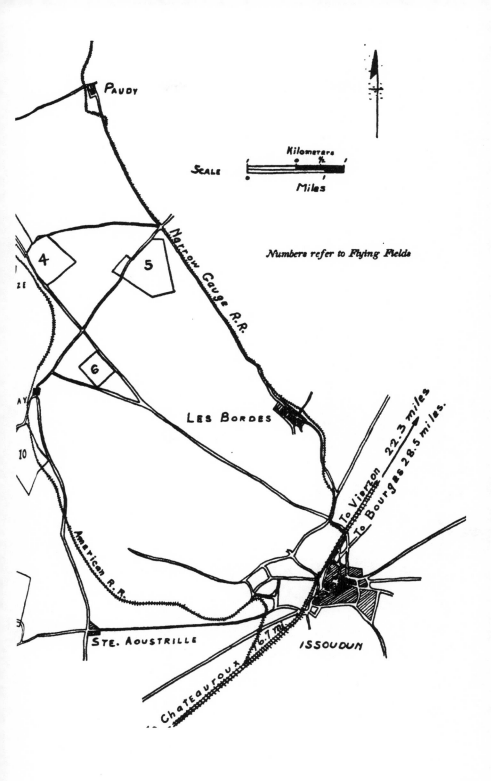

The First Aviation Instruction Centre established near
Paris had early been abandoned, possibly because it was
too near Paris. The Second Aviation Instruction Centre was
built up from the old French airdrome and flying school
on the plateau across the river at Tours. It was gradually
enlarged to meet the needs of the American service, and
for a long time was the principal place for the preliminary
training of flying cadets. For this purpose it was equipped
with the old-fashioned Caudrons. Later on it was developed
entirely as a school for training aerial observers, and as such
was most successful under the very competent direction of
Lieutenant-Colonel S. W. Fitzgerald.

The story of Issoudun, where the Third Aviation Instruction Centre was located, is one full of lights and shadows.
Located on the arid plains between the villages of Vatan
and Lizaray, the camp was some seven miles west of the
historic town of Issoudun, made famous by Balzac. It was
right in the heart of France, about twenty-five miles north of
Chateauroux, about sixty-five miles due south of Orleans,
and twenty-five miles west of Bourges. It was not far from
two of the largest American supply depots, Gièvres and
Romorantin. The land was of clay mixed with small shaly
rocks. The soil was so poor that villages and farmhouses
were relatively few and far between. This gave the large
open spaces necessary for the flying fields; but the ground
was so impervious to water that it did not dry readily and
was frightfully muddy for months at a time. In order to
reach the selected location, an American railroad nine miles

in length was built to connect with the French lines near the town of Issoudun.

The "Third A. I. C.," as our post was usually called, consisted of a main camp containing headquarters, hospitals, instruction barracks, quartermaster stores, aero supply warehouses, repair shops, sleeping quarters for about 4000 men, and an assembly and test field; and within a radius of five miles a dozen other fields, covering all together about fifty square miles of French territory. We had over a thousand airplanes and could accommodate about the same number of students. There were nearly 5000 enlisted men on duty, a number which was soon increased until there were all together about 8000 persons, including officers, men, Chinese laborers, and German prisoners, occupied in keeping this school in operation. Our function was to take aviators who had received their preliminary flying training elsewhere and give them advanced and special training, thereby fitting them to become pursuit, observation, or ferry pilots, as the needs of the war and the abilities of the pilots might indicate. More than 2000 pilots were graduated here.

One's first impressions of Issoudun depended entirely on how one approached it. To the enlisted mechanic of a squadron arriving at night after a long and tiresome journey in a freight car, it must have seemed like getting into any other American camp where there was plenty of mud under foot, a group of rough board barracks all around, and the satisfaction of knowing that total ignorance of French was not going to spoil the comfort of his billet. On the next day, or rather the next Sunday afternoon, when he found that he was many miles from an interesting town, it was not so amusing.

It was my good fortune to see Issoudun first from an elevation of about ten thousand feet. In May, Major Spatz, then Commanding Officer, had kindly flown me over from Tours. Fortunately, I did not know that he had recently been the victim of two bad accidents and had crashed two machines in succession on landing. Otherwise, I might not have taken such pleasure in my ride! Seated for the first time in my life in the front seat of a small Nieuport, I greatly enjoyed my first cross-country view of France from the air. After passing for some distance up the lovely valley of the Cher and over some extensive wooded areas, we came at last in view of widespreading plains. As we drew nearer I made out little groups of hangars here and there, and finally realized that an interesting gray patch, colored somewhat differently from the surrounding plain, was a group of buildings that included the main barracks, shops, and headquarters of the Third Aviation Instruction Centre.

It was always a pleasure to take a visitor up and show him our camps and fields from an airplane, for it was by far the easiest way to give him an adequate idea of the extent of our plant and the admirable way in which Colonel Kilner and his assistants had laid out the fields so as to utilize all the available air space within easy reach of the main repair shops. For this reason we were keenly disappointed when Assistant Secretary of War John D. Ryan, then in charge of the Army Air Service, arrived on his first and only tour of inspection, and declined to go up. We had arranged to have a very comfortable DH-4 prepared and ready for this purpose, and had detailed to it the most experienced and conservative pilot on the post. We hoped that Mr. Ryan would thus get a comprehensive idea of his largest flying school. I remember that he gave as his reason for not caring to go up that he had made the rule that civilians must not be taken up in army planes, and he felt that he ought not to break his own rules!

It was also a keen disappointment to be visited at night by one of the most influential members of the Senate Military Affairs Committee. He arrived after dark, and left before midnight. There were so many things that one would like to have had him see and personally understand! Of course, there were many other places in France which needed his attention worse than ours did, but that did not allay our dissatisfaction with his nocturnal tour of inspection.

To the visiting officer who came into our camp by motor car there was nothing very comprehensive or picturesque. It was not nearly as striking as the average military camp in the United States, nor one-quarter as impressive as the splendid aviation fields at home. Aviators arriving from Ellington Field or Dayton were rarely enthusiastic about it. It had grown from very small beginnings, and had been built of whatever materials Colonel Kilner could get hold of. The barracks were of various sizes and kinds. The shops were of different vintages. The hangars were a medley of canvas, steel, and imitation concrete.

The first sign that caught the eye on entering from the highway was POLICE, PRISON AND LABOR OFFICER. The fact that a few minutes later one found one's self on the corner of "Broadway" and "Fifth Avenue" only partially alleviated the shock one had received from the sign at the entrance. We tried to be neat and soldierly. So we were greatly pleased when a visiting Brigadier-General of Cavalry told us that our men saluted more snappily than those in any camp he had visited in France. And we tried to be as efficient as possible, but we had no time to go in for handsome outward appearances, and the original plans had not contemplated thrilling the natives by any display. Nevertheless, when we really managed to get a visiting officer up in the air, it was a pleasure to see the surprise and satisfaction on his face as he looked around over fifty square miles of territory and noted the evidences of American energy and enterprise.

So far as I know, the only General Officer ever to arrive at Issoudun by airplane was General Harbord, when he was in command of the Services of Supply. He came down from Tours one day on a short tour of inspection and was piloted by Colonel Kilner, then Chief of Training. General Harbord took a keen interest in aviation and sent the following paragraph about our pilots to the editor of the *Plane News*, our local paper :

In War, as it is being waged on the Western Front, the heir of the Knights of other days is the pilot of the pursuit plane. The fighting pilot, like the Knights of old, goes forth to individual combat, where

two may meet but one alone depart. The greatest of Knights were the
finest men, and let America's crusaders ever uphold this tradition—
chivalrous, clean and fearlessly fighting until we wipe from the earth
this scourge of German *Kultur*.

Colonel Kilner made us frequent visits by air, and enormously increased the enthusiasm of the pilots for Air Service management by his own personal enthusiasm for flying and fearlessness in travelling about France wherever he
needed to go by air instead of by road. He had had several
crashes in his career, both in Mexico and California, as well
as in France, and he was thoroughly familiar with the psychology of discomfort following a bad crash, but this never
induced him to accept the excuse of being "too busy" to fly,
or of claiming that it was so important that he reach a given
point on time that he could not afford to take the risks of
aerial transportation. I know from personal experience after
two bad crashes how easy it is to accept the belief that one
is not feeling well enough to fly. Everybody knows that one
ought not to fly except when feeling well!

In administrating the Third Aviation Instruction Centre
I followed the general principle of giving the heads of departments, and in particular the Commanding Officers of
the outlying fields, the fullest measure of responsibility, expecting certain results, but not directing the details or the
methods by which these results were to be achieved. Where
results did not materialize, where inspection disclosed unsatisfactory conditions, where criticism did not bear fruit,
the responsible heads were quickly removed and the best

General Harbord's Arrival at Issoudun

Reading from left to right—Major T. G. Lanphier, Major-General J. G. Harbord, Colonel Walter G. Kilner, Lieutenant-Colonel Hiram Bingham

men available put in their places. On the other hand, where results were satisfactory, encouragement was given to those who were responsible for the results, their recommendations for promotion were almost invariably accepted, approved, and forwarded, and their wishes and desires were given the utmost possible consideration.

Every day at noon there met with me my chief assistants, including the Post Executive Officer, the Post Adjutant, the Chief Aeronautical Engineer, the Construction and Maintenance Officer, the Officer in Charge of Flying, the Chairman of the Medical Research Board, the Commanding Officer of the Hospital, the Post Quartermaster, the Commanding Officer of Student Officers, Commanding Officers of outlying fields, the Liaison Officer, the Police, Prison and Labor Officer, the Post Disbursing Officer, the Personnel Officer, and the Officer in charge of Aerial Gunnery. At this meeting every one had a chance to report progress, to air his grievances, and to become familiar with the successes and failures of the others.

Special stress was laid on the fact that my staff officers, visiting outlying fields and speaking in the name of the Post Commander, must give their instructions through the Commanding Officer of the outlying field, who was personally responsible to the Post Commander in the same comprehensive manner that the Post Commander was responsible to the Chief of Training at Headquarters. This method of administrating a post that included nearly 6000 enlisted men, 450 German prisoners, 250 Chinese coolies, and from 1100 to 1400 officers, most of them student officers, proved to be satisfactory. The Inspector-General, in his report to the Commanding General, S. O. S., dated November 26, 1918, on the subject of his inspection of the Third Aviation Instruction Centre, took occasion to commend the Post Commander "for the efficient condition of this Centre."

He also spoke of the competition between the fields which was used to maintain a high standard of efficiency and said, "A spirit of friendly rivalry exists which has kept up the interest of the personnel since the signing of the Armistice." President Lowell of Harvard University once published in the *Atlantic Monthly* an article on the importance of competition as a stimulant for undergraduate activities, both physical and mental. Ever since reading it I have been a sincere believer in the value of competition as a spur to high endeavor.

The nature of the Nieuport plane, which was the only one available in large quantities for training purposes, was such as to require a graded course, as will be described in another chapter. It was not an ideal course, but was, I believe, the best that could be devised in view of the equipment available. However, the principle of having a large number of small fields under semi-independent commands, each using two or three hundred enlisted men, and doing a certain amount of repairing, and using the main field for assembly and rebuilding and for the principal warehouse, hospital, quartermaster, etc., worked out extremely well.

These fields were generally about two miles apart, so that

the air was not crowded even when there were several hundred planes in commission and a thousand students being taught. Daily meetings of the Commanding Officers of the fields, frequent meetings of Engineer Officers, Officers in Charge of Flying, and Supply Officers enabled proper co-ordination to take place and homogeneous planning to be carried out. I believe that the ideal aviation training centre consists of a central plant easily reached by road and air, and a dozen surrounding fields where preliminary, advanced, and specialized flying and aerial gunnery are taught.

My duties at Headquarters were greatly facilitated by the skill and long army experience of Captain Lester Cummings, who was my first Adjutant, and who later took charge of preparing squadrons for departure. My second Adjutant was Captain William V. Saxe, whose success was due to his unselfish zeal for whatever work was assigned him, combined with unusual charm of manner and unfailing courtesy. It was most fortunate for me that Major Tom G. Lanphier, a veteran of Chateau-Thierry, was completing his flying training just as I arrived. His ability to command had been evident on the Aquitania, where I had been impressed by the way he handled the troops at life-boat drill. His familiarity with the workings of every field on the post, his skill as a pilot, and his loyalty made him an ideal Executive Officer. He afterwards took command of the post.

CHAPTER XII

TRAINING AVIATORS

THE plan for Issoudun was that it should be used chiefly as a place where pilots already fully trained in the United States should have a "refresher course" before being sent to the Front. Due to the lack of advanced training planes in the United States and the fact that it was practically impossible during the continuance of the war for our pilots to do much more than get their preliminary training and "acquire their wings" before coming to France, it became necessary to develop at Issoudun a complete course in advanced flying and in aerial tactics. This was also made necessary because so many hundreds of cadets had been sent to France without any flying training at all, and could secure only preliminary instruction at the French schools or at our own Second Aviation Instruction Centre at Tours.

The history of the Training Department shows a marvellous growth. For its details I am indebted to Lieutenant Thomas Ward, who had been a member of the celebrated First Reserve Aero Squadron, and whose knowledge of the complete story of Issoudun was second to none. Very little flying was done in the fall of 1917, but in December the records show 1117 hours of flying for the month, which was increased in January to 2812; February, 3414; March, 4205; April, 7392. There was a slight falling off in May and June, due to various causes, chiefly the great difficulty of keeping the Nieuports in commission during the warm, wind-

less days of the late spring. In July the flying time increased
to 9350 hours; in August to 12,510; falling off in September
to 9562, but under the very able leadership of Captain H. C.
Ferguson breaking all records in October with a total of
17,113 hours for the month. In November, after the Armistice was signed, the pressure let down and we flew only
10,041 hours. Captain Ferguson, first as Commanding Officer of Field 5 and later as Officer in Charge of Flying, showed
remarkable ability, determination, and initiative.

In October and November, 1917, there had been a great
deal of wet weather, and the clay-covered fields of Issoudun
were converted into oceans of mud. Attempts to fly caused
much breakage of propellers until Captain Rickenbacker,
who acted as Engineer Officer and was the first student
graduated from the school, invented a mudguard which
prevented the wheels from throwing mud and stones directly
into the propeller. Incidentally, it was quite appropriate
that the first graduate of Issoudun should later become the
leading American ace.

It may be interesting to note at this point that another
well-known ace, Captain Douglas Campbell, was the first
Assistant Officer in Charge of Training here. The fifth to
graduate was Captain Hamilton Coolidge, who had a splendid record at the Front with eight Huns to his credit when
he was killed by a direct hit from an anti-aircraft gun.
The seventh graduate was Lieutenant Quentin Roosevelt,
who was at one time Post Quartermaster, Supply Officer,
and Transportation Officer, and after he had completed his

training, took charge of training at Field 7. He had his father's wonderful courage and fine enthusiasm.

At the beginning no definite course of instruction was laid out. Most of the teachers were French pilots, who naturally used the ideas then in vogue at the French schools which they had attended. Their methods were better adapted for French than American aviators. The course at Issoudun was not thought out on paper beforehand by a theorist, but was gradually evolved under the most strenuous conditions imaginable and contained ideas derived from a very considerable number of the best American pilots in France. With a true sense of the importance of having the best possible teachers and a keen realization of the old adage that "a stream cannot rise higher than its source," it was early determined to retain only the very best American pilots for teachers and instructors. Each man that went through the school was jealously watched by those in charge of the work at the different fields, and if they saw unusual qualities in him, he was promptly requisitioned as a member of the staff. Of course this was very hard on the individual. Occasionally it worked backward. In one case an unusually good pilot, knowing that he was being selected as a teacher, deliberately broke the flying rules on the last day of his course in order to spoil his record. He knew that we would not want a man for a teacher who had a bad record in the school, and he thought that he would be sent to the Front if he was not good enough for a teacher. He was promptly assigned to an unattractive ground job.

Issoudun: Field 7

Men who did not obey the rules were not wanted at the Front.

With true American devotion to high ideals, the great majority of the first-class pilots selected as instructors cheerfully gave up the chance of becoming aces themselves in order to perfect the output of the school and thus to help increase the total number of American aces at the Front. In order to prevent our self-sacrificing instructors from getting stale, a few were allowed to take turns in going to the Front for a month at a time. This gave them new ideas and new experiences. When they came back to the school they had the advantage in every case of having successfully brought down one or more Huns. This increased their prestige with their students and let them feel that they had had their chance at a little real action. Occasionally, pilots who had been at the Front for six months or more and who were *tired out* were sent back to the school as teachers. Those who have been in the teaching profession know that a teacher who is tired is seldom very effective. These pilots were no exception to the general rule. Two or three of them were unusually good, but our experience with the majority led us to believe that the best instructors were not those who had become unfitted for duty at the Front, but those who had learned the importance of teaching and were glad to take advantage of a few weeks at the Front to increase their efficiency in the game for which they were preparing others.

With such a splendid staff as was gradually built up by following this policy, it was only necessary to show each man that his ideas would be welcomed and to allow him to put into practice his own theories of teaching in order to develop a very thorough course of study. Since it in no way rested on the ideas of a non-flying general staff, nor on the preconceived notions of one or two flying officers, nor on the arbitrary decision of a small group of outside experts, it was most flexible and was constantly undergoing change and improvement.

The problem of training a pilot who had received his preliminary work on a slow flying Caudron was much more difficult than that of one who had been trained on a Curtiss JN-4 H. No man was kept back by reason of the awkwardness of his fellow students. Every pilot was encouraged to go ahead as fast as possible, or rather as fast as our supply of the most advanced type of planes permitted. In the beginning of his course, however, it was necessary for the student to remain assigned to a section until he had completed the preliminary groundwork of aerial gunnery and motor instruction and had passed through the course in Rouleurs on Field 1.

At some of the French schools the Rouleurs were especially built "penguins," which were guaranteed not to fly. At Issoudun, however, we were accustomed to use what we could get. In this case the best thing available was a Morane monoplane from which the ailerons had been taken, and which was equipped with a 40 to 50 H.P. Gnome motor.

Many of the boys who had learned to fly in the States could not understand why they were put on non-flying

Rouleurs before being sent up in the air. Some of them, in fact, managed to get by Field 1 without really learning what the work there had to teach them. Later they had to be sent back from one of the advanced fields because they were unable to make proper use of the rudder when taking off, taxying, or landing. They were finally ready to admit that the rudders of small fast planes, designed for successful use in the air when travelling at more than one hundred and twenty miles an hour, are not large enough when the plane is going over the ground at only twenty-five to thirty miles an hour. The pilot must use his rudder very gently in the air, but very roughly on the ground. If he does not thoroughly understand handling the small rudder of the fast scout planes, it will be almost impossible for him to make them roll straight on the ground. Most of our advanced planes were short-bodied Nieuports equipped with rotary motors. As I have already said in speaking of the troubles of our cadets, the Nieuports were extremely fond of making a violent and unexpected turn on the ground — the *cheval de bois*.

The lower left wing of the Nieuport has a slightly greater angle of incidence than the corresponding wing on the other side. This is in order to aid the pilot in overcoming the effect of the torque of the rotary motor. It causes the left wing to drag a bit, and this makes it more difficult to roll straight on the ground. This tendency is still further increased in landing on a field that is not quite level (and few French fields were really level). If in landing you happen to light on one wheel with greater force than on the other, the tendency of the Nieuport to turn abruptly and unexpectedly is very marked. It will readily be seen that it was very necessary for the student to understand thoroughly the use of a small rudder when operating on the ground. We found the cranky, non-flying "clipped" monoplanes very useful for this purpose.

Students were also encouraged to study the action of the motor before starting on their first ride, and to keep the application of power as steady as possible, since the slip stream of air from the propeller acting on the rudder is the force that causes the latter to become effective.

The student's first trip was straight across the field, towards a soldier who was stationed at the far end, whose duty it was to help him turn round and to start his motor in case he stalled it, as frequently happened. The student was not accompanied by a teacher in his wild ride. It was the duty of the teacher to watch carefully the cause of any difficulties and observe whether the student was avoiding trouble by going too slow, or was really learning to make proper use of the rudder. The second trip was made at a higher rate of speed, but with the control stick pulled well back and the tail held firmly on the ground. When the pilot had succeeded in making a good round trip with the tail skid helping to keep him straight by plowing through the field, he was told to get the tail off the ground for a few rods and then "make a landing."

It was possible to run these "buses" at about forty miles an hour without having them leave the ground except by leaps and bounds, but unless one gave a sharp kick on the rudder and then instantly brought it back to neutral at the psychological moment, the tendency to travel in anything but a straight line was made manifest. When the student started using the elevators in order to get the tail off the ground, he generally began to think less about the importance of instantaneous action on the rudder. Or he forgot the small size of the field, and this spelled trouble.

I never shall forget my fifth trip across the field, when, having acquired some confidence in my ability to keep the pesky thing on a straight line, I overran the limits of the somewhat restricted area, rolled into a ditch, and turned upside down. There were a number of rules posted on the bulletin board at this field, which every one was supposed to digest before taking his lessons. One was: "Do not overshoot the field, as you will only crash and will not learn anything!" Obviously, students occasionally forgot this rule.

Another was: "Never raise the tail of a machine unless told to do so by an instructor, and then only when coming into the wind—never with the wind." This rule was occasionally disregarded by high-ranking pilots from the regular army who scorned to listen to the instructor, and who, consequently, caused extensive repairs to be made to the unfortunate Rouleurs. The students' confidence in their ability to taxy at a rapid rate was considerably lessened by the number of accidents—not serious, although quite humiliating—which they saw while awaiting their turn. It was

not uncommon for several of these queer looking birds to be
flat on their backs at the same time.

After having satisfied the instructors at Field 1 of their
ability to use the rudder, the students walked over to Field
2, where dual control machines, operated by experienced instructors, were ready to give them their first experience in
actual flying in France. On this field we used the 23-meter
Nieuport. That is to say, the total wing surface' was 23
square meters. To one accustomed to the Curtiss JN-4, the
very small lower wings and the absence of perpendicular
struts made the ship seem quite fragile.

The 80 H.P. Le Rhone motor used on these machines
had a comparatively short life—forty hours being considered a good average. Once the student learned to handle it,
however, he became very fond of this light and relatively
quiet French engine. Three or four Le Rhones acting together did not make as much noise as a single Liberty motor;
nor, it should be added, did they produce as much power.

To one accustomed to the American stationary internal
combustion motor, like the Curtiss OX, the operation of the
French throttle required study and practice. The throttle
consists of two levers called "manettes." The motor is fitted
with an external mixing chamber or carburetor, the mixed
gasoline and air being sucked in through the inlet valve.
By opening the small manette, the flow of gas to the jet is
regulated. The large manette is actually the throttle con-
trolling the mixture of gas and air. It was very important
for the student to understand the use of both manettes.

Field 2: Instructor and Student starting on a lesson

Field 2: Nieuport 81, 23-meter, 80 H.P. Le Rhone motor

He also had to learn to keep his left hand constantly on them while flying. It finally became second nature to him to keep adjusting them so as to make his motor run smoothly. His reaction to "skipping" or "popping" came to be immediate and instantaneous.

We tried to teach the operation of the manettes as thoroughly as possible before the student went to Field 1. While there our students got practice in keeping the left hand always on the throttle to prevent its slipping and thereby changing the speed of the propeller. American trained students, having learned to rely on the Zenith carburetor of the Curtiss engine, found it difficult to learn that the manettes needed constant attention. Furthermore, students from the United States, where the throttle is usually on the right-hand side and where the importance of using the French type of switch for the magneto had not been emphasized, found it useful to familiarize themselves with those peculiarities while still on the exciting Rouleurs. Yet it was difficult to tell whether the student had really taken it all in until he began to fly in the dual control machines. As a matter of fact, many of the students had to be instructed all over again on a motor located for this purpose back of one of the hangars on Field 2.

Even the instructors, however, did not always agree as to the best method of operating the manettes! In order to enable their discussions to be thoroughly understood by all parties, a special set of manettes was fastened to the fireplace in the attractive club-room which had been con-

structed for the use of instructors on this field by Captain
T. C. Knight, the Commanding Officer of Fields 1 and 2,
who was particularly successful in working out the various
problems that arose on these fields.

The length of time which a student had to spend on
Field 2 depended entirely on himself and his ability to learn
rapidly and to demonstrate his efficiency not only to the instructor to whom he was assigned, but also to another first-
class pilot known as the tester, who gave him his final
examination. If he failed to satisfy the tester that he had
mastered the intricacies of flying the 23-meter Nieuport,
he was sent back to his instructor for further lessons.
Each instructor was allowed to follow his own ideas to
a very considerable extent, although all were obliged to ride
in the front seat. Some used the telephone and some found
that the students did better when left alone, and when they
were not trying to listen to the telephone and "feel" the
ship at the same time.

The 23-meter Nieuport is not very stable in the air, and
if the pilot tries to climb too rapidly or fails to nose down
when he develops motor trouble, the plane quickly stalls
and falls sideways, generally going into a spin. If this oc-
curs near the ground, the result is disastrous; if at an elevation of six or seven hundred meters, it is generally possible to come out of the spin before reaching the ground.

Since most of our students had received their preliminary training with a stationary motor, they found it difficult
to understand the gyroscopic action of the rotary motor,

which inclines to pull the nose of the plane down into a spin if it is not held level on a turn. In flying the JN-4 we used to be told to nose down on the turns so as to avoid losing flying speed. This tendency of the Curtiss trained pilots had to be overcome before it was safe to let them fly with a rotary motor. American trained pilots were also inclined to fly with too little rudder. I remember receiving a striking lesson from the Chief Instructor at San Diego, who was sure I used my rudder too much and consequently made me fly about the field with my feet actually off the rudder bar, guiding the machine solely by use of the ailerons. One cannot do that with the Nieuport 23. It requires the use of the rudder at all times. Furthermore, the rotary motor makes the technique of a right-hand turn quite different from that of a left-hand turn.

I mention these matters in some detail because many people found it difficult to understand why, after a pilot had earned his wings in the United States, it was necessary to give him instruction in a dual control machine in France. At times considerable pressure was brought to bear upon us to let the American trained pilots go directly into the fastest and smallest scout planes without giving them the instruction just described. We felt that this would be in some cases inexcusable homicide. On the other hand, some of the men who were "born pilots" needed less than an hour's instruction on Fields 1 and 2 before they were able to go on to Field 3.

After the pilot had satisfied the instructor and the tester

that he could take his Nieuport off the ground in the desired direction without having it turn away from the wind,
that he knew how to climb on his first turn, throttle his
motor down so as to secure maximum efficiency in level
flight, make his turns without losing any elevation, avoid
"skidding" (caused by too much rudder and too little bank),
avoid "slipping" (caused by too little rudder and too much
bank), make "three-point landings" with the wheels and
the tail skid hitting at the same moment, and, by the proper
use of his rudder, overcome the tendency of the Nieuport to "cheval," he was given a card that admitted him to
Field 3.

At Field 3 he found a 23-meter Nieuport not fitted with
dual controls, but intended for solo flying. The absence of
the instructor in the front seat not only made the machine
lighter and enabled it to leave the ground more quickly
and climb faster, but also had a psychological effect in making the pilot realize that he had no one but himself to depend upon. This ship is an excellent machine to use in
carrying single passengers and landing in small fields. It
does not glide far, and therefore does not cause the embar-
rassments that occur when using the DH-4. However, it has
a very considerable tendency to make violent turns while
gaining flying speed and before leaving the ground. Furthermore, it is not easy to keep it rolling smoothly in a straight
line when you land. Nevertheless, after overcoming the effects of two bad crashes in this cranky little ship, I became
very fond of it personally and used it almost entirely when

inspecting from the air during the last three months of my stay in France, although I should have preferred an Avro.

The work at Field 3 consisted in making the student as familiar as possible with the Nieuport 23 and giving him plenty of confidence. He was required to make a sufficient number of landings to overcome his dread of unexpected turns. His air work was carefully watched to make sure that he was equally good on both left-hand and right-hand turns. He was required to make spiral turns of more than 45° to determine whether he was able to use his elevators as a rudder and his rudders as an elevator when banking over to that extent.

His instruction in cross-country flying depended to a certain extent on what kind of planes we had. At various times the 15-meter Nieuport, the 18-meter, and the 23-meter were used for this purpose, depending on the number of ships in commission. The course was designed to familiarize the pilot with the difference between flying over France and flying over the United States. Most of our fields in America were so located that any one with average intelligence could find his way back to the field without the use of a map or, if required to use a map, would be left in no doubt whatever as to his whereabouts. In France, however, with its large number of small towns and villages that looked very much alike from the air, its great number of straight, white roads leading in every direction, its crazy-quilt design of small cultivated fields, bewildering in their similarity and complexity, the chance of getting lost in the air even while using one of the excellent French maps was very considerable. The shape of the forested areas was the most important thing to learn. Our pilots were fond of telling the story of a champion cross-country flyer from the United States who had never had any difficulty with map reading and who scoffed at the idea that it was necessary for him to learn anything additional in this subject at Issoudun, getting totally lost on his first cross-country flight. He flew until obliged to land because he was out of gas. He finally had to telephone from some distant point to have somebody come and rescue him. In the United States he had flown by roads and large rivers. In France there were too many of the first and too few of the second.

In addition to this cross-country work at Field 3, students were given an hour or so with an acrobacy instructor in one of our few Avros. The student was put into all sorts of strange positions in the air to test his air sense, to give him confidence in the ability of a plane to right itself when certain definite rules were followed, and to determine whether there was anything radically wrong with his power to overcome dizziness and keep his head level under trying circumstances. If the instructor found a pilot deficient at this point, he was sent over to the hospital to consult the Medical Research Board. Advanced physical tests sometimes showed that the pilot was not fully competent and should never have been passed for training as an aviator.

While undergoing their instruction in motors and in the work on Fields 1, 2, and 3, the pilots lived in the Main Bar-

racks, near the Guard House. After graduating successfully
from Field 3, they were sent over to Field 9, several miles
to the westward, for further instruction. This field, under
the careful oversight of Lieutenant Molthan and Captain
Oliver, was equipped with 18-meter Nieuports, that is, the
wings measured 18 square meters in area. In 1915 and 1916
this machine had been very popular at the Front. It was
faster than the 23-meter, but was less able to glide slowly
and therefore had to be landed at a higher speed and required
more skilful handling. The general appearance was similar,
although the upper wings were smaller. The struts of the
23-meter have an outward slope, while those of the 18-meter
are vertical. While the 23-meter was far more delicate to
handle than the JN-4 or the Caudron, the 18-meter was
still more so. The motor was the same as that used in the
23-meter.

Since these ships were not adapted to taking up passengers, all instruction had to be given from the ground. It included lectures, partly in the nature of repetition in regard
to the use of the rotary motor, partly in regard to field requirements and traffic signals, and as to the necessity of keeping in good physical condition. The work on the flying field
was divided into three parts: a landing class in which the
student received opportunity to make from ten to thirty landings; a spiral class in which he made all kinds of turns, including what are known as "tight spirals" where the wings
are practically at an angle of 90° for part of the turn, and an
air work class. The instructors watched the students through

field-glasses, and later explained to them the nature of their mistakes. If it was found that a student did not readily accustom himself to the more delicate and speedier type of ship, he was advised to go in for reconnaissance or bombing piloting rather than to continue the course in pursuit and combat flying.

Just as certain athletes are more skilful as acrobats and gymnasts than others, so some pilots seem to be better adapted for the more spectacular though no more useful work of pursuit and combat. Due to its exciting character, we found great difficulty in persuading young pilots to abandon their ambitions and learn to be good reconnaissance pilots. It requires great skill, unusual courage, and plenty of gray matter to make a good reconnaissance pilot, but it is not necessary that one should be a first-class acrobat. It makes less of an appeal to the average boy.

As a result of the air work and spiral class on Field 9, the men who showed less ability in rapid and delicate manoeuvre as acrobats were taken out and sent over to Field 10, which was equipped with DH-4 planes and where a special course was arranged to train pilots for observation squadrons. Those pilots who satisfied their instructor of their ability as acrobats, however, passed from Field 9 to Fields 4, 5, and 6, and took up their lodgings at Field 5.

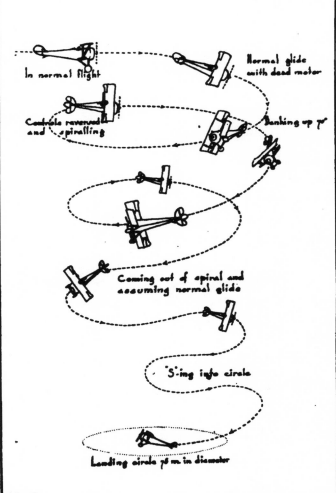

SPIRAL

In normal flight

Normal glide with dead motor

Controls reversed and spiralling

Banking up 70°

Coming out of spiral and assuming normal glide

S'ing into circle

Landing circle 75 m. in diameter

No. 2

CHAPTER XIII

ADVANCED TRAINING FOR PURSUIT PILOTS

IT is not my intention in this chapter to furnish a manual whereby a pilot can learn to do stunts or become a good military aviator. On the contrary, since the science of aviation is so very new and the art of flying has been practised for so few years and aerial tactics are scarcely more than a few months old, the object of setting down these details is historical rather than practical. Many of the pilots that went through the course will probably find that at the time they went through things were not exactly as set down here. I have tried to portray the system as it was at the time the Armistice was signed. A few years from now, many of these manoeuvres and formations will undoubtedly seem very crude and extraordinary. The pilots who are born this year will look upon us, who strove to the best of our ability to give the most advanced course of flying in the world, as foolish old idiots. At the same time, some of them may be glad to see how we did it, and their fathers may be glad to be reminded of how it was done in November, 1918.

Fields 4, 5, and 6 were under the very competent direction of Captain St. Clair Street, a most conscientious and successful commander. These fields were equipped with the 15-meter Nieuport, using the same motor as the 18-meter and the 23-meter. While not quite as small as the Baby Nieuport, it was the smallest practical avion that the Nieuport Company produced, and it was probably the most difficult plane to land. It was used extensively at the Front in 1916, but proved to be almost too delicate. Consequently, we believed that when a student had mastered this plane, he could feel confident of his ability to master readily any other type that might be assigned to him at the Front or anywhere else.

On Field 5 instruction was given in taxying, taking off, and landing. Due to its small wing spread and short body, the 15-meter Nieuport lands very fast and is difficult to handle on the ground. The landing class always offered a good deal of excitement to the spectator and caused much trepidation in the hearts of newly arrived pilots. It was a long cry from a JN-4 to a 15-meter Nieuport. With a JN-4, to level off too far from the ground meant usually a disagreeable pancake and something of a shock; to level off a 15-meter Nieuport too far from the ground meant a crashed plane and a chance of serious physical injury. Field 5 was also used to give the students experience in landing near a designated mark and plenty of facility in getting familiar with straight flying on this delicate little plane.

While living at Field 5 the pilots did spirals and acrobacy on Fields 4 and 6, where it was necessary for them to perfect their ability to make both right- and left-hand turns, to learn to locate other planes in the air during flight. and report the number of planes that they had seen, to execute the dreaded tail spin and learn how to come out of it safely, to make tight spirals, half rolls, and side-slips — in a word, to show their nerve, willingness, and ability to do exactly as told and to follow instructions without fail.

VRILLE OR SPIN

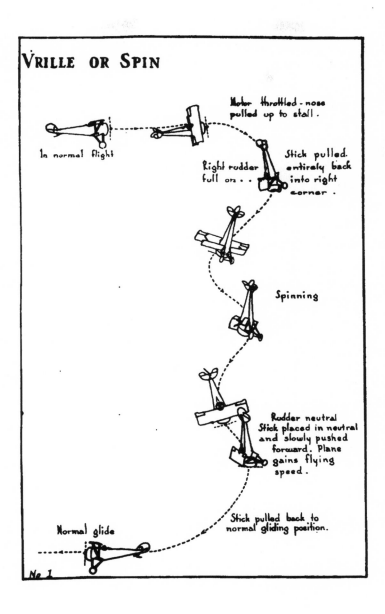

In normal flight

Motor throttled - nose
pulled up to stall.

Right rudder
full on . .

Stick pulled
entirely back
into right
corner .

Spinning

Rudder neutral
Stick placed in neutral
and slowly pushed
forward. Plane
gains flying
speed.

Stick pulled back to
normal gliding position.

Normal glide

№ 1

In the air work class on Field 4 the student was instructed how to make spiral turns at a bank of approximately 65°. He was expected to make continuous figure 8's at an elevation of one thousand meters or more. The object of this was to familiarize him with the new ship and enable him to make his turns correctly. In the right-hand turn the torque of the rotary motor has a tendency to pull the nose down, while in the left-hand turn this tendency is reversed. Consequently, he was instructed to use very little rudder in making a right turn but to go into the turn by banking the plane over slowly. When the desired amount of bank is reached, the stick is pushed back sufficiently to keep the plane from side-slipping, while the rudder is used to hold the nose up. With the left turn, on the contrary, the rudder is used to keep the nose down. Great care had to be used to do smooth figure 8's with this type of plane without getting into a vrille or spin.

One of the most important things that a pilot had to learn was how to get out of a spin. In order that he might have sufficient experience in doing this, and to make it safe for him to run the risks of getting into a spin while executing some other manoeuvre, it was necessary to teach him first how to get into a spin at will. Instruction as to how to use the controls so as to secure these results was given by an instructor in an airplane on the ground. The student was then expected to go through the same performance smoothly and accurately until he had satisfied the instructor that he thoroughly understood exactly what action of the controls would produce with speed and certainty a spin and what action would bring him out again. He was then told to take his plane up to an altitude of nearly five thousand feet before beginning anything.

The spin or vrille was executed by throttling down the motor, holding up the nose of the plane until its flying speed was almost lost, then kicking the right rudder violently over and pulling the stick sharply back and to the right. This caused the plane to fall immediately into a vrille or "spinning nose dive." In order to come out of the spin, the rudder is at first placed exactly in neutral, then the stick is brought into the neutral position and pushed slowly forward. This causes the plane to stop spinning and start a straight nose dive. After flying speed has been attained by the nose dive, the plane is gradually pulled up to a level flying position and the throttle opened.

The chief danger is that the student in his excitement will over-control and send the plane into a reverse spin or else will push the stick too far forward and turn a somersault, coming out of the spin on his back. Consequently, it was very important to see that the student went up high enough so that he had plenty of room to come out of any queer positions into which he might get before falling too close to the ground.

Personally, I should have been extremely glad to have been able to avoid the risks due to the necessity for teaching pilots aerial acrobacy in single seater machines, by using more Avros and perfecting the student's acrobacy in that extremely manoeuvreable dual control machine, but we had to use the planes that we could buy in France. Shortly after

VERTICAL VIRAGE

Shown as seen
from above.

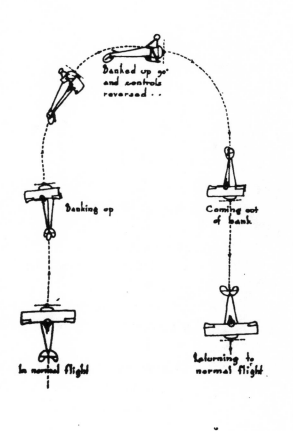

Banked up 90°
and controls
reversed . .

Banking up

Coming out
of bank

In normal flight

Returning to
normal flight

No. 3

the Armistice was signed, we began receiving from England Avros we ought to have had months before. In order to allow for a greatly enlarged programme, an excellent field was prepared and named Field 12, and was devoted entirely to Avro work under the direction of Lieutenant Raymond A. Watkins. The system known as the Gosport System, developed by Colonel Smith Barry and based on sound flying principles, was to have been used on this field in the work of transforming pilots from the training they had received on JN-4's, Caudrons, and Farnams. Unfortunately, due to our inability to secure enough Avros and our determination to use to the limit every plane we could secure from the Supply Department in Paris, we were unable to take advantage of our belief in the effectiveness of the Gosport System.

We all without exception would have preferred to have Avros for the larger part of our training. In this matter we were in entire agreement with the opinion of Colonel (later Brigadier-General) Lee, of the R. F. C., who told us in Washington in December, 1917, that the Avro was the best training plane that Great Britain had developed during the war. To show us what it was like, he had one sent over from England and gave frequent flights in Washington that winter. Yet some of our more experienced pilots were loth to admit the necessity of adopting a British training plane, and we never secured the full advantage of this information so generously given us by the British Aviation Liaison Officer.

In the class in spirals on Field 4, students were sent to an altitude of about four thousand feet and required to make

four good tight spirals to the left and one to the right with
a dead motor and land inside of a circle seventy-five yards
in diameter. The spirals were supposed to be completed at
an elevation of about two thousand feet, and pilots were
instructed to S down into the field from that altitude. To
execute this manoeuvre properly, the engine is throttled
down and a normal glide assumed, then the plane is slowly
banked over to an angle of about 70°. After passing the
45° point the controls become reversed, the stick, acting
on the elevators which now become rudders, is pulled back
until it is tight against the seat. The rudder is used as an elevator to hold the nose of the plane at such an angle as will
insure sufficient speed without stalling and on the other hand
without descending too fast. When S-ing into the field
after completing the spirals, it was necessary to use a fast
glide in order not to stall the plane on the sharp turns.

After satisfying the instructor of his ability to do tight
spirals, the pilot was next taught to do vertical banks or
virages, beginning at an elevation of about five thousand
feet. The movements of the controls in this manoeuvre are
the same as those in tight spirals, except that the plane is
banked over to 90° and the speed is increased to a point
where dizziness is brought on very rapidly.

After this the pilot learned the renversement, the quick-
est method of doing an aerial "about-face." This manoeuvre
is performed by first pulling smartly on the stick and then
turning the plane over on its back with a sharp, quick kick
on the right rudder, at the same time throttling the motor.

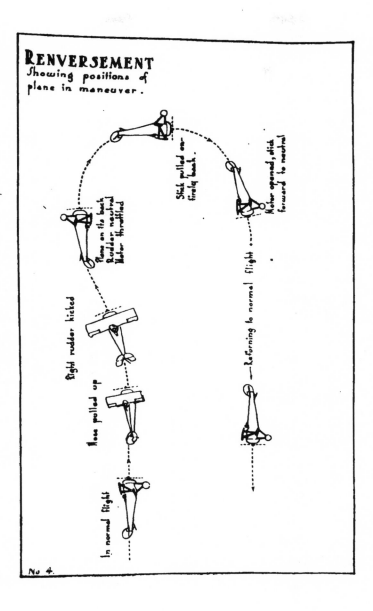

RENVERSEMENT
Showing positions of
plane in maneuver.

No. 4.

Just as the plane comes over on its back, the rudder is kicked sharply back into a neutral position and the stick pulled back into the seat, which causes the plane to come out into a normal glide.

The course of instruction at Field 5 was completed by learning what are known as "wing slips." When once in a wing slip, the plane falls very rapidly sideways and is controlled by a slight pressure on the stick and rudder. To get it into the wing slip, our pilots were taught to bank the plane over slowly, reducing the motor gradually and putting on reverse rudder so as to prevent the plane from diving, and at the same time pushing the stick slightly forward in order to overcome any tendency to spiral. To come out of the wing slip, it is necessary to push the rudder down so as to cause the plane to dive, and pull in the stick as though coming out of a spiral.

To follow all these instructions in detail in the small single seater Nieuport when they knew that some of their friends had already been killed in attempting to execute these manoeuvres, involved an amount of courage that is not understood by the average soldier on the ground. At the same time it was absolutely necessary for the flyer who wished to become a good pursuit pilot to do exactly as he was told and carry out his instructions to the letter.

The pilot who was able to master these various evolutions, quickly and safely, had nothing to fear from the air. The pilot who could not do it, but who had kept his inability from the knowledge of his previous instructors, was likely to meet with very serious and often fatal consequences. It was better for the Service that these fatal consequences should not happen in the course of combat at the Front; but it was very hard on the morale of the students that these fatalities overtook their friends on the flying field. One of the instructors in acrobacy — a remarkable pilot and the most painstaking and successful of teachers — told me it had been his painful duty to help remove eight bodies out of crashed planes on the acrobacy field alone.

With the perfection of modern methods of physical examination for aviators, it ought to be possible to prevent most accidents of this kind by taking poor pilots off the flying list before they reach this point. In many cases, however, the young pilot is too proud to admit that he is not physically fit to do this type of aerial acrobacy, and labors under a mistaken idea that by sheer will power he can provide what is lacking.

A considerable amount of weeding out occurred at Field 5, and every effort was made to prevent students from continuing in their combat training if they gave evidence of physical or mental inability to meet its requirements. Those who passed successfully went on to Field 7, which was furnished with the same type of plane equipped with larger and more powerful engines. Here the 120 H.P. Le Rhone took the place of the 80 H.P. This field, under the able direction of Captain (later Major) R. S. Davis, was one of our very best fields. It was the only field that succeeded in developing a band of its own — a band, by the way, that

WING SLIP

In normal flight   Banking up

Vertical
Starting slip by
pushing stick for-
ward giving 'up'
rudder and throt-
tling motor

Slipping

Dropping nose
by giving 'down'
rudder

Spiralling by
pulling stick back

Normal flight

Controls placed in nor-
mal flying position .
Motor opened . .

No. 5.

made excellent music, and greatly helped the men at Field 7 to be keen about their own organization. Both Fields 5 and 7 maintained very high morale among their officers and enlisted men. They took excellent care of their students, and endeavored to keep up their interest as they went along. When the weather prevented regular flying hours, every effort was made to encourage indoor baseball, handball, and boxing.

In addition to becoming familiar with a more powerful motor, the principal instruction at Field 7 consisted of practice in formation flying and the tactics of patrols, both offensive and defensive. Beginning with the simplest kind of formations, the pilot was gradually made familiar with the latest forms of aerial tactics as fast as they were brought back from the Front. We were helped by aviators who had engaged in actual combat with the enemy, and who had learned all that both friends and foes had to teach, in those famous battles in the air that formed the most spectacular part of the modern battlefield.

It was early borne in upon us that the aviator who was a grandstand player did not last long against an enemy formation. The successful pursuit pilot must curb his individual daring and his love of taking a sporting chance. Team play, coöperation, and the weight of numbers were all essential. As the war went on, fighting in the air became more and more a matter of maintaining successful formations intact under all circumstances. It will thus be seen that formation flying was one of our most important subjects and one that required skilful teaching and the closest application of all students.

It generally took about half an hour for the pilot to accustom himself to the new plane. Then he was given four hours' work in a small group of three or four to become familiar with the requirements of keeping his place in formation under all sorts of conditions. Then four hours in flying in a larger group, followed by four hours of work involving offensive and defensive tactics, and two hours of patrol at an altitude of about 15,000 feet.

There are several methods used in forming a patrol. Where there is a very large field, the patrol can be formed on the ground and the take off can be made in the desired formation. At the Front, however, many of the airdromes were small, and few of them large enough or good enough to make this feasible. Consequently, the desired formation was usually achieved in the air by one of two or three methods. The method generally followed at Field 7 was for the leader, before taking off, to acquaint each member of his formation with the following facts: the place over which planes would rendezvous; the altitude at which the patrol would form, generally about 1500 feet or high enough to prevent serious accidents, but not so high as to waste time or make it difficult for members of the patrol to find one another; the general direction which the leader would take after the formation was made; the probable route which he intended to follow; the way in which his plane was marked, usually by a streamer placed on right or left wing, depend-

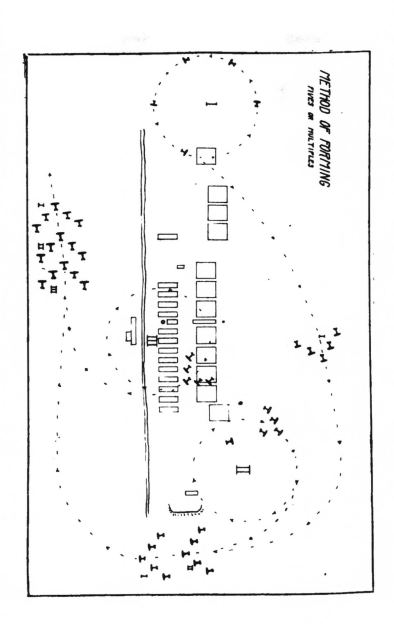

METHOD OF FORMING

FIVES IN MULTIPLES

ing upon whether the pilots were to use right or left turns
while forming the patrol. Patrols were formed as nearly over
the hangars of Field 7 as possible, in order that the instructors might the more readily note which pilots failed
to get into formation quickly and observe the cause of their
mistakes.

After each pilot of the patrol had received his instructions,
he took off as soon as possible without delaying or interfering
with the others, got his altitude, and proceeded to the designated rendezvous. As soon as he arrived at this place,
always maintaining the proper altitude, he began to make
circles in the specified direction. The leader was instructed
to wait for all of the patrol to form before starting out. As
soon as he saw that all were there, he gave the signal of
"attention" by rocking his plane from side to side.

In directing the manoeuvres of aerial patrols in the future,
we may expect that the use of the wireless telephone will
materially change many of the tactics which were common
at Issoudun in November, 1918. At the same time it is well
to remember that the enemy by powerful counter wireless
can render the successful operation of such means of communication extremely difficult and perhaps impossible.

The leader was instructed to keep a straight course until
the formation was in good order behind him, to make it as
comfortable as possible for all the members of the formation, and to govern his own speed by that of the slowest
plane in the patrol. Our pilots frequently had trouble in
learning to join their formations without taking too much

time and without getting lost. The most common fault was making the turns too wide. The pilots who arrived at the rendezvous first would grow tired of waiting, and would tend to form wider and wider circles over a large area, which made it difficult for the leader to get them together quickly. Another trouble was the tendency to keep climbing unconsciously to a higher elevation than that designated as the level of the first formation. Equipped with a more powerful motor than he had used before, and engaged in trying to see which of the hundred or more planes which might be in the air at that time belonged to his formation, it was very easy for the inexperienced pilot to keep climbing unless he frequently referred to his barometer.

Another difficulty was that of forming in a strong breeze, when the planes tend to make elongated curves unless the pilots take particular pains to make sharp turns when flying with the wind. In the face of these and kindred difficulties the best pilots soon came to the fore. As for the others it was often necessary to signal to the leader from the ground to start his patrol without waiting for those who were "lost, strayed, or stolen."

Pilots in formations for instructional purposes were numbered as follows:

> *Leader No.* 1,
> *First pilot on the left, No.* 2,
> *First pilot on the right, No.* 3,
> *Second on the left, No.* 4,

and so on.

In general, No. 2 was instructed to fly 50 meters above and behind No. 1, and at an angle of 45° to his left; No. 3 the same distance above and behind No. 1 and at an angle of 45° to his right; No. 4 and No. 5 took positions relatively similar to the left and right respectively of No. 2 and No. 3. Thus each member of the formation was 50 meters behind and above the pilot immediately in front of him and at a constant angle of 45° from him, no matter how many planes comprised the patrol. If at any time during the patrol the leader was obliged to drop out, No. 3 took his place.

The last man on the left was the "rescue man." It was his duty to watch any machine that fell out of formation and follow it down, but he did not land except in case of emergency. If everything was found to be satisfactory and the pilot whom he had followed down did not need assistance, the rescue man was instructed to ascend again and rejoin the formation, which he was supposed to find circling overhead. If the pilot whom he had followed had crashed and appeared to need assistance, it was the duty of the rescue man to land and render all possible aid. On observing this, the remainder of the formation was instructed to return to Field 7 and report.

The course in formation flying was graded. At first, in making simple turns, the leader was directed to give no signal, but to start gradually, at the same time speeding up his engine in order to assist pilots on the inside of the turn to execute the manoeuvre without stalling or losing flying speed. Pilots on the inside were told to throttle down as fast as possible and cut in slightly toward the leader in order to avoid being obliged to make too sharp a turn. They had to be careful not to approach too close to the arc described by the leader in order to avoid getting into the wash of his propeller. Pilots on the outside of the turn had to speed up their engines in order to negotiate the turn as fast as possible and at the same time maintain their positions. When the leader desired to change the altitude at which the patrol was flying, he did so slowly and deliberately, particularly in the early part of the training. He tried to avoid any tendency to run away from his formation. He had to keep track of the members of the patrol, and if necessary slacken speed in order to permit stragglers to catch up.

After our students had advanced far enough to be adjudged competent to gauge distances and to fly simple formations correctly with easy turns, they next undertook to learn various offensive manoeuvres in which they were obliged to execute sharp turns, at the same time always retaining their position in the formation in order to keep the patrol well knit together as a unit ready for offence or defence. In making these fast, sharp turns, all pilots were instructed to keep their position even though those on the inside were obliged to slow down almost to the point of stalling. Until the pilot could fly by instinct he was very likely to stall and fall into a spin while attempting to make the sharp inside turns of the advanced patrol manoeuvres. Here, however, the confidence which he had obtained in passing through the advanced work in acrobatic flying at Field 5 came to his as-

RIGHT ANGLE OR CROSS-OVER TURN

sistance and gave him that assurance which was necessary in order to have him learn aerial tactics.

The "cross-over" or 90° turn was considered advantageous for small patrols of three machines. In this manoeuvre each plane turns individually in its own place ; the inside pilot climbing on the turn and the outside pilot diving slowly to avoid danger of collision. Machines No. 2 and No. 3 cross so that each has approximately the same distance to cover. Instead of one getting ahead of the other, the formation remains the same. It has the advantage of enabling a right turn to be made quickly and at uniform speed.

Later on, in order to teach the pilots to fly in formation, automatically, without having to devote conscious attention to the coördination of eye and hand, the patrol leaders were sent out with particular orders to execute steep and unexpected dives and climbs, violent change of speed, and "archie dodging."

The Taylor stunt or right-about-face necessitated prearranged signals. The leader did a renversement or half roll while the other members of the formation did sharp right or left turns depending on their respective places. This manoeuvre was considered excellent practice in getting together rapidly and without loss of altitude.

The importance of constantly increasing the size of the unit was recognized and patrols of fifteen or more planes were occasionally attempted. It is well known that group flights of this nature were extensively used by the enemy during the summer of 1918. So thoroughly did the Ger-

mans appreciate the value of preponderance of numbers
in aerial fighting that they built more hangars than were
actually necessary for the number of planes in commission
at a given time. This enabled them to concentrate a large
number of machines at a given point within a very few
hours and without the necessity of waiting for the removal
of hangars and machine shops. A large group of hangars
empty yesterday, occupied to-day, could thus serve as a
base for very large formations early to-morrow morning.

Our large groups generally consisted of an agglomera-
tion of units of five planes each, the different units formed
in different locations at slightly different altitudes; the leading unit forming at the lowest altitude and the unit which
was to be the last in the group formation at the highest altitude. The disadvantage of attempting the use of very large
groups is the possibility of one poor pilot being able through
his eccentric flying to break up the entire formation. This
only emphasizes the great need for careful and thorough
instruction and the futility of trying to rush pilots to the
Front without their having acquired complete mastery of
the art. A man can be taught to fly in a few days of good
weather, but it is a matter of months before he becomes
sufficiently skilful in the art to make certain that he will
not break up a large group formation by erratic flying, poor
judgment, or getting rattled through having to give his
attention to too many things at once.

A defensive manoeuvre called the "Lufberry Show" was
named for a very brilliant ace from Wallingford, Con-

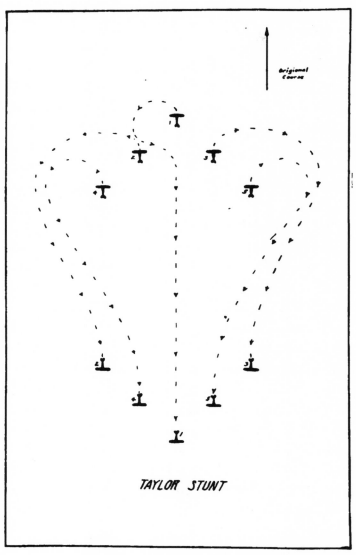

Original
Course

TAYLOR STUNT

necticut, who was killed at the Front. The formation when attacked instinctively formed itself into a milling circle, milling round and round so that each plane protected the rear of the plane in front and was itself protected by the plane behind. In order to form this circle, the last plane on the designated side speeds up, flies opposite the leader, and starts the circle, followed by the next to the last plane on that side until the leader is reached, when he is followed in natural order by the planes on the other side of the formation. As soon as the circle has been completed, the leader again assumes direction of the formation, sets the pace, narrows or widens the circle, gains or loses altitude in accordance with his judgment, and finally breaks the circle and gives the signal for reassembling.

The importance of this milling circle was dwelt upon with great emphasis by pilots who returned from the Front shortly before the Armistice was signed. It seemed to be the most effective way in which a small formation could escape successfully from the attack of a larger group. The chief danger lay in the possible adverse action of the wind, which might take one deeper and deeper into enemy territory while one was milling around, unless the leader took pains to elongate his curves toward home.

Leaders of formations were held responsible for having the formation fly at the designated altitude, and for observing ground signals, reporting the number of planes seen in the air, the towns over which they had taken their patrols, and the fact that at the end of two hours in the air the patrol

was reasonably near Field 7 and not so far away as to be
obliged to make forced landings through lack of gas and oil.
The members of each formation were also questioned as
to what they had seen happening on the ground, as well as
concerning planes which they had passed in the air. A pilot
can hardly get too much practice in formation flying, since
it forces him to fly by the feel of his plane rather than by
watching his instruments and observing the action of the
nose of his plane as compared with the horizon.

Captain Davis and his staff of instructors at this field,
owing to their conscientious effort to perfect their students
in the intricacies of securing the proper formation in the
air, executing manoeuvres with precision, maintaining their
places in the formation, and learning to judge distances accurately, produced excellent results.

An interesting device for teaching pilots to judge distance
correctly was a dummy ship staked out on the ground beyond the line of hangars. Students were obliged to indicate
required distances from this ship at various angles until
they had acquired the ability to place themselves at exactly
the specified angle and distance from the key ship.

It was learned at the Front that one of the chief factors
of success in aerial fighting is the character and ability of
the leader of the patrol. Unusually good eyesight, quick
judgment based on experience and prudence, ability to
think quickly and correctly in the face of great emergency,
coolness and courage in time of danger, and finally, a high
degree of skill in carrying out his manoeuvres so as to facil-

LUFBERRY SHOW

itate the correct functioning of the patrol—such are the qualities which make a great flight commander.

In the early days of the war we heard a great deal about individual combats in the air. Fonck, the great French ace, is said to have won most of his victories by sudden and unexpected attack alone on a solitary adversary, whom he had been able with his extraordinary vision to spot from afar and whom he had stalked as the Indian stalks the deer. The Indian must get to leeward of his quarry in order that its keen sense of smell may not enable it to detect his presence. The falconlike Fonck must get between his adversary and the sun in order that his quarry may be unable to see him and so escape from that terrible diving attack in which the pursuer, travelling at a rate of two hundred miles or more an hour, is upon him before he is even aware of his presence in the sky. This kind of aerial fighting has always appealed to newspaper readers and to pilots, but it has proved to be very expensive. Fonck is one of the few who survived this plan of aerial warfare, and it is said he was never outnumbered in a combat.

The average pilot, however, must owe his safety and his efficiency as a fighter to his ability to form a perfectly working cog in the machine of the patrol. It was said that our pilots who passed successfully at Field 7 wasted less time at the Front in acquiring the ability to fit into squadron manoeuvres and in learning new tactics than the pilots of any other army.

After completing the work in formation flying at Field 7,

students were sent to Field 8 to learn aerial combat. We were extremely fortunate in having at this field several of the very best combat pilots in existence. During the summer of 1918, Captain Robert Austin, the leading combat instructor, repeatedly demonstrated his ability to out-manoeuvre the best British and French aces that we could induce to visit the school. His flying was without flaw. He did not take such risks as did the British aces, and never went in for stunts near the ground or any unnecessary performances, but when combating against an opponent he showed an uncanny ability to out-guess the other's next manoeuvre and to keep his enemy always at his mercy.

The wonderful record that our graduates made at the Front and their success in sending down far more enemy planes than they themselves lost, was due in part to their thorough training in formation flying, but in very great measure to the confidence which came from having engaged in combat against Captain Austin and the members of his staff.

It was on Field 8 that a pilot had an opportunity to use every bit of the flying ability which he had acquired in all his previous experience. Some of the American trained pilots, who had flown too long on the old type of preliminary training planes, found it difficult to accustom themselves to the rapidity of manoeuvre demanded by the instructors at this field. While it was necessary that the pilot should have a good foundation in ordinary flying before coming here and should be able to do aerial acrobacy with skill and confidence, it was also essential that he should not have acquired any bad habits. The good combat pilot must be able to fly in any direction and in any attitude with supreme confidence in his machine and in his ability to put it in any desired position. He must be extremely alert. He must have formed the habit of seeing every visible plane in the sky and of knowing by instinct its approximate location at any given moment. It was said that the remarkably long life of Fonck at the Front was due to his constant inspection of every sector of the air. Probably seventy-five per cent of the pilots shot down at the Front were the victims of surprise attacks, and had no idea that there was an enemy in the immediate vicinity until he was so close that it was impossible to escape.

It was here on Field 8 that the aggressive spirit of a good polo player or of a first-class football player placed him in the front ranks of the combat pilots. The sluggish flyer is likely to leave himself open to attack by an aggressive pilot. The active, energetic, aggressive fighter is not only more likely to gain the advantage of offensive tactics, but will also be more likely to spot his enemy first and gain the benefit of position. The American boy is particularly good in games requiring quick judgment and correct action. This trait made him excellent in meeting the rapidly changing conditions of aerial combat. There were no hard and fast rules that could be laid down as to how to win out in a "dog fight," as the rough and tumble aerial combats were called. "If a Hun gets on your tail and you see the tracers coming close, you will most likely do some acrobatics that you never have done before." "In this work a steady hand, a cool head, and an all-seeing eye are the essential features of safety. Add to them ability to fly and skill in using the machine gun, and your results spell success." So we were told by pilots from the Front.

All the planes used on Field 8 were equipped with camera guns built like a machine gun, but shooting pictures instead of bullets. The pictures register the position of the enemy at the moment that the trigger is pulled. In this way it is possible for the instructor and the student to see what would have happened in actual combat. Examination of these pictures illustrates the tendency of one pilot to shoot when still at too great a distance for effective work, of another pilot to overshoot the mark, and of a third to fail to make sufficient allowance for the speed of the opposing machine.

In actual aerial gun fire, from six to ten bullets are fired in every burst or volley. This burst will have a spread of about thirty feet. If the gun is properly directed, the enemy plane will pass through this thirty-foot fan with a good chance of being hit in some vital spot. The camera gun takes but one picture for a burst, but that picture shows just what portions of the enemy plane would have come under gun fire, since it shows the direction in which the plane was flying and the distance of the plane at the time the shot was fired.

Any one who has ever done any target practice knows the importance of being able to learn the exact results as soon as possible after firing. When the student arrives at the stage where it is advisable for him to use an actual machine gun, he can aim at a target on a lake or on sand. In either case he is able to see at once, by the splash of the water or the little clouds of dust, exactly where his shots are hitting. The main drawback is that he is not firing at a rapidly moving airplane, but at targets which under the most favorable conditions are only able to move in an area of two dimensions instead of three. With the camera gun, on the other hand, the aviator can fire at an airplane which is going through all the gyrations of aerial combat. He then can descend, have his pictures immediately developed, and see the results of his judgment and skill. Failure to allow for deflection, forgetfulness of the fact that both gun-platform and target are in rapid motion, over-confidence, or the reverse, are plainly shown in the permanent record of the pictures. Good shots were just as plainly recorded—and more likely to be preserved than the others!

The first work at Field 8 was to train a pilot in the use of sights on his gun. Small parachutes were used. These were released at about ten thousand feet, care being taken to see that they were not dropped over territory where other machines were flying in large numbers. The greatest danger from a parachute is that it will get tangled up in the tail of the plane. Consequently, the best method is to release it when making a tight spiral or a skid with the motor off. In either case the draught, being athwart the ship, will carry the parachute away from the tail.

Shooting at the parachute was considered the best way of

beginning, because it involved less danger than shooting at another plane. When two pilots worked together, one acted as a target for the first half of the period and the other for the second half. The quarry was ordered to fly steadily in a given direction while the other pilot practised shooting at him from directly behind, from the sides, above and below, so as to secure practice at all angles and be obliged to make widely different allowances for direction and speed. It was advised that the attacker dive at his target many times, taking pictures only when sure of his results. Furthermore, pilots were encouraged to use the full allowance of their time, even though something happened to their target.

It was related of Lieutenant Luke, whose short life at the Front was full of an extraordinary number of victories over the Hun, that he never came in unless he had to, and that he was constantly borrowing some one else's plane—so greatly did he appreciate the truth that *practice makes perfect.* It was said that his death was due to his fondness for fighting alone and his dislike of formation flying. His record is more fully given elsewhere.

Practice in avoiding surprise attack was taught as follows: A pilot was sent out to patrol the road between two towns. His orders were to patrol his designated territory until he saw his adversary and then to engage in combat. Naturally, it was the object of the attacker to employ all the rules for successful attack, namely, to make use of the sun, mist, and clouds so as to approach without being seen and to keep between his quarry and the sun when delivering the final shot. His object was to be directly in the area in which the quarry would have the greatest difficulty of seeing anything.

As soon as sufficient practice had been obtained in single patrols, groups were designated to patrol between given points and other groups were told off to attack them. The instructions were that members of the patrol should fly well apart, avoiding close formations, and that each member of the formation should S to and fro so as to have a clear vision of the entire sky. The first member of the patrol to sight the opposing group was directed to leave his place in the formation and signal to the leader. When the attack was made, each member of the patrol was directed to pick out an adversary and combat with him, taking care to avoid collision with other planes. After making one shot with his camera gun, each pilot was directed to attempt to withdraw as fast as possible to one of the boundaries of the patrolled area. The pursuing pilot was directed to cease pursuit as soon as his adversary had reached this rendezvous. The escaping pilot was then directed to circle at an agreed altitude and wait for the other members of his group. On their arrival they formed again and continued as before.

It was expected that in this course at Field 8 a pilot should learn to sit tight in his plane in such a manner as to be able to use his gun sights without moving about in his seat; to use his sights quickly and accurately, as instinctively as a trapshooter firing at clay pigeons; to handle his plane intuitively in all manoeuvres and be able to bring it out of any given evolution in the desired position with relation

to his opponent; to keep his eye constantly on the enemy
and fly by the "feel" of his ship; to make successful aggressive attacks under various conditions; to manoeuvre
out of a difficult position and turn the tables on his opponent; to acquire a falconlike ability to see everything in the
sky above and below; and to spot his quarry from afar.

The pilot who was able to satisfy Captain Austin of his
ability to do these things had no reason to fear that he would
be out-manoeuvred by any Hun whom he was likely to
meet. Of course, if through carelessness or misfortune he
became separated from his formation and was attacked by
superior numbers, his ability to engage in successful combat
was of small importance compared with the speed of his
ship in getting home.

At the time the Armistice was signed, Captain (later
Major) Harry L. Wingate, who was in charge of the field,
was extraordinarily successful in overcoming the difficulties
of keeping in commission a large number of the monoplanes and other types of small scout machines which were
in use at this field, and which received very severe handling
in the course of aerial combat work. Constant inspection of
machines after they had come in from flight, a high morale
among the enlisted mechanics, and a splendid determination to overcome every obstacle at no matter what cost, enabled Captain Wingate to graduate from fifteen to twenty
men every flying day at his field. Considering the type of
planes that he had to work with and the severity of their
use, this was a remarkable achievement.

While still living at Field 8, the student received instruction in aerial fire at Field 14, which was built especially for this purpose. The work consisted of shooting with Vickers Machine Guns mounted on type 24 Nieuports and using the Victor gear. The targets were on the ground, and consisted of trenches, silhouettes, and condemned machines, with shot screens so placed as to register hits when the shooting was made with proper deflection. During the course each student fired from eight hundred to one thousand rounds in the air, and by being able "to see the dust fly" attained confidence in using his sights and proved that he had a sufficient knowledge of deflection to engage successfully in aerial combat at the Front. Diving at ground targets requires nerve and confidence, but proved not to be as dangerous as had been supposed. There were no casualties at this field. Captain George W. Eypper, who had entire charge of the work in Aerial Gunnery after Major G. Bonnell went to the Front, carried on as successfully as his predecessor.

CHAPTER XIV

OBSERVATION AND NIGHT PURSUIT

TWO new problems arose in the summer of 1918. The first was the necessity of teaching observation pilots to fly DH-4's; the second was the demand for pilots who could undertake the dangerous work of night pursuit. When the DH-4's with the Liberty motor began to arrive from the United States, conditions at Field 7 were such that there seemed to be more room there, and a better chance of successful operation without interference with the regular work of the field, than at any other point. In the mean time Field 10 was secured, and especially prepared to meet the need for a large field devoted entirely to instruction on DH-4 planes. This was the only plane that was being manufactured in the United States for use at the Front. While not at all adapted for combat work, it was probably originally intended as a two-seater fighter. As a matter of fact, it was used by observation and bombing squadrons.

The training of observers was carried on at Tours at the Second Aviation Instruction Centre. Here at Field 10 we attempted the instruction of observation pilots, and aimed to give them some knowledge of what the observer was trying to do. There was a ground course, planned to cover from two to five days, and meant to give the pilot an elementary knowledge of the work carried on in an observation squadron. It was given by officers who had seen service at the Front, and who were able to impress the student with the importance of the work. This was all the more necessary because the

View of part of Field 10 and a D.H.-4, Liberty motor

average pilot, longing for the excitement of pursuit squadron activity, was inclined to look with little favor on the actual routine that was before him. Lectures on the organization of the ground forces, intended to give familiarity with methods of attack and defence used by both artillery and infantry; lectures on interpretation of aerial photography, intended to teach the pilot the value of the photographic work done on his missions; and lectures on the methods of coöperation with the other branches of the Service were given from time to time.

Tactical and strategical reconnaissance; a thorough explanation of the use of the compass and its importance in cloudy or foggy weather; explanation of the other instruments used in aerial navigation; interpretation of things seen on the ground and their respective importance; studies of the organization and actual experience of observation squadrons; the kind of preparation needed for an artillery mission; a pilot's duties on a photographic mission; the importance of contact patrol; lectures on the Liberty motor and the use of the somewhat complicated set of instruments in front of the pilot's seat in a DH-4, were given as well as possible under the circumstances.

Due to the pressing demand from the Front that observation pilots be sent up immediately, and due to the large number of crashes of the DH-4's, flown by inexperienced pilots, it was felt that every available minute of flying weather should be taken advantage of, even at the cost of missing some of the important lectures. This was very dis-

couraging for the highly trained observers and aerial photographers who were detailed to the work of ground instruction at Field 10. The demand from the Front, however,
was so insistent, and the mortality among DH-4 pilots so
extraordinarily high, that it was necessary to give our students all the actual flying instruction possible.

The first part of the course consisted of ninety minutes
of dual control work with an instructor, verified by a practical examination with a tester in which the student had to
demonstrate his ability to make forced landings and to get
his plane out of the various skids and slips into which it
was thrown by the tester.

After satisfying the instructors of his ability to use the
Liberty motor correctly, and to handle the DH-4 satisfactorily, he was required to make a dozen good landings from
an elevation of about one thousand feet and to practise sharp
banks and figure 8's at an altitude of about twenty-five hundred feet. This elementary air work, covering about three
hours, was followed by practice in spirals, first loose spirals,
later tight spirals, with the machine banked up to 90°; and
finally about four hours in formation flying. It was not a satisfactory course, but it was the best we could do under the
circumstances, considering the imperative demands from
the Front.

None of this work in DH-4's should have been given in
France. The pilots came from America, the ships and motors
came from America, so did the gas, oil, and spare parts —
everything, in fact, that was used at the field. All this had

to be brought across an ocean infested with submarines. Better fields for the work could easily have been found in America, much nearer to the source of supply of both men and machines. I suppose that for the sake of encouraging our citizens the Administration thought it was better to say that one hundred and fifty DH-4's had been sent to France, than to say that they had been sent to an American training school. Of course, the public did not know that the one hundred and fifty sent to France for training purposes could have been used more effectively at home and at far less expense. By sending them to France, it added to the total of machines shipped overseas—a total that was never large enough to satisfy American public opinion.

The difficulties of operating these heavy ships on a wet French airdrome were enormous. The necessity for bringing over so much material, including gas and oil, to do what should have been done in America was most unfortunate. It would have saved time, money, and men, if those DH-4's, instead of being sent to American training schools in France, had been used for the instruction of our personnel at home and only enough sent to the training schools in France for use in a refresher course. At Issoudun we ought not to have been required to do more than see that a pilot already trained on American DH-4's had a chance to learn the latest wrinkles as taught by officers just back from the Front, before being sent there himself.

Night Flying was practically unheard of before the war. Gradually the use of night bombers became practicable, and both Paris and London were treated to frequent nocturnal visits. The answer to this was the development of night pursuit flying. It is difficult for a pilot to imagine any greater risk than being expected to take up a delicate pursuit plane at night. It had to be done, however, and Field 7, with its large expanse of open country, offered the best location. It was regrettable that the necessity of night work interfered to a certain extent with the sleep and rest of the men who were carrying on the regular duties of the work in formation flying, but this was unavoidable. It was one of our greatest disappointments that the Armistice was signed just as our night pursuit pilots were receiving the finishing touches of their training in coöperation with the Searchlight Company.

Hunting the Hun in the dark was a favorite sport of the late Captain Armstrong, of the R. A. F., Commanding Officer of the first British Night Pursuit Squadron at the Front. He himself had a record of having brought down more than fifty Hun machines, including the gigantic five-engine Gotha.

One day I was crossing the street from my quarters to my office, when the unaccustomed sound produced by a plane looping near the ground called my attention to the extraordinary antics of a Sopwith Camel. It made loop after loop over Headquarters, missing the roofs of the buildings by only a few feet, finally coming so close to the ground as to cause

Used on Night Flying: Sopwith Camel

Nieuport 33, 18-meter, 80 H.P. Le Rhone motor

us all to hold our breaths as the marvellously skilful pilot pulled his ship out of a loop within a few inches of the ground, fairly touching the long grass. Then the machine was pulled straight up into a "zoom" of unparalleled magnitude. It stalled, fell like a leaf, fluttering from side to side, recovered, made a tight spiral incredibly near the ground, lit as gracefully as a butterfly, and hardly rolled more than a few inches. Then a small dog bounded out of the cockpit, from the pilot's lap to the ground, while the pilot himself with a novel under his arm and a smile on his face walked nonchalantly across the airdrome. Thus did Captain Armstrong announce his arrival.

One of the greatest differences between the Royal Air Forces and our own was that they believed in encouraging morale and stimulating their pilots to recklessness by such exhibitions as these, even though the most skilful pilots occasionally met their death in this fashion. Captain Armstrong himself was killed shortly after the Armistice while stunting too close to a hangar.

The American Air Service held that the advantages of such recklessness were more than offset by the increased chances of losing valuable lives. The war did not last long enough for us to determine which was the proper method. There is no question but that there was a far higher morale among the pilots in the British squadrons than in our own. This was due to various causes. Furthermore, I do not believe that the type of pilot that was being graduated from Issoudun during the summer and fall of 1918 needed exhibitions of this kind to make him willing and ready to take all necessary chances when he went after the Hun.

Captain Armstrong was the most graceful and skilful flyer that I have ever seen. He was not quite as good in aerial combat as our own Captain Austin, as was shown in a famous twenty-minute struggle. We were most fortunate, however, in being able to secure his services in starting our instruction in night pursuit.

Planes for night pursuit work are equipped with navigation lights,—one at the end of each wing, one on the tail, and one inside the cowl,—all of which may be turned on or off at the pleasure of the pilot. There is also a signalling light placed under the seat of the ship for signalling to the ground. This is used to give a code letter to the operator of the field lights, so that when the pilot gets ready to land after circling the field, the landing light is flashed on for his benefit. In order to avoid accidents in the darkness, each ship is given a number, and is not supposed to land except when that number appears in the ground lights on the landing field. In addition to the signal lights on the ground, there are two powerful searchlights, used as landing lights, placed along the line of direction of the wind. Planes leave them on the right when taking off and landing. Gradually the students became accustomed to landing with less and less light and to taking off in the darkness without any lights at all. Finally, they acquired sufficient skill to make good landings with the landing light on for only thirty seconds. This practice was essential because of the necessity of having as little light as possible showing on the airdrome at the Front. The position of the field is constantly shown by one small red light on the ground.

Half a dozen of the most skilful pilots that we could secure, under the able leadership of Captain R. Melin, were selected for this training. They began practising landings at night in an Avro with Captain Armstrong in the instructor's seat. After being given a sufficient number of landings and flights to enable them to get accustomed to night flying in a delicate, highly manoeuvreable plane, they kept on practising until they gained sufficient confidence to fly on dark nights without having to worry about the technical side of the art. Our students were so good that it took only from six to ten flights with the instructor before they were ready to go solo on the same machine. Then followed from ten to twenty-five more landings on the Avro until the pilot was confident that he knew where the ground was and had learned not to misjudge the few things which are visible even on dark nights. The Avro is an ideal machine for this purpose.

After the student had shown the necessary proficiency on the Avro, he was sent up in the Sopwith Camel, a single-seater machine equipped with a 120 H.P. motor, the machine preferred by Captain Armstrong as being most effective for night pursuit. In the Camel the student practised landing fifteen or more times until he acquired the necessary skill. In connection with practice in landing, the students were sent up to do the usual air work, utilizing from ten to twenty-five flights in this way in accordance with their own individual difficulties in mastering the problem of correctly going through manoeuvres without being able to see the horizon. Thus the students gradually came to be able to execute the same acrobatics at night as in the daytime. During this stage, also, they were given experience in flying in the searchlight,— a very trying performance at first. They also had practice in avoiding it; and in sending the necessary signals.

After the technique of night flying in small pursuit planes was mastered (owing to the scarcity of Sopwith Camels we also used the Nieuport, type 28), the most interesting part of the work began, namely, practice in attacking night bombers. The night bomber is picked up by listening devices, his position is given to the searchlight operators, and the pursuit pilot is sent up to the known elevation of the night bomber and into his approximate location. When the pursuit pilot has reached his appointed position, he gives the signal with one of Very's lights. Immediately the searchlights, directed by the listening devices, are turned on the night bomber, who is then held in the powerful rays. The pursuit plane comes up in the blackness behind until he is a little below and directly in the rear of his prey, and shoots from a distance of about twenty yards and at an angle of about 10° below the night bomber. He has plenty of time to fire deliberately and with care. Captain Armstrong used to say that the results were so satisfactory as to be "hardly sportsmanlike"!

As a means of offsetting the successful use of the large night bombing planes there is no doubt that the night pursuit squadrons were eminently satisfactory. In fact, it was expected that the enemy would soon have copied this development to an extent which would have made the use of the great Handley Page night bomber extremely precarious. The inability of a huge, heavily weighted, bombing plane to manoeuvre with sufficient rapidity to dodge the agile scout was sure to be his undoing, particularly as there would be no friendly searchlights in the enemy country to enable him to see the scout and open fire on his assailant. The answer would be to place searchlights on the bombing plane itself, although that would make it an easier mark.

It was a bitter disappointment to Captain Melin and his group of excellent pilots that the Armistice was signed in the very week that they were perfecting their ability to coöperate with the searchlight companies. After they had secured the necessary experience at the Front, they would have been used as instructors to develop future night pursuit squadrons.

CHAPTER XV
THE "PLANE NEWS"

OUR weekly paper, of which we were very proud, and on which we depended for all sorts of inspiration, both serious and humorous, was called the *Plane News*. Started under the auspices of Colonel Kilner in November, 1917, and printed by hand on an ancient mimeograph, it laid claim to being the first newspaper of the American Expeditionary Forces that was entirely edited and printed by soldiers. Seeing the advantages of being able to brighten a despondent community by this weekly budget of news and good cheer, Miss Givenwilson, then Directrice of the Red Cross Activities at Issoudun, secured the funds wherewith a real press and printing-office were established in camp. During 1918, this little paper steadily grew in influence and importance, although from time to time its personnel had to be changed, owing to the exigencies of military service. By the middle of the year it had become recognized as the official organ of the American Air Service in France.

Shortly after my arrival, Lieutenant H. M. Ogg, who had been acting as officer in charge of the *Plane News*, was ordered away and his place was taken by Captain Leo R. Sack, who had had plenty of journalistic experience in Washington. As a newspaper man, Captain Sack thoroughly appreciated the importance of having the paper run in such a way as to be read by the largest number in order to do the greatest possible amount of good. Under his guidance

Extra   Plane News.   Extra

Vol. 1, No. 46   On Active Service, France, October 9, 1918   Price 25 Centimes

PASSED BY CENSOR

MAJOR-GENERAL HARBORD ON "FLYING" VISIT TO 3rd A. I. C.--

PEACE MOVE ANSWERED BY NEW ALLIED PUSH AT FRONT

COMMANDING GENERAL OF S. O. S. IN RECORD FLIGHT FROM HDQRS.

Is Piloted by Col. W. G. Kilner in Liberty Plane to World's Finest Air Post

LT.-COL. BINGHAM RECEIVES CHIEF

First Time in Military History Man of Such High Rank Risks Long Cross-Country Flight

Major-General James G. Harbord, Commanding General of the Service of Supplies, American Expeditionary Forces, and second only to General Pershing, flew from Headquarters S. O. S. to the 3rd A. I. C. this morning. Col. Walter G. Kilner, Chief of Air Training, U. S. Air Service, piloted the machine.

The flight was made in record time in a Liberty plane.

Lieut.-Colonel Hiram Bingham, Post Commanding Officer, and staff received the officials, and conducted a tour of inspection.

The First Air Service Band was on the field at the time of his arrival.

ATHLETIC MEETING TONIGHT

At 8 o'clock tonight Athletic Directors of all organizations will meet at the J. C. A. Hut No. 2. The Athletic Director has called this special meeting for the purpose of discuss-

---

GENERAL TERM "AIR SERVICE" TO DESIGNATE TWO BUREAUS

Common Name to Include All Divisions Including Theory, Active Service and Production.

In a recent issue of the Official Bulletin the War Department authorizes the following:

"In a recent communication received at the offices of Maj. Gen. W. L. Kenly and Mr. John D. Ryan, from the Adjutant General's Office, it is stated that hereafter Air Service will be the general term including the Division of Military Aeronautics and the Bureau of Aircraft Production.

The officers and enlisted men of the Division of Military Aeronautics and those serving in the Bureau of Aircraft Production shall be known as members of the Air Service, Military Aeronautics, and Aircraft Production, respectively.

The chief of the Bureau of Aircraft Production will hereafter be addressed as the Director of Aircraft Production, and the chief of the Division of Military Aeronautics, as the Director of Military Aeronautics."

AMERICANS, BRITISH AND FRENCH DRIVE FROM CAMBRAI TO MEUSE

U. S. Senate for Rejection of All Dealings With Germany, Austria and Turkey

As it is answer to the German's cry for peace, the Allies have launched a new and vigorous offensive extending on a wide front. The British operating between Cambrai and Saint Quentin, a front of twenty miles, have, with the help of American forces from North Carolina, South Carolina and Tennessee, penetrated the enemy territory to a depth of more than three miles and have taken many towns and hundreds of prisoners.

On the right flank of the British-American attack the French have simultaneously thrown heavy forces against the enemy with extraordinary results.

"IT IS UP SOME MORE"

Henry Watterson, blind editor of The Courier-Journal, and editor of The Courier-Journal, Louisville, Ky.,--John-son, write PLANE NEWS. --The boys want mail from home and the

---

In the sector of the Meuse river other American forces have forced the enemy to give up bridgehead stronghold and have the opposing forces well under way in a hurried retreat.

The entire line from Cambrai, south

the *Plane News* increased in size, circulation, and influence. As a means of raising our spirits and keeping us steadily at work in the face of great difficulties, it was of supreme importance to the camp.

The *Plane News* was most fortunate in having on its permanent staff two artists of first-class ability and ingenuity — Sergeant George D. Alexander and Private Timoleon Johnston. Their series of cartoons depicting various features of camp life and aviation experience were enjoyed by thousands every week. The associate editor was Private Gene D. Robinson, whose *Epistles of Peter* rank high as keen comment on the conduct of the war veiled in humorous vein. Of a trip to Paris he wrote as follows:

A guy should get a taxi without talking to the driver, as the metres run on just the same when you're talking. Always have your home address in your pocket, as the ride may be finished in an ambulance. Don't ask the driver where you are going, as he will figger that you want to tour the city anyway and the only place he won't take you is the top of the Eiffel Tower, but he will add that on the bill anyway. The taxi will finally stop when it runs out of gas and if the name of the street is Rue de Bill it's probably the place you're bound for. Pay the bill and if he says anything tell him that he need not deliver the car to you, but to keep the money anyway.

If you go in a café at 11 o'clock the waiter will get around about 1 o'clock. There is nothing on the menu to eat, no matter how careful you read it, and when the food comes you don't know whether to salt and pepper it or to use a nut cracker. While you are studying, the waiter will ask for a tip because the clock strikes 2 o'clock. Tell him to bring you the leaf of a tree, a limp dish rag with icing, something sweet and slimy on the scalloped tail of a high geared snail, and he will say something in French, probably that his daughter sprained her ankle while taking a violin lesson, but outside of that everything will be lovely.

I guess I will close now as I got to be in a battle today, which may decide the war, and I wish you would send them ten bucks you owe me Steve.

Yours 'til Germany goes Democratic,   PETE

Occasionally we got a letter, the publication of which in the *Plane News* helped to cheer everybody up, such as the following from Colonel Kilner:

I desire to commend the work of you and your Staff at the 3rd A. I. C. in the training of pursuit pilots. Officers at the Front state that the pursuit pilots now being received at the Front are the best that have ever been turned out, and are highly pleased with their performances. Request that you convey this commendation to all concerned.

Editorially, the *Plane News* remarked:

Such positive proof of the effectiveness of the school is gratifying. All along we have felt that we were on the right track, and that the pilots that were graduated from the school to the front, would reflect high credit on their country and on the Air Service.

Only the fittest survive here. But if they cannot make good here, why send unfit pilots to the front where the life or death of thousands of doughboys depends upon their efforts?

It is pleasing to know that the "pursuit pilots now being received at the front are the best that have ever been turned out" and that officers "are highly pleased with their performances."

With every officer and man and every student officer at the Third A. I. C. on his toes to make good, and all working with energy and enthusiasm that can not be equalled, there is every reason to believe we will continue to send the "best pilots" to the front.

From time to time the *Plane News* would raise the ambitions of our pilots by printing articles concerning work done by graduates of the school after they had gone to the Front. Here is an article of this type about Lieutenant Frank Luke, Jr., who won undying fame in his few weeks at the Front:

Luke is gone, but the memory of his exploits will remain long after this war is forgotten.

As a balloon strafer he had no equal and he seemed to take a keen delight in this most dangerous of aviation combats. His plan of attack was simple. A German balloon would be located and Luke, with several other pilots, would climb into the clouds and when at a point above the balloon he would dive out of the clouds, followed part way down by the rest of the formation, whose particular part would be to start a "dog fight," with the Fokkers protecting the balloon.

Luke would continue his nose dive regardless of the archies that would by this time be sprinkling the air with their shrapnel souvenirs. When within a few hundred feet of the victim he would let go a burst of incendiary bullets. Immediately there would be a flash of flame skywards; two figures would shoot earthward and two parachutes would gracefully open up like a lady's fan—the show would be over quicker than it takes to tell it. Luke would immediately zoom up and join the "dog fight" if it still continued, but generally it would be over by the time he gained the same altitude, one side or the other having been defeated.

Luke's greatest feat and one that probably will never be equalled, was on September 18th when he brought down three planes and two balloons in twelve minutes. Most of Luke's victories were shared by pilots in his flight who held off the Fokkers while Luke got the balloons. The officer who teamed with Luke and who shares the most victories with him is 1st Lieut. Jos. F. Wehner, 27th Aero Squadron, of Lynn, Mass., who has to his credit seven balloons and two planes—Lieut. Wehner has since been shot down, the last seen of him was on September 18th fighting five Fokkers while protecting Luke.

In the operations office of the First Pursuit Group, to which Luke belonged, is a large piece of cardboard fastened on the wall, at the top printed in one inch letters are the words: "Hall of Fame," and underneath are the names of the pilots who have brought down one or more German planes or balloons. After each name is a small facsimile of an iron cross, each cross meaning a victory. There are eighteen of these crosses after Luke's name. They were placed there in the short space of seventeen days, another record that will probably never be equalled.

The last heard of Lieut. Luke was on September 29th, when he dropped a note to an American Balloon Squadron stationed near Verdun, which read: "Watch for burning balloons." Shortly afterwards two German balloons were seen to go up in flames. Luke did not return; he was entirely alone on his last expedition; no one saw him go down and how he came to his end will probably never be known. The official record reads as follows:

"Second Lieutenant Frank Luke, Jr., Phoenix, Ariz., 27th Aero Squadron, First Pursuit Group. Record: 14 balloons, 4 planes. Missing since Sept., '18."

We often had occasion to remind our students of the fact that Luke had had considerable difficulty in the first part of the course, and had been sent back once or twice for failing to satisfy his instructors. He was the kind, however, whom nothing could discourage, and he would take every opportunity to secure all the instruction and practice in flying that could possibly be obtained.

The *Plane News* was particularly useful in the trying days after the fighting had ceased. One of the schemes it helped to develop in order to make time pass more rapidly was thus described:

Field 9's Team in the Plane Assembling Competition
End of Part I, Wings removed and packed Plane ready for shipment on truck

Plane Assembling Competition
Field 8's Team half through Part II, reassembling the Plane

A new sport, one that can be played only on a flying field, sprang into popularity here last Saturday when teams of airplane mechanics, working against time, demonstrated to a huge crowd on the Main Field, just how fast an airplane can be dis-assembled and subsequently completely rigged ready for the pilot.

The initial contest created keen enthusiasm and the rooters cheered the workers on their work with the same spirit that fans encourage the progress of baseball, football and track teams. The interest created is especially gratifying as this combination of work and play had not been tried out before. The contest also demonstrated how fast American Airplane Mechanics can work, as the slowest team finished in better time than it was anticipated would be necessary for the winning team.

The ship used for the initial contest was the Nieuport, type 27, with a 120 horse power Le Rhone motor.

Too much credit can not be given the men comprising the competitive teams, whether they be of the winning one or the last to finish, for the "pep" displayed and particularly the ingenuity in tools and special equipment used as time savers — as all sorts of jigs and special tools were to be seen. Inquiry of the engineering officers of the various fields brought out the facts that they were the tools regularly used on the fields and were the results of the ideas of the mechanics engaged in different work. Nothing in the way of tools being furnished by the government for this work, it being up to the mechanics themselves to design and make tools to save time, and the results of Saturday's contest speak only too eloquently as to how they have met the emergency.

The contest was won by the team from Field Eight, composed of the following:

Ship Crew — Sergeants First Class Harry F. Woodring and Chas. F. Polson, Corporal Harry Bearcroft and Privates First Class Michael Dolphin and Frank L. Lacher. Motor Crew — Sergeants Aaron I. Rose, Bernard J. Gorman and Henry R. Clark.

Total time consumed for the four operations was $97^1/_5$ minutes. This includes the penalization of $1^1/_5$ minutes on the first operation.

The second team was that of Assembly and Test, composed of the following:

Ship Crew — Sergeants First Class C. Winkler, C. W. Misfelt and T. W. Reardon and Sergeants R. W. Lyon and A. J. Johnston. Motor Crew — Sergeant First Class G. W. Puryear, Sergeant R. S. Johnson and Corporal F. R. Moore.

Time was 103 minutes for the four operations.

Third to finish was Field Five, teams comprising the following:

Ship Crew — Sergeants First Class Jesse Parcell and Albert Busk and Sergeants Frederick Gordon, Chester Tidland and John Downey. Motor Crew — Sergeants First Class Theodore Holmes and Wm. H. McMahon and Sergeant Bueren Manwiller.

Time 104 minutes.

The total operation of which time is given above, was composed of four separate operations. First being that of disassembling the ship, lashing the wings to the side of the fuselage ready for transporting. Second operation, that of reassembling the ship, lining same ready for flight, safetying all bolts, nuts and turnbuckles so that it would pass inspection. These two operations were done by what we have called "Ship Crews," composed of five men. The third and fourth operations were, namely, the taking out of the motor, and installing of the motor in the ship, including starting of same. This was handled by what we have called "Motor Crews," composed of three men.

The following is a table of figures showing the time taken by different crews for the different operations, and it will be interesting to note that it was anyone's contest up until the last moment:

First Operation —

Field Fourteen, 13 minutes.
Field Eight, $13^1/_2$ minutes.
Field Seven, 15 minutes.

Second Operation —

Assembly and Test, 25 minutes.
Field Seven, $31^4/_5$ minutes.
Field Eight, $37^1/_2$ minutes.
Field Five, $37 /_5$ minutes.

Plane Assembling Competition
Part II, reassembling the Plane

Plane Assembling Competition
End of Part III, taking out the motor

Third Operation—

Aero Repair, 13⁴/₅ minutes.

Field Eight, 15¹/₂ minutes.

Field Fourteen, 18²/₅ minutes.

Field Five, 18⁴/₅ minutes.

Fourth Operation—

Field Five, 29²/₅ minutes.

Field Eight, 31 minutes.

Assembly and Test, 33⁴/₅ minutes.

The second contest of the series will be staged this afternoon on the Main Field with Nieuport 23-meter planes, equipped with 80 horse power Le Rhone motors. Cash prizes of 200 francs for the first and 100 francs for the team second under the wire will be given by the *Plane News*. The *Plane News* also has provided for the purchase of banners for the winners.

The second contest aroused keen competition, and further reductions were made in the time for the four operations. The sporting editor of the *Plane News* wrote this report:

Spurred by the presence of a large crowd and two bands, the Main Field and Field 7 organizations, 300 francs prize money and the desire to hang up a record, Air Service mechanics staged a real sporty exhibition of the new sport of disassembling and assembling an aeroplane on the Main Field Saturday afternoon.

Minutes were clipped off the records made on the previous contest and it is believed that the winners ran up a record for 23-meter Nieuports that will stand for some time to come. The increasing number of ingenious tools which have been made by the different crews were quite noticeable. There were very few penalties considering the time taken for the entire four operations and all expectations have been surpassed. There is no doubt that the Airnats of this center would be able to hold their own against any and all competition.

Results of Saturday's contest are as follows:

First—Field Two A, 1 hour 2 minutes 40 seconds.

Second—Field Seven, 1 hour 7 minutes 10 seconds.

Third—Aero Repair, 1 hour 8 minutes 45 seconds.

Probably the most remarkable thing to take place in the way of fast workmanship was in the third operation, where the Aero Repair took out the motor in 11 minutes.

The Field 2 A team which won the first prize of 200 francs donated by the *Plane News* was composed of the following men: Sgts. Marson, Brindell, Rust, Pierce, McFadden and Cpls. Hawn, Dotson, and Muhler. Field 7's team which won the second prize of 100 francs was composed of men from the 37th, 640th, and 173rd Squadrons; M. E. Cambell, Sgts. Bowman, Barbee, Peck, Yepsen, Phelps and Chauffeurs Hamilton and Lewis.

Before closing this brief account of the activities undertaken by the *Plane News*, I must give one more of its interesting stories about Issoudun.

The bravery and daring of American aviators is not confined to active service at the front, as the following remarkable experience of a student pilot at this advanced training center will prove: The moniteur was giving instructions, and upon the day the accident occurred, the moniteur, as usual, rose in the air ahead of the pilot, who followed, and the two planes quickly sought an altitude of 5000 feet. Then began a series of manoeuvers, the moniteur demonstrating for the benefit of his student. The Lieut. suddenly dove at the instructor, expecting him to get out of his line of flight. Through some miscalculation or misjudgment of distance, the moniteur held his plane too near the diving plane, and the engine head of the student's plane collided with his wings. With one wing crushed, and with such force of momentum that it was impossible to gain even a fraction of control, the moniteur's plane dropped like a stone to the earth, resulting in the instant death of the instructor.

A peculiar feature of the accident was the cutting of the engine's fastenings of the student's plane to such an extent that the engine dropped from its place and fell to the ground. The result was the destruction of any resemblance of balance, and the plane wobbled

Plane Assembling Competition
Beginning of Part IV, putting the motor back in position

Plane Assembling Competition
Cheering the winning Team from Field 14. The riggers of this Team in the foreground, having finished their work, Parts I and II, are watching the motor mechanics complete Part IV

uncertainly on unsteady wings. Seeing and grasping the situation instantly, the pilot steadied the plane against a probable fall by shifting his body so as to counter the loss of balance and so succeeded in keeping the plane on a fairly even keel. Then started a series of glides controlled by the shifting of the weight of his body, that for coolness and daring have few parallels.

Seizing a moment when the plane rode at an even keel, the student mounted quickly upon the fuselage at full length and again steadying the machine, he started his descent to the ground, with no control except the weight of his body against a counter inclination of the unbalanced plane to flutter into a fall. Any panic or nervousness upon his part would have resulted in death, and knowing this and realizing that the odds were heavily against him the lieutenant manipulated the controls of the plane, and worked his bodily balance control as calmly as if he was ten feet from the earth. The ground gradually shaped into a recognizable view, and with his admirable coolness the lieutenant glided to earth with a landing worthy of a finished pilot. The remarkable nerve and firm determination of the pilot had won the day—and saved his life.

The whole daring performance had been observed by the pilot of another plane which had followed the wounded plane downwards, unable to give the slightest aid. The pilot of the second plane was wearer of the Croix de Guerre and had fought air battles at the front where scenes of reckless daring and paramount bravery were commonplace to him, but he later stated that the feat of the student pilot was one of the most remarkable for coolness and bravery that he had ever witnessed.

CHAPTER XVI

THE ENGINEERING DEPARTMENT

TO the average person, a flying school is a place where flying is taught, but to the enlisted man on duty at a flying school, it is a place where wrecked planes are continually being repaired. Young pilots are always making errors in judgment that result sometimes in damage to themselves, but more often in damage to the airplane.

Crashes that occurred on the airdromes of outlying fields were taken care of by the engineering department of the field concerned. Those that occurred on cross-country flights or in the area between the fields, and which had to be rendered first-aid by our field service department, were brought in to the main field and turned over to the aero repair department, under the direction of Captain Duncan Dana. If the crashed plane proved to be a total wreck, it was carefully salvaged, all the precious bolts and screws that were so hard to obtain in France during war times were rescued, and everything that could be used again was turned into the supply stores from which planes were rebuilt.

In the airplane repair shops, work was repeatedly held up through lack of raw material. Dope and cloth for the wings, well-seasoned spruce, ash and laminated wood, glue, sheet aluminum, steel cables for wing bracing, paint, and varnish were often unobtainable for weeks at a time. In particular, the only glue we could secure for long periods was of very poor grade and not waterproof. Furthermore, the shortage of airplane spare parts was so serious at all times, and the difficulties of procuring them from the French manufacturers were so tremendous, that it was only by making these parts from such raw material as could be obtained and constantly using old parts of crashed airplanes that sufficient material was secured to keep the planes repaired.

There was an excellent wood-working shop in which spare parts for machines of all types could be turned out. Spars, struts, and longerons were made for all types of planes. Wings were entirely rebuilt, landing gears, or undercarriages, as the English called them, were constructed out of partly new and partly salvaged materials. Altogether, our central repair shop was able to rebuild and turn out "as good as new" more than twenty airplanes every week. Our engineer officers estimated that this shop saved the Government more than $100,000 a week through its skill in manufacturing planes and spares out of salvaged materials and from a limited supply of spruce sent from the United States.

One of the departments which always interested our visitors was the propeller repair shop. There is nothing on an airplane which must be more exactly balanced and more carefully made than a propeller. "Props" represent a high degree of very skilled labor. At the same time they are extremely vulnerable and subject to constant breakage. A bad landing frequently causes a plane to stand on its nose or capsize. In either case the propeller is almost sure to be broken. A forced landing on soft ground, no matter how skilfully the pilot may bring his plane to earth, is likely to

mean a somersault because the wheels cannot run fast enough
over the soft ground to accommodate the forward motion of
the plane. This means another propeller gone. In starting
off from a muddy field—and all fields in France are muddy
during a good part of the year—a certain amount of mud is
thrown up from the under-carriage. If this strikes the rapidly revolving propeller, it is almost sure to nick it in such
a way as to make the plane vibrate. There must be a new
"prop." Even the celebrated Rickenbacker mud-guards,
which were invented by the first engineer officer of the
school, who later became our Ace of Aces, failed to prevent
all danger from this source, although enormously reducing
propeller fatalities.

Broken propellers had always heretofore been regarded
as of no further service. Since a propeller costs from $200
up, it can be readily seen that here was a source of great
expense. At Issoudun, however, it had meant more than expense. Propellers simply could not be bought in sufficient
quantities to provide for the enormous loss due to those
muddy, rock-strewn fields. Accordingly, during Colonel
Kilner's régime, every broken propeller had been carefully
saved and the wood used to patch those which were not
damaged too seriously. Provided two-thirds of a blade was
left practically intact, our skilled workmen had learned how
to replace the other third, and to do it in such a way as to
make that part of the propeller stronger than it had been
before. In fact, it was the proud boast of the sergeant in
charge of this shop that some "props" had come back eight

or ten times to be repaired, but that the damage had never occurred in the place which he had mended, but always at a new point. About twenty-five propellers were turned out of this shop every day as good as new. The saving here to the Government was rarely less than $25,000 a week. The men took great pride in the circumstance that for many months this was the only flying school that was able to save large amounts of money in this way.

Oil that had been fouled by usage in the motors, and which in the old days would have been thrown away, was collected and used in our little foundry as fuel with which to melt aluminum. This enabled us to cast new pistons at a time when they were unobtainable in the market. Not only pistons, but many other things were made in this little foundry, including piston pins, piston rings, bushings, etc.

The motor repair department, under the very efficient management of Captain Charles W. Babcock, maintained a wonderful record. There was practically never a time when flying had to be postponed for want of a reliable motor. Most of our motors were Le Rhone 80's and 120's. Their normal life was forty or fifty hours of flight. After a motor had had fifty hours in the air, it was taken out of the plane and sent to the machine shop for a thorough overhauling. It was completely stripped, every part carefully gone over and cleaned, new parts substituted if necessary, and an effort made to rebuild the motor as good as new. After reassembling, it was sent out to the test department and thoroughly

tested. Careful records were kept each day of the progress
of motors through the shop, and the men took particular
pleasure in striving to better these records. Shortly before
the Armistice was signed, 119 motors were turned out of
the shop completely overhauled in one week. This week's
work included eight Liberty motors and one Hispano Suiza,
in addition to one hundred and ten Le Rhones.

Work in the motor repair and machine shop had been
delayed at the start by the presence of unintelligent and
insufficiently instructed personnel, and by the absence of an
adequate supply of spare parts. The manufacture of spare
parts was hindered by the fact that wire, steel, and sheet
metals could only be obtained in very small quantities and
with extreme difficulty. At the time of my arrival the
machine shop was doing well, and there was less complaint
of the character of enlisted personnel. The system of organizing squadrons in the United States was at first especially poor. Men with absolutely no qualifications as mechanics were listed on the squadron organization as tin-
smiths, coppersmiths, and expert motor mechanics, although
in civil life they had been salesmen, clerks, and farmhands.
One mechanic's qualification was having "driven a Ford
occasionally." Men were rated as expert machinists whose
only experience with machinery consisted in feeding stock
into one end of an automatic machine and pulling the finished product out at the other end. Such poor and super-
ficial methods of trade testing had been used that it had
been necessary at Issoudun to reclassify squadrons in their

entirety, and to organize courses of instruction and training for men who had been rated as experts in their lines, but who had no real conception of the fundamental principles of the trade they professed. The men were anxious to learn, however, and by the middle of 1918 were very proficient. As time went on, the enlisted personnel arriving from the United States improved as a result of the better training received in America or England.

The sheet metal department was kept busy preparing gas tanks and cowls. We had a great deal of trouble with the tanks in the French planes. The straining incidental to acrobatic flying frequently caused them to leak. Turning an airplane upon its nose often damages not only the propellers, but also the cowl or hood of the engine.

A large part of the flying in an advanced school of this sort must be done at a sufficient elevation to enable the pilot who accidentally stalls and gets into a spinning nose dive to come out of it safely. Consequently altimeters were in great demand, and were difficult to secure. Our instrument department was constantly repairing those we had, and also standardizing the tachometers or revolution counters, on which the young pilots depended in such large measure for their safety. An old experienced pilot hardly needs a " rev. counter " to tell him whether his motor is turning up as it should. But an inexperienced pilot must never leave the ground without assuring himself by means of this delicate instrument that his power plant is going to be able to get him safely over the trees.

It was also continually necessary to repair magnetos and to rebuild spark plugs. In one week in October our shop turned out 143 magnetos and 2140 spark plugs.

Rough landings also caused great damage to the landing gear. Sometimes the pneumatic tires were the only things to suffer. Then again the wheels themselves would give way under the effects of a bad "pancake." Our shops did not allow this to interfere with flying, however, and in one week we turned out as many as 290 wheels and 350 newly vulcanized tires. In this way our mechanics enabled us to overcome the difficulty of purchasing supplies and the delays incident to transportation over submarine-infested waters.

One of the greatest difficulties faced by our repair and supply departments was the wide variety of our machines. This had been rendered necessary by the scarcity of the most desirable types and our determination to use anything that would fly. It was hard to keep all in commission. At the close of the day, September 9, 1918, out of 1002 machines on hand there were only 519 in commission. For the important combat work at Field 8, more than two-thirds of the planes were out of commission. On Field 7, considerably over half were in the hospital. Yet the training on these two fields was of enormous importance, and required the fastest and best machines. The demand from the Front that we turn out pilots during October was greater than at any other time during the history of the school. It will be remembered that we broke the best previous flying record by over 5000

Issoudun: Assembly and Repair Hangars on the Main Field
In the distance are the Motor Repair and Aero Repair Shops. In the foreground on the right
are drums of gasoline and castor oil

hours during this month. Yet so efficient was our engineering department under the able leadership of Major Victor Pagé, that on October 20, Field 8 had less than one-third out of commission, while Field 7 had 99 machines in commission and only 6 out of commission. Out of a total of 979 machines, there were 628 in commission — an improvement of more than 100. Of course, after the Armistice we were able to improve this record because it was not necessary to push the training at such speed. On the last day of November, out of 1109 machines then on our books, there were 951 that needed no repairs. Field 8 had 54 machines in commission — 17 in repair ; Field 7, 134 machines in commission and only one undergoing repair ; Field 5 had 113 in commission and not one out of commission. I mention these fields particularly because they used the lightest and most delicate types of planes, and it had always been very difficult to keep them sufficiently supplied with flying material. This fine record was due largely to the extraordinarily good morale among the enlisted men on these three fields, who responded eagerly to the splendid leadership of Captain Street, Captain Davis, and Captain Wingate.

Great credit should be given to the officers and men of the engineering department for their unfailing devotion to duty, for the ingenuity they developed in inventing new tools, devising new processes, and meeting emergencies as they arose. Major Pagé, who had long been a recognized authority on internal combustion motors, and who came to be acknowledged as the best aeronautical engineer in France, was able to instil great enthusiasm in his staff. His expert knowledge gave them confidence in his judgment, while his tireless energy and fearless honesty inspired them with a determination to double their efforts.

CHAPTER XVII
IMPORTANT ACCESSORIES

A FLYING School needs more than repair shops. It requires a Test Department, Supplies, Doctors, Letters from Home, and the ministrations of the Red Cross.

After a new airplane arrived from the manufacturers and had been assembled, or after a rebuilt plane had been sent out from the aero repair shops, or whenever a flyer found fault with his plane and claimed it was not fit to fly, it was immediately turned over to one of the officers of the test department. This department, organized under Captain (later Major) W. M. Conant, Jr., stood between the engineering department and the training, or flying, department. The testers had to be not only expert flyers, but born mechanics with an intuition for "trouble shooting."

It was frequently their duty to take up types of planes that they had never flown before. It was their every-day duty to be the first to decide by experiment whether a plane would fly, and whether it had been carefully constructed. Of course, they first determined by visual inspection that the plane had been properly put together, was properly rigged, and appeared to be safe for flight. But they then had to determine by actual flight whether the plane would fly according to the high standards maintained by their department.

Captain Conant had a remarkable record. He had flown every type of ship at the school and had never made a poor landing, although many times obliged to make forced landings. At the Front he would have had a wonderful record as an Ace, but he cheerfully accepted the inevitable fate of being obliged to utilize his skill in making the training of aviators as safe, and the planes as mechanically perfect, as possible. Like Captain Austin and so many of our best pilots, he sacrificed fame for greater service.

One of his permanent occupations was looking for new testers to meet the needs of the constantly growing school. He looked for men who seemed to possess the flying instinct and whose ability was natural rather than mechanical. He insisted that his testers be thoroughly familiar with aerodynamics, and at the same time have a large amount of practical common sense. As a result of his skill in selecting men, the testers of Issoudun came to be known as a body of extremely hard-working pilots, cool, finished, accomplished flyers, who had absolutely no fear of the air, and to whom stunt flying was merely one of the easiest ways of determining whether a plane was fit to fly. In fact, no plane was O.K.'d for flying until a tester had put it through various severe manoeuvres and determined that it was mechanically ready for the use of student pilots.

To the test department was due the credit for the fact that so few students at Issoudun lost their lives through mechanical defects in our airplanes. The very severe strains brought to bear on planes engaged in combat practice on Field 8 were occasionally responsible for accidents that occurred after a considerable period in the air, and in flying for several periods after the test department had O.K.'d the ship. Otherwise, no one was killed by a faulty plane. It was, of course, impossible for the testers to make sure that each of the thousand or more planes at the school were O.K.'d before each flight, but in the case of newly assembled planes, or those newly repaired after being damaged or reported as not flying properly, their skill in inspection and testing left nothing to be desired.

After the Armistice was signed and the necessity of rushing our finished product through at the highest possible speed was eliminated, orders were given that the test department should make frequent inspections of all ships brought out to the lines for flying, and check up on the inspection made by the local officer in charge of flying. There were no enlisted mechanics in the test department. It was composed entirely of officers who ranked as inspectors, and who pointed out to the engineering officers or their representatives the faults that needed to be remedied. It had been the custom in the past for the testers to be a branch of the engineering department and under the control of the Chief Aeronautical Engineer. I came to believe, however, that it was better policy for them to belong to a separate department and for the Chief Tester to be on a parity with both the Officer in Charge of Flying and the Chief Engineer.

It must always be borne in mind that an aeronautical engineering department likes to keep up a high record of performance in turning out rebuilt motors and planes. It must also be borne in mind that a training or flying department likes to break records in the amount of flying done and the number of students graduated. Consequently, it is of particular importance that a department, whose sole interest is to see that accidents do not occur from mechanical defects, should come with power between these two departments and prevent the acceptance by the flying department of any machine that had been repaired too hastily, or the continued flying of any machine of which a student complains.

Every one who came to visit Issoudun was shown our aero supply warehouses, in which we all took the greatest possible amount of pride. Organized by Captain H. B. Close, they were improved and extended by Lieutenant (later Captain) Selmer J. Tilleson. We were obliged to use so many different types of planes, and to have on hand such a very great variety of aeronautical supplies, that if Lieutenant Tilleson had not succeeded always in being able to find the desired article, no one could have blamed him. But to keep hundreds of thousands of spare parts, listed under more than 30,000 separate headings, in stock and always be able to locate any one of them at a moment's notice and to tell exactly how many had been on hand the day before, was an achievement that deserved extraordinary commendation. Fortunately, we had no Handley Pages, for a single Handley Page airplane is itself composed of 100,000 parts; but we did have seventeen types of Nieuports, four types of Morane monoplanes, three types of Spads, besides sundry Sopwiths, Caudrons, Voisins, and Avros, and the American DH-4. Nevertheless, Lieutenant Tilleson's warehouses were models of neatness and orderly arrangement, which evoked the envious admiration of other supply officers.

One of our principal difficulties was in securing a sufficient supply of gasoline. It was a considerable time before the army officers who controlled the distribution of gasoline tank cars came to a proper realization of our needs. The fact that they had sent us four tank cars, each containing 6000 gallons of gasoline, "less than ten days ago" seemed to them a sufficient answer to our wail that we should "have to stop cross-country flying this afternoon on account of lack of gas" unless more was immediately received. They finally learned that on good days we frequently did more than 1000 hours of flying, that each hour of flying meant from 12 to 20 gallons of gasoline, depending upon the type of motor used, and that the multiplication table proved that we were likely to use up more than two tank cars every good day. Captain Leo Sack, our efficient liaison officer, was fortunately very convincing and most persistent. When his friends finally mastered this problem, and grasped what it meant to keep one thousand airplanes supplied with power, we had no more trouble.

We sometimes felt that the supply officers in Paris did not treat us as generously as they ought, considering the fact that we could not furnish pilots as fast as they were needed at the Front unless we had the equipment with which to do it. They were much nearer to the Front than they were to our school, however, and they naturally felt that the demands of the Front for machines and spare parts

should take precedence over ours. In general, we agreed with
them, but on one point, namely, our supply of Spads, we always felt they were mistaken. If they had supplied us with
an adequate quantity of the machines which were actually
in use at the Front, we could have taught our pilots to avoid
many of the mistakes which caused the extraordinary destruction of Spads in the fighting area. However, we never
succeeded in persuading them of the value of this invest-
ment. Spads were destroyed at the Front so rapidly that
there was never any surplus left to send to the schools, so
that our pilots did not receive their final instruction in the
planes which they were actually to use in pursuit squadrons until they had left the school and reached active squadrons where fighting rather than teaching was the principal
matter in hand. Naturally, they crashed a good many, and
in a region not as well equipped with repair shops as the
Third Aviation Instruction Centre. We should have been
allowed at least twenty-five out of the hundreds that were
secured from the French.

Intermediate Quartermaster Depot No. 5 was located
on our main field, and was in charge of Major Charles W.
Godfrey. His experience in successfully feeding thousands
of troops in New England during the first year of the war,
when he was in the Commissary Branch at Boston, stood
him in good stead. He came to us at a time when provi-
sions were very difficult to secure. The needs of our rapidly
growing army at the Front had to be met first, as was right
and proper, but that did not make it any easier for the hard-

*Issoudun: The Main Barracks, the "Y," the Red Cross
and the Quartermaster buildings*

*Issoudun: Foreground: Our prize bakery, where the Q. M. turned out
10,000 loaves of fine white bread daily*

*Next to the bakery are the Q. M. warehouses. In the distance, at the left
the Hospital, at the right Headquarters*

working mechanic in our shops and hangars to go hungry, or to be denied the regular supplies of food and clothing as laid down in army regulations.

Major Godfrey, by his wonderful enthusiasm and self-sacrificing attention to the smallest details, and also by his willingness to risk official displeasure in order to accomplish ends which he felt were justified by the needs of our soldiers, made us all have a high regard for the Quartermaster Department. He took an intense and personal interest in seeing that the Mess Sergeants made a proper use of Government rations, that the cooks understood how to conserve fuel and at the same time get good results with field ranges, and that his own bakery, which turned out 10,000 loaves of excellent bread daily, should have every facility that it deserved. He also saw to it that the men were well shod. Commanding officers of outlying fields found to their surprise and delight that the rules which our Quartermaster found it necessary to make were intended to give them the best possible service, and that whenever these rules worked hardship, a word from them resulted in prompt changes.

Major Godfrey's first ride in an airplane was at night with one of the most daring pilots of our night pursuit group. He seemed to feel that his experience was not as enviable as some of us thought it ought to be. He never was quite sure whether the twinkling lights which he saw in the darkness were stars or camp lights. He insisted that it was really very thrilling, and we did not doubt him, for we knew the pilot.

When an aviator has been given a properly tested machine, well fitted with gas and oil, when he is suitably clothed, fed, paid, and housed, he thinks he is ready to fly. Generally, he forgets the importance of medical attendance until "something happens." Camp Hospital No. 14 was located in the main camp. It was under the direction of Major William G. Noe, who was in command of an adequate force of surgeons and enlisted men, but who was inadequately supplied with army nurses and ambulances. There were some 500 beds in the hospital. At the time of my arrival, about one-third of them were occupied by wounded or gassed soldiers from the Chateau-Thierry sector.

When the "flu" epidemic struck us, strenuous efforts were made to combat its spread. Our barracks, like those all over France, were greatly crowded. The men slept in bunks built in sections of four, two men sleeping on the upper tier and two on the lower. Orders were given that bunkmates must sleep head to foot, and not side by side. This immediately lowered the rate of new cases, since no man, by coughing at night, could infect his bunkie. Rigid rules were enforced regarding keeping barrack windows open in all sorts of weather. Buckets of water were kept on the stoves so as to provide a moist atmosphere, the use of common drinking-cups was forbidden, and men were sent to the hospital as soon as they gave signs of having a cold. During the worst of the epidemic, we were admitting to the hospital from sixty to seventy-five new cases a day; but so

skilfully did our medical officers handle the situation, that
out of a camp containing over 7000 men, we lost only thirty
as the effects of the "flu."

It was a most fortunate circumstance for my administration of the Third Aviation Instruction Centre that Colonel
William H. Wilmer and his Medical Research Board arrived from the United States early in September. I will admit
that when a telephone message came from the Assistant
Provost Marshal at Issoudun railway station announcing
the arrival there of a "dozen Staff Officers," visions of a
visitation from G. H. Q. for purposes of inspection filled me
with dismay. I had been in command of the post only about
a week or ten days, yet I realized how many adverse criti-
cisms could be made, and I wished that these General Staff
Officers had postponed their visit until a little later. When
our new arrivals turned out to be Colonel Wilmer and his
staff, dismay was changed to delight, as every one will realize who had an opportunity to become acquainted with that
most distinguished member of the medical profession and
his friends.

In the United States it had been found advisable to appoint
so-called "flight surgeons" at each of the flying schools.
These men had been carefully trained in the pioneer laboratories at Mineola and were familiar with the latest results
of research into the physiology and psychology of the pilot.
Not only did they learn the effects of thin air on his reactions
and what might be expected to happen to any individual pilot through lack of sufficient oxygen, but they also had

studied most thoroughly the special physical characteristics
of those who found it difficult or impossible to learn to fly.
Many of the specialists who had taught these flight surgeons were on the Medical Research Board which was now
established at our camp. They came provided with the very
latest apparatus, and with special instruments intended to
facilitate the physiological determination of a student's apti-
tude for aviation.

Two members of the Board were asked to serve on all
investigations connected with serious accidents to our pilots.
Their skill and knowledge soon brought out the fact that
the majority of accidents were caused by defects in the physical condition of the pilots. To be sure, a number of accidents are always traceable to apparent disobedience to orders. Sometimes the disobedience is direct and unequivocal,
as when two brilliant pilots, arriving in the course of their
instruction at the combat field, decide to disobey instructions
and, disregarding all caution, display their ability by combating at a low elevation. This experiment sometimes resulted disastrously.

On the other hand, there is another type of disobedience
of orders which is due to physical condition rather than to
moral or mental delinquency. This arises when a pilot is
told to go to a certain altitude, stall his machine into a spinning nose dive, and then put all of his controls into neutral.
If these instructions are obeyed, the airplane automatically
comes out of the spin and into a steep straight glide from
which the pilot can easily proceed to recover control with-

out endangering himself or his ship. Occasionally, however, it was apparent to the instructors that the pilot disregarded his orders and failed to put his controls into neutral, thereby causing the plane to stay in the spin until it crashed to the ground.

The experiments of the Medical Research Board, and particularly those conducted by Lieutenant-Colonel Henry Horn, demonstrated with unerring fidelity that those pilots who reacted improperly after being spun in a swivel chair were physically unable to carry out their instructions. When they attempted to thrust the joy stick forward into a neutral position, they actually pushed it to one side so that the aileron controls were not in neutral. On the other hand, Colonel Horn discovered by a thorough examination of our best pilots, including those who by reason of their great skill had been chosen as instructors or as testers of new machines, that they were able to react perfectly to the tests of the whirling chair. Not only did they overcome the effects of this dizziness in one-third or one-half the time required by an average person (and thereby place themselves in the class of whirling dervishes), they also had no difficulty in immediately putting the controls in neutral, notwithstanding the effects of a prolonged spinning in the chair.

So firmly did I believe in the ability of the Research Board to prevent accidents due to inherent defects in the physique of the aviator, that instructions were given to place in the hands of incoming pilots an article by Lieutenant-Colonel Rowntree, who was Colonel Wilmer's right-hand man. This article urged frequent consultation of the Medical Research Board by flyers who were feeling ill, or "not feeling fit," or feeling insecure in their work, or when their flying records were poor, or after an accident. Instructors were directed to consult the Board whenever they saw that their students were in one of the above classes, or whenever they themselves desired information as to the type of work for which a flyer was best suited, so far as this could be determined by physical examination.

Considering how many delays the flying cadets had suffered in the past and how many handicaps they had had to overcome in their efforts to get to the Front speedily, it was not surprising that some of them regarded the Medical Research Board with suspicion. They soon came to realize, however, that it was the object of Colonel Wilmer and his colleagues, especially the flight surgeon, Major R. R. Hampton, to assist pilots to become more efficient, and not to remove them from the flying list.

We all of us came to the conclusion that it was not fair either for the army or for the pilot himself, that he should assume unnecessary risks. Ordinary risks were great enough in all conscience, but the danger was much increased when those attempted to fly who were not fit. We endeavored to impress on our pilots the fact that they could not expect to be successful in the air unless they kept themselves fit. They were urged to go to bed early and to get at least eight hours of sleep. We made every effort to see that all pilots took some physical exercise daily. Although the flyer is out of doors a

great deal, his occupation is actually a sedentary one, and far
more fatiguing to his nerves than to his body, so it was all
the more important to encourage outdoor sports. Each field
commander was requested to report at officers' meeting each
day how much exercise had been taken in the preceding
twenty-four hours by the pilots under his command. It was
significant that the fields which did the best work found
the most time for exercise, or took it in the most violent form.

Colonel Rowntree reported that a large number of flyers
consulted the Board for digestive disturbances. The ladies
of the American Red Cross also reported that the instructors who flew a great deal seemed to be frequently "off their
feed," while others had abnormal appetites and ate five or
six meals a day. The Medical Research Board came to the
belief, after a careful study of the food problem, that aviators should avoid heavy foods in the early part of the day.
Sugar and starches, breads, cereals, fruits, and vegetables
were advised, even though these constituted but a small part
of the regular army ration. Heavy foods, such as meats and
fats, which have been proved by experience to be essential
for infantry and other troops engaged in heavy manual
labor, were recommended in great moderation. It was particularly advised that such foods should not be eaten until
after the day's flying was over.

An aviator's life is very abnormal. A student aviator crowds
such tremendous experiences into such a small portion of the
day, he is so frequently left with plenty of time on his hands,
albeit greatly fatigued by unusual nervous strains, that there

is no question which worries the commanding officer of a flying field more than the development of proper habits by his student pilots. In the tropics, where men get fatigued easily and have more leisure than they do in the temperate zone, I have noticed a strong tendency toward intemperance. Not only intemperance as regards the use of alcohol, but intemperance in other things, including gambling and the use of cigarettes. The same is true on a flying field, with this difference, that indulgence in bad habits is likely to cause errors in judgment that lead to fatal accidents in the air.

So much of a pilot's work is done alone, so deeply must he draw on his own powers of endurance and self-respect, that he particularly needs the kind of cheer that comes in Letters from Home. Irregularity in the delivery of mail matter was not confined to the Air Service. Every one in the A. E. F. suffered from it more or less. One day a letter would arrive that was only three weeks old. This would be followed a few days later by one a month old, and then on the next mail would arrive two that were six weeks old. Of course the difficulties were enormous, and the suffering was not serious, in most cases.

At Christmas time the mail service seemed to improve, and our standard packages, "9 × 4 × 3 inches, weighing not more than 3 pounds," must have been given special consideration, for a large percentage of them were only a month *en route*. They had to be mailed in the United States before the 20th of November, and most of them arrived before the

25th of December. One day a member of the staff brought in a letter to Santa Claus, but did not tell me who wrote it. It contained the following paragraphs :

DEAR SANTA :

If you happen to have anything lying around loose that doesn't weigh more than three pounds, and which isn't more than nine inches long, four inches wide, and three inches thick, it will get to me all right if you will paste the enclosed coupon on it and mail it at your own post office. I think that would be better than to try to bring it over with your reindeers.

I 'm not saying that your reindeers are n't good ones, you understand. I never saw better ones. But some folks are likely to be misled by the size of those packages. A package $9 \times 4 \times 3$ is a little thing, not as large as two bricks, and it would n't hurt you half as much if it fell on your head. But if you figure out the bulk for two million people you 'll see that it is nothing to be sneezed at, even by your reindeers, no matter how well they can sneeze.

Two million of those packages placed end to end would make a string 284 miles, 29 rods, 1 foot and 6 inches long. Leaving out the jog where the toolshed stands, they would make a pile three feet deep all over my Dad's farm. They would fill 100 good sized freight cars. It would take a good team of reindeers eight years to haul them from Morestown to Lake City. If you could put one of those packages down a chimney every minute, and worked eight hours a night at the job, it would take you 11 years, 1 month, 21 days, 5 hours, and 20 minutes to get rid of them all.

Nevertheless, the idea was an excellent one. It did away with the likelihood of overcrowding the mails with cumbersome and perhaps useless "gifts," and it brought good cheer to an enormous number of those who were thinking that it would be nice to have Christmas at home.

Finally, nothing helped toward the success of the Third
Aviation Instruction Centre more than the American Red
Cross. As early as October 3, 1917, Miss Irene Givenwilson
and a few other ladies from the Red Cross stepped off into
the "sea of mud" and took possession of a small section in
one of the three barracks. They opened a temporary can-
teen, and were soon cheering the men with hot coffee and
sandwiches.

From this little beginning the Red Cross gradually grew
until its rooms and buildings covered nearly an acre of our
camp. The men who spent the terrible winter of 1917–18
at the post were all unanimous in their opinion that the
Red Cross did more to keep up their spirits than any other
agency. The influence of those splendid Christian women,
the cheering smiles with which they greeted all comers, the
tremendous energy which led them to work from early
morning until late at night at whatever job came to hand,
did more to keep pure Americanism alive in that corner of
France than everything else put together.

Among other things the Red Cross erected a laundry, a
barber shop, and a comfortable bath house. By taking turns,
the squadrons would get hot showers at least once a week. A
tailoring and repair shop were greatly appreciated by the
hundreds of flying officers and enlisted men. A technical
library and an officers' club were early established. Miss
Givenwilson, Miss Amy Brewer, Miss Gertrude Hussey,
and Miss Potter were chiefly responsible for creating this
little bit of the homeland where kind words and encouraging

Extra! Extra!

Plane News.

Vol. I, No. 31   On Active Service November, 11, 1918   25 Centimes

HOSTILITIES CEASED!

Armistice Between Fighting Armies Effective at Eleven O'clock This Morning

TRAINING OF PILOTS HERE WILL CONTINUE WITHOUT INTERRUPTION

Hostilities between the Allies and Germany have temporarily ceased according to official announcement from American Headquarters. Here is the announcement.

American Official Communique, Nov. 11, 1918.

In accordance with the terms of the Armistice, hostilities on the fronts of the American Armies were suspended at 11 o'clock this morning.

Rec'd at 1:50 p. m.

NO STOPPING HERE

This does not mean that the War is over. It means that a temporary truce has been declared. The War may be resumed and it may not. But the American Army is taking no chances. Training of all branches of the service will continue without interruption.

Here at the 3rd A. I. C. student officers will be trained as heretofore, the only difference being that more time will be spent on their training and physical care.

The number of Aviators, according to the General Staff, is insufficient for the size of our Armies. If hostilities should be resumed this evil will be remedied.

smiles for each soldier could be had for the asking. They were well assisted by a score of others, rays of sunshine in a dark valley. After the departure of the veterans, the work was ably carried on by Mrs. Elsie Cobb Wilson and Miss Peck, who were most successful in alleviating those severe attacks of the blues and homesickness which afflicted so many of our men after the Armistice was signed and before orders came to leave for the port of embarkation.

A few days before Christmas a very welcome present in the shape of the following letter came from General Patrick, the head of the American Air Service in France.

AMERICAN EXPEDITIONARY FORCES

U. S. AIR SERVICE, PARIS

OFFICE OF CHIEF OF AIR SERVICE

17th December, 1918

LIEUTENANT-COLONEL HIRAM BINGHAM,

Commanding Officer, Issoudun

MY DEAR COLONEL BINGHAM:

As the school at Issoudun is about to close you will soon be relieved from your present duty as its Commanding Officer and returned to the United States. Before your departure I desire to place on record my hearty appreciation of the excellent work you did while in command of this, our largest training centre in France. The results achieved speak for themselves and evidence the interest you took in your work and your power to inspire those who were working with you.

May I add that I was just about to recommend your promotion when the Armistice came and all advancement was stopped. While

it was thus impossible to bestow upon you this well earned evidence
of work well done, I want you to be assured that in my opinion it
was your due.

Very truly yours,

(Signed) MASON M. PATRICK,
Major-General, U. S. A.
Chief of Air Service

I sent a copy of this letter to Colonel Robert M. Danford,
then Brigadier-General, who had been my commanding
officer in the days of the "Yale Batteries" at Tobyhanna.
It was to his remarkable ability as a military instructor
that any success I may have had at Issoudun was due.

On Christmas Day my orders came to go home, the best
present any one could ask for. The next day I left Issoudun
and, on January 1, 1919, sailed from St. Nazaire.

After a few weeks of duty in the office of the Director
of Military Aeronautics in Washington, I received my discharge on March 8, 1919, just two years from the time I
began to fly in Miami.

CHAPTER XVIII

SHOULD THE GENERAL STAFF CONTROL THE AIR SERVICE?

THE wisdom of a General Staff must always depend on two things: first, the practical experience, in the field, of the officers composing it, and second, their studies of the accumulated wisdom gained in previous wars. In the American Air Service in 1917–18, we received no help from anything of this kind. While probably every officer of the General Staff had had practical experience in handling infantry, in the care of cavalry, in the use of artillery, or in the building of roads and bridges, not one of them knew the nervous fatigue of piloting an airplane or how it feels to have engine failure over wooded, hilly country, or the difficulties of aerial observation when the air is blowing by at a hundred miles an hour!

They had been able to assimilate the wisdom of centuries regarding the requirements of a foot-soldier—what food, clothing, and discipline best met his needs. They had been able similarly to secure centuries of experience with mounted soldiers and knew the needs of cavalry, but they had no experience to guide them in making adequate rules for the care, training, and discipline of aviators or aviation mechanics. The science of aeronautics and the art of flying were too recent to have received the attention they deserved from the older and wiser heads on the General Staff.

When I went on duty in Washington in May, 1917, I took it for granted that the War Department had carefully considered how to utilize an Air Service to the fullest extent. It was amazing and very disconcerting to learn that the General Staff of the Army had apparently made no plans for the part which aviation was to take in the war. The programme of studies outlined for the first Officers' Training Camps contained no reference to the Air Service. The War College had published some useful pamphlets, copied from the French and British, on coöperation with artillery. Yet, so far as I could discover, no effort was made to teach our thousands of new officers anything about the progress that aviation had made on the Western Front during 1916, nor what they might expect the Air Service to do, nor how to communicate with airplanes by ground panels, nor what the proper function of the Air Service was.

The newspapers at that time were full of exciting stories of the aerial combats and victories of the Lafayette Squadron. From what I could learn by conversation with our line officers, these aerial combats constituted the spectacular, and bombing planes the useful, end of the Air Service. Observation squadrons and liaison with artillery and infantry were practically unknown to the average line officer.

It is hardly necessary to say that there was equal unpreparedness in many other branches of the Service. Still, it must never cease to be a source of amazement to our descendants that, while the great nations of the world had been fighting for their lives for two years and a half, and ordinary common sense would have seemed to have dictated the necessity of preparing for the day when we, too, should get thrown into the gigantic conflict, so little should have been done of what is known as "General Staff Work."

We did not know until we had been at war for several months what kind of airplanes we were going to use, how many we should need, how many flying schools we were going to have, where they were to be, what were the best locations, what system of training was to be followed, or how many men we were to train. So little thought had been given to the matter, and so small had been our conception of the probable number of pilots, that, for several months after we entered the war, the bulletins of the War Department referred to in an earlier chapter offered commissions as First Lieutenants to those who could pass the examinations for Reserve Military Aviator. The law provided an increase in grade to those who could pass the more severe tests of Junior Military Aviator. As it seemed obvious that no one should be sent to the Front who was not a fully and completely trained military aviator, many of our ambitious young pilots believed that by the time they were ready to fly over the lines, they would rank as Captains.

When the provision for granting increased rank and pay to aviators was passed by Congress, it was thought necessary to offer these inducements on account of the extreme danger of the service, and the high mortality among the best known aviators in this country during the years 1910–12. It was felt that any one who was willing to undertake this dangerous training ought to be specially rewarded. As long as we had an Air Service consisting of one fly-

ing school and a small assortment of experimental airplanes,
a few of which could fly a short distance, the provision was
undoubtedly wise. But when we were faced with the necessity of having several hundred pilots, and the probability
of having several thousand, it might have been foreseen by
an adequately prepared General Staff that the bulletins in-
viting young men to enter the Air Service should not make
it appear that it was our plan to flood the Air Service with
Captains. Only Central American armies are supposed to
have an excess of rank at the top.

Most of the aviators in the French service were non-
coms, although they enjoyed the social privileges of officers.
Many of the aviators in the German Air Service were non-
commissioned officers, although the observers were nearly
always officers. In the British Air Service, practically all
pilots were commissioned officers, and it was felt that the
splendid morale of the Royal Flying Corps and the remarkable record which its pilots had made on the Western Front
in 1916 were due largely to this fact.

The American Air Service adopted the last plan. General
Pershing, however, soon came to the belief that the rank of
second lieutenant was high enough for most of his pilots;
yet until October, 1917, there was no provision by law for
second lieutenants in the Signal Corps. Consequently, the
tens of thousands of young men whose applications poured
in during the first six months of the war had every right
to believe that when they passed their tests, they would
become first lieutenants. Most of them, furthermore, natu-

rally expected to be able, before long, to pass the Junior Military Aviator test and become captains. The fact is that the exigencies of the Service and General Pershing's refusal to permit any except regular officers of the permanent establishment to take the Junior Military Aviator test resulted, as has been pointed out, in great disappointment and much loss of morale among what had been the most enthusiastic and keenest group of young men in the army.

Logically, of course, it was not to be expected that our squadrons would be composed chiefly of captains. It would have been bad for the rest of the army and bad for the men themselves, had such an event occurred. In fact, it was so obviously ridiculous that it became all the more regrettable and almost inexplicable that the War Department should have for so many months offered First Lieutenancies to all those who could pass the easy Reserve Military Aviator test. Perhaps it is true that this is only one of many instances in which our persistent refusal to prepare for war led us into making serious blunders, but there was none which caused more unhappiness or greater loss of *esprit de corps*.

The situation as far as it concerns extra "flying pay" is quite different. The statement is frequently made by old army officers that in time of war aviation is no more dangerous than any other branch of the Service. There was a strong effort on the part of General Pershing and the General Staff to persuade Congress of this during the early part of 1918, and to alter the law so that Military Aviators would not receive an increase either in pay or grade. The Military

Affairs Committee of the Senate refused to consider the proposal, but General Pershing achieved his purpose so far as France was concerned by refusing to permit any reserve or temporary officer to take the examinations for Junior Military Aviator. For many months he also refused to issue the orders necessary to place pilots "on flying duty," thereby preventing them from getting even the 25 per cent increase in pay that was permitted to Reserve Military Aviators. Later on this was changed, although with evident reluctance.

Since the grade of Junior Military Aviator carried with it an increase in pay of 50 per cent, and the grade of Military Aviator, attainable after three years as a Junior Military Aviator or for distinguished service at the Front, carried an increase in pay of 75 per cent, there was naturally a great deal of resentment felt by the pilots who were doing the most flying against the relatively few regular officers whose administrative duties prevented them from flying more than just enough to warrant them in drawing their flying pay, but who, through their grade as Junior Military Aviator or Military Aviator, were paid two or three times as much for the small risks they ran as were the ordinary pilots who were taking their lives in their hands every day.

Had General Pershing and the General Staff contented themselves with asking that the law be changed regarding the increase in rank, and explained the disadvantages of having too many high ranking young pilots, there would probably have been no objections raised; but when the Mili-

tary Affairs Committee learned from foreign flying officers
on duty in Washington that both the French and British
Governments gave extra pay to their pilots, the insistence on
the part of the General Staff that pilots did not run unusual
risks met with unanimous disapproval. It was only one of
the results of that lack of expert knowledge of military aeronautics and lack of sympathy with the difficulties of aviation which pervaded the General Staff during 1917–18.

Speaking of risks, it may be of interest to refer to my own
experience. My first instructor in an army machine was
Captain Roger Jannus, a pilot of long experience, great skill,
and remarkable devotion to duty. He was killed while in the
course of a practice combat near Field 8 at Issoudun. His
machine caught fire in the air, probably from a gasoline
tank which had become leaky owing to the strains and con-
tortions of combat flying. Captain Jannus was too experienced a pilot to have taken up an imperfect machine, and
no one could have foreseen the accident which happened to
him after he had been combatting with an instructor about
three-quarters of an hour. My second instructor was Captain H. Taylor, who was the officer in charge of flying at
Mineola when I went there to take my Reserve Military
Aviator tests in August, 1917. He was a very experienced
pilot and devoted to his work. I had not been flying at Mineola but a few days when he was killed while giving a lesson
in spiralling to the pupil whose turn immediately preceded
mine. The student was seriously injured, but eventually
recovered. It was an extremely hot day, and I have since

had occasion to notice that accidents in the air always increase during extremely hot weather, possibly as the result of fainting or vertigo.

My third instructor at Issoudun was more fortunate, and lived to achieve a brilliant record at the Front. My fourth instructor, Lieutenant Ott, was killed at Issoudun, while endeavoring to bring his ship out of a dangerous position into which it had been thrown by an inexperienced student in the back seat. My fifth instructor, and the one who succeeded by his patience and skill in giving me a sense of confidence in the tricky Nieuport 23, was Lieutenant Blanchard. He was an unusually painstaking pilot, a faithful instructor, and a very competent aviator. After several months of teaching at Issoudun, he was sent to the gunnery school at St. Jean des Monts to perfect himself in actual firing before going to the Front, but was killed by being thrown from his machine when diving at a target. When it is remembered that these men who gave their lives at flying schools were not beginners, or poorly trained pilots, but experts in the art of flying, it seems incredible that any one should begrudge the pilot his additional pay.

A recent article in the *Philadelphia Press* calls attention to the very heavy loss suffered by the French Air Service. During the four years of the war nearly 2000 French pilots and observers were killed at the Front; 1500 "disappeared," which means that some were killed, others were taken prisoners; nearly 3000 were injured, and *about* 2000 *were killed while on duty at school or depot* in the Zone of the Interior. On the day of the Armistice, the French Air Service had about 13,000 available pilots and observers. The very heavy proportion of losses compared to the size of the service is self-evident.

It is an interesting commentary on human nature and on the utility of a combined civilian and military control over the army that the members of the Senate Military Affairs Committee, none of whom were flyers, should have been more ready to sympathize with the Army Aviator than were the officers of the General Staff.

Not only in rank and pay, but also in such minor matters as spurs and blouses, was the General Staff's attitude shown. As has already been stated in a previous chapter, during the first year of our participation in the war, the General Staff insisted that an aviator who wore boots must wear spurs as well as wings! At last the humor of it struck somebody, and aviators were allowed for a few months to wear boots without spurs. This was too much for the old cavalry officers, however, and in December, 1918, the former rule was restored!

As regards the blouse, we made many efforts to be allowed to wear a coat made with a collar that was safe and comfortable, like those worn by Allied aviators. Our naval aviators were successful. We had not been at war more than three months before they secured the authorization of an attractive and sensible uniform with roll collar and appropriate insignia, a uniform several times referred to by foreign officers in my presence as the smartest uniform in Europe, and one that undoubtedly gave the naval flyers additional prestige and improved morale. Notwithstanding the promptness of the navy in realizing that the aviators could not be expected to be either comfortable or efficient in a high-standing collar, the General Staff of the army absolutely refused to permit the military aviator any deviation from the snug fitting neck-band which helps the infantry soldier to stand stiffly erect on parade.

Our uniform was designed for the kind of fighting that the American Army had been accustomed to on the Mexican border and in the Philippines. Nothing could be more effective for that sort of fighting than our service hat and the thick flannel shirt. In France, however, it was necessary to fight in a blouse or coat, although this had been designed chiefly to be worn on parade. Even the old conservative staff officers could see that it was impossible to wear our service hat under the very necessary steel helmet, so the sacred hat was soon given up in favor of a cloth cap. Why a more comfortable form of blouse was not provided for the ground troops, I do not know. That it was denied to aviators was undoubtedly due to the fact that no members of the General Staff had ever had to fly over the lines or in a crowded area near a big flying school where it is necessary to turn the head from right to left, back and forth, continually, in order to make sure of avoiding other airplanes, either enemy or friendly.

At school we permitted our students to wear sweaters under their flying equipment instead of the regulation blouses. Even so, however, they were frequently subjected to serious reprimands if they were seen by old regular officers, "improperly clad and contrary to regulation." At the Front, however, it was different. The aviator who went over the lines ran a very good chance of being taken prisoner in case he was forced to land because of engine failure or being shot down. Naturally, it was necessary for him always to be clad in the uniform of an officer. Some squadron commanders permitted their pilots to wear non-regulation blouses patterned on the English model, with roll collars. This caused censure and complaint on the part of those whose duty it was to uphold the regulations and see that they were carried out. Other pilots who crossed the lines wearing the regulation collars frequently came back with necks cut and bleeding, owing to the necessity of turning the head incessantly in order to avoid surprise attacks of enemy airplanes.

This may seem to be a small matter, and hardly deserving of so much attention. The truth is, however, that it made the young pilot feel that the army took no interest in his welfare. The General Staff failed to recognize that this supremely voluntary service, from which it was so easy to escape if one felt so inclined, required plenty of encouragement, and the zest that comes from intense pride in an organization. It was well known that the British and French armies treated their aviators with the utmost consideration, permitting them great freedom and recognizing that the extremely hazardous and nerve-racking nature of the daily service over the lines required a different form of discipline.

The additional fact that our own navy had acknowledged the special uniform requirements of an aviator made it all the harder to understand why the General Staff refused to give us more consideration. It is worthy of note that Major-General Brewster, the Inspector-General of the American Expeditionary Forces, in May, 1918, personally recommended a change in the uniform regulation in order to give the aviators what he felt they justly deserved. His recommendation, however, produced no result.

It was frequently felt by the officers of the American Air Service that the army as a whole, particularly some of the older staff officers, were so jealous of the extraordinary interest which Congress and the American people took in aviation, and were so resentful of the unfortunate amount of advertising which the Air Service received (through no fault of its own), that they took satisfaction in declining any requests for special consideration. The fact remains, that the Air Service, composed largely, as it must be, of high-strung, venturesome boys willing to take unheard-of risks in their enthusiasm, and facing extraordinary dangers even in the ordinary course of their daily drill and training, needs intelligent, sympathetic consideration.

The General Staff must prepare for the future by requiring its officers to fly, or by including among its members a relatively large number of pilots and observers, so that there will be just as sympathetic an understanding of the Air Service as there is of the Cavalry or Field Artillery. There will be no excuse for not having on the General

Staff men like Colonel Walter G. Kilner, who received the Distinguished Service Medal for his remarkable work in organizing aviation instruction in France, knows the whole problem of Military Aeronautics from top to bottom, and who did more towards the success of aviation in France than any other officer in the American Expeditionary Forces. Furthermore, there should be men on the Staff like Colonel Robert M. Danford, now Commandant of Cadets at West Point, who believes that all artillery officers should become aerial observers, even if they cannot learn to fly themselves. In the past, all officers of field artillery were "mounted" officers and wore spurs; in the future, they should all be able to wear the wings of a pilot or an observer. The eyes of the artillery must be under the control of the same general officer who directs the activities of the guns themselves. In other words, it would be folly to divorce Military Aeronautics from the army. Our military aviators must be trained by army officers, who have themselves learned the peculiar difficulties of this new branch of the Service.

Plans for military airplanes will undoubtedly be presented by members of the arm that is going to use them; but the actual manufacture and production of airplanes need not be under military control any more than the manufacture of arms and ammunition as carried on at such great plants as Winchester's and Colt's.

Personally, I agree with such authorities as Admiral David Beatty, that an Independent Air Force is a mistake, and that the army and the navy should each control the training and the operation of their own aviators. The *Aircraft Journal* for November, 1919, contained the following digest of an interview with Admiral Beatty, which is most significant.

Admiral Beatty stated that he had supported the creation of the Royal Air Forces, for the reason that at the time it was the only way he could get the personnel and material he needed in the Grand Fleet; he thought that a young and new service would be keen to make a reputation with the two older services (Navy and Army) by being particular not to let anything interfere with Naval and Army Aviation needs. In that way, with production centralized, they would get by the troubles they were having for supply of material. But that was his idea during the war; now that the war is over, he does not consider the R. A. F. organization a proper one, as far as it applies to the Navy and Army; the phrase " Navy and Army and Air " is an attractive one but it is n't sound in each profession — Navy and Army — and there should be no independent fighting force in the air. . . .

He considered that the value of the Independent Air Force for England was somewhat overrated: results of the war showed that damage by bombing, both physical and moral, was not as great as expected; for example, in spite of the tons of high explosives dropped on Bruges there was surprisingly little damage. The moral effect of the bombing wears off, for the population gradually becomes accustomed to it. Referring to the organization requirements of the United States, he said that with our geographical position there was no excuse at all for an independent fighting Air Force. But he does believe that a separate Air organization to control all aviation production is desirable, for England or any other country.

CHAPTER XIX
THE FUTURE OF AVIATION

WITH increased knowledge as to the possibilities of aviation, other departments of the Government will more and more desire to own and operate their own planes and dirigibles. The Post-Office Department has its own problems, which are even now being successfully worked out. Similarly, the Forest Service will desire to use small dirigibles to enable their forest rangers to cover large reservations quickly and effectively. In the course of time the Department of Agriculture will undoubtedly wish to use airships to make rapid surveys of large crop areas. The Navy Department will continue to control the seaplanes and dirigibles which are now such indispensable adjuncts of the modern battleship. The Treasury Department will need to use the air just as it uses the water for revenue cutters, in order to prevent the breach of those laws, the observance of which the Treasury Department is particularly interested in. The Department of Justice will need a certain number of fast planes in order that its special agents may make rapid visits to those places that require immediate investigation.

In considering the future, we must remember that the air has become one of the routes of travel, and that its use as such is going to grow, just as the use of our navigable streams has increased since the days of Fulton, and the uses of the ocean have multiplied since the days of Prince Henry the Navigator and the commencement of scientific navigation. To be sure, aviation is only in its infancy; it must not be expected that its future will be smooth and lacking in incident.

The man-in-the-street has been watching the progress of aviation during the past ten years with varied emotions. At first he showed great interest in the progress of an art which was made of practical utility by the patient scientific experiments of the Wright brothers. Then, after noting with dismay the large percentage of well-known flyers who were killed, his enthusiasm waned and he was inclined to feel that perhaps, after all, man was not intended to imitate the birds. A few of his friends bought airplanes that did not fly, or at any rate which could not be made to fly by the purchasers, and he learned to discount the statements of airplane manufacturers. He discounted them so far, in fact, that unless he was fortunate enough to come into personal contact with Curtiss Flying Boats at Miami or Atlantic City, his faith was dead. His lack of interest was reflected in the small size of the appropriations which Congress saw fit to make for the development of aviation in the army and navy. This feeling of discouragement was further enhanced by the disputes and "scandals" connected with the administration of the Army Aviation School at San Diego.

Then came the war and the achievements of the celebrated Lafayette Squadron. The man-in-the-street began to read of aerial victories, and came to believe that the war could be won in the air, if enough money was spent. His imagination visualized a cloud of American planes over Germany. His enthusiasm reached such a pitch that the largest single appropriation ever made for aviation in all its history, $640,000,000, was passed almost without discussion, and practically unanimously, by a Congress which reflected his superlative optimism.

The newspapers which he read in the fall of 1917, as he rode home from his day in the street, gave him a tremendous sense of comfort in the thought that we were soon to overwhelm the Huns in the air. Then came unaccountable delays. Skepticism and disappointment took the place of optimistic enthusiasm. Dismay followed, and in the summer of 1918, the man-in-the-street threw his aviation ideals overboard, shrugged his shoulders, and decided that somebody had sold him a gold brick. So completely did he turn his back on his former belief, that he refused to read about what had been really accomplished before the Armistice was signed; or, reading it, declined to be "fooled a second time."

The fact that he had expected more than was humanly possible did not help him to appreciate the miracle that had actually been performed. In a year and a half the Army Air Service had grown from having 224 airplanes of doubtful value, "a magnificent retrospective museum," as a visiting French aviator remarked, to over 17,000, a large percentage of them the best in the world for the purposes for which they were intended. We did not manufacture all of the 17,000, nor did France or England manufacture all the ammunition they used. The point is—we had them!

There were other achievements that the man-in-the-street might have been proud of. He believed in the Rolls Royce motor, but thought the Liberty motor a failure. He ought to have been interested to learn that England, with all her faith in the Rolls Royce, was only able at the end of the war to *make* ten a day, while we were *manufacturing* 150 Liberty motors every twenty-four hours. This took time to develop. It always does take time to put a new motor on a production basis. He did not know that in order to manufacture a Liberty motor on a typical American quantity production basis, it was necessary to make 3000 separate tools, gigs, and fixtures.

With his skepticism and his lack of technical knowledge, he did not understand why England and France were eager to purchase Liberty motors. He doubted the statement that they were willing to take all we could spare them. The chief reason was that the Liberty motor is remarkably efficient. It weighs 100 pounds less than the Rolls Royce and develops 100 horse power more! It is not surprising that the first motors to succeed in crossing the Atlantic Ocean were Liberty motors; while the Rolls Royce got "red hot" and Mr. Hawker had to look to a chance steamer for aid.

With regard to airships and balloons, the man-in-the-street knew very little, or he would have taken even more pride in the American Air Service. From being able to make two balloons a week when we went into the war, our capacity increased so that when the Armistice was signed, we were actually making 70 balloons a week. But that was not the principal thing, although the presence of these kite balloons was an important factor in winning the war on the Western Front.

We probably never shall know just how many of our military secrets were known to the Hun, nor just how far this knowledge, and what it meant in terms of the spring campaign for 1919, led him to sign the Armistice in the fall of 1918. It may have been that the knowledge of our ability to begin inflating our balloons with non-inflammable gas, a gas which could not be exploded by the fire of incendiary bullets from Hun airplanes, had something to do with his decision that the game was not worth the candle. The fact remains that we had learned to produce helium gas in quantity, and that the first shipment was made in November, 1918.

The aerial observer, riding steadily in the basket of a kite balloon, had proved to be more useful in the control of artillery fire than his brother in the observation airplane, who was continually dodging anti-aircraft fire — to say nothing of the attacks of hostile planes. The balloon filled with hydrogen made a relatively easy mark for hostile planes, and it took only one bullet to send it down in flames, while the observer escaped in a parachute. Had it been filled with helium, he would have been able to stay up almost indefinitely. And the observer would have given a good account of himself by using machine guns, firing from a relatively stable platform against the attacking airplanes, whose guns were firing from a platform moving at the rate of more than 100 miles an hour.

Helium, as the gas next lightest to hydrogen and with 95 per cent of its lifting power, was not known to the man-in-the-street, and would not have interested him, for when we entered the war helium cost $1700 a cubic foot. To have used it on the Western Front in the same quantity that we used hydrogen would have cost us $34,000,000,000, or more than all our Liberty Bonds combined. The knowledge of what we might do if we could produce it at reasonable cost led to such earnest investigation on the part of our scientists in Washington, that a method was discovered whereby helium could be extracted from natural gas in Texas or Oklahoma at the cost of 10 cents a cubic foot. Instead of $34,000,000,000, it would then only have cost $2,000,000 to replace hydrogen in our balloons over the lines. These things should have encouraged the man-in-the-street. As he becomes conscious of them, they will eventually lead him to take a new interest in the possibilities of aviation and the future of the Air Service.

The extraordinary success of the British dirigible in hunting submarines and keeping on their trail until they were put out of business is now one of the open secrets of the war. The dirigible, more easily than the fast flying airplane, could pick up the oily trail of the submarine, locate various oily surfaces, examine them at its leisure, "stalk the submarine to its lair," and finally direct the destroyers where to drop their depth bombs most successfully. In the matter of

Coast Defence, it would seem as though dirigibles were far more successful than seaplanes.

In the pursuits of peace time, the possible activity of dirigibles, both small and large, has scarcely been given due consideration in America. The possibilities of a small dirigible are enormous and but dimly appreciated. If one is willing to run the risk of fire and use hydrogen gas, a portable gas-making machine has been perfected which enables one readily to make hydrogen from a wayside stream. If one prefers to use helium, it can be compressed into tubes that are feasible for transportation. Furthermore, the leakage of helium is not as great as that of hydrogen. A skilful aeronaut can find landing places for a dirigible in many regions where landing in an airplane is absolutely out of the question.

The use of dirigibles in exploring large flooded areas and making prompt reports regarding the extent of the flood has been suggested. Imagine what an enormous saving could be effected by prompt, accurate reports of its description at a time when telegraph wires are down and communication by railroad or automobile has been seriously broken.

Their use in crossing desert areas, where full advantage can be taken of prevailing winds and where, by sailing low, a large amount of data can be collected with the minimum amount of risk and delay, should be considered. It frequently happens that important mines are located in the midst of mountainous deserts which are very difficult of access. A case has been brought to my attention of a miner in Alaska who lost $100,000 because of his inability to go over the

trails during the winter season. He would have been willing
to pay $25,000 for that transportation which would have
been entirely practicable had a dirigible and its crew been
available.

In exploration in the Amazon Valley we have always been
hampered by the extreme density of the jungle and the necessity of keeping near the great watercourses. There are
thousands of square miles within easy flying distance of
navigable rivers, thousands of square miles of totally unex-
plored country which the explorer who has a dirigible could
photograph, map, and investigate, from a low elevation in
the air, to his heart's content. To attempt to do this in airplanes would mean the necessity of flying at great eleva-
tions in order to increase the margin of safety in case of
engine failure and make it possible to glide to some safe
landing area upon a navigable stream. On the other hand,
a small dirigible operating from a motor boat on a river
could make journeys of hundreds of miles over absolutely
unknown regions with a very small amount of danger. Owing to the dirigible's ability to float low over heavily forested
country, a tropical botanist or a practical forester skilled in
the commercial features of the Amazon basin could locate
at very little expense the important groves of mahogany or
rubber which do so much to make the tropics profitable in
commerce.

Should Commercial Aeronautics be under a separate
branch of the Government? At the Sixth National Foreign
Trade Convention, held in Chicago in April, 1919, repre-

sentatives of the largest and most powerful exporting manufacturers and merchants of America adopted the following resolutions:

Realizing the unquestioned advantages of having the speediest possible mail and express service in enabling American enterprise to
compete successfully in securing the specifications and requirements of
our foreign contracts, this convention urges prompt Congressional
consideration of suitable plans for developing aerial navigation. The
establishment of the necessary aids to such navigation, the investigation and development of the fundamental principles of commercial
aeronautics, the promotion of airship service to distant countries, are
matters which demand the prompt establishment of a separate department of the government. One of its chief duties should be to provide the necessary information which will make possible the use of
aerial navigation as an aid to foreign trade.

The development of foreign trade depends in large measure
upon pleasing the foreign customer. When his need arises,
he gives his order to the man whose integrity he respects,
who can deliver the goods most promptly, and whose standing in the local community is at a high level. Agents of
American goods abroad have in the past been at a disadvantage, owing to lack of proper banking facilities, lack of
adequate ocean transport, and lack of prestige due to the
absence of our flag on the best passenger and freight lines.
These things have been largely remedied, and our European
competitors know that at least American banking facilities
and American steamship lines have improved during the
war to such an extent as greatly to assist the American exporter. Consequently, they are naturally turning to the pos-

sibilities of Aviation as a means of passing us in the race and securing the most attractive foreign contracts.

If the foreign buyer knows that his order must go by steamship mail from Buenos Aires, the greatest city of the southern hemisphere, or from Hongkong or Yokohama, those great markets of the Far East, before they can be delivered to our factories in America, a process that will take about three weeks in time as compared with three or four days if he sends the order to Europe by a British dirigible airship like the R-34, it will be hard to secure that order if he is in a hurry. Furthermore, if he knows that he can secure from Europe specifications or missing parts by airplane express within a week or ten days from the time he sends for them, while it would take him from six weeks to two months to get the same service from New York, it will be very difficult for the American exporter to secure his order.

Our British cousins have a knowledge of export trade and how to develop it that is second to none. Even during the darkest days of the war, the British Air Ministry was studying the problems of civil aerial transport. They have been experimenting with rigid dirigibles for several years. They sent a sample over here in 1919 to prove that the thing was feasible. The R-34 and ships of her type which are being built in England to-day can go anywhere in the world, provided there are proper terminals, and provided there are occasional ports to which they can repair in time of stress, and where they may ride safely while taking on supplies of gas and oil. As soon as they can be sure of sufficient aids to aerial navigation and proper docks that will not endanger the safety of these expensive but speedy aircraft, England and France will have lines of rigid dirigibles and seaplanes established between the principal cities of Europe and the great foreign markets in South America and the Far East.

Of course it will take time to develop these terminals, but England is steadily working on the problem while we are making little or no attempt to progress in that direction. After years of experimentation, England has learned how to build a successful rigid dirigible which can cross the Atlantic in less than forty-eight hours, without endangering either passengers or crew in case of engine trouble. We have developed no rigid dirigible in this country, nor, so far as I know, are there any under construction. It seems as though we were asleep to the possibilities of aerial transport. There is no question that England's foreign trade is going to be tremendously boomed by her far-sighted study of civil aerial transport and by her present attention to rigid dirigibles. When these great airships are seen in foreign ports flying the British flag and offering quick connection between British manufacturers and their foreign customers, we shall find effective competition to be very hard sledding. If we wait until we actually see and feel the effects of the British aerial international transport, it will take us years to catch up, and in the mean time the position of our competitors will be more and more firmly established.

History is curiously repeating itself in this question of

foreign transportation. One hundred years ago, steamers were just being tried out. The first one to cross the Atlantic was an American — the steamer Savannah. She took thirty days to cross the ocean, while our clipper ships often did it in half that time. Our experienced exporters, instead of having vision and doing all in their power to establish American lines of steamers, were contented to rely on our attractive clipper ships and to brag about their performance, while England gradually developed lines of ocean steamers, and we one day woke up to the fact that our clipper ships were out of date and that England had the coaling stations, the foreign agents, the necessary terminals, and the technical knowledge to enable her to push our ocean-going commerce out of the foreign ports where it had once been so well known. Are we about to do this all over again? Are Americans willing to be content with having made aerial navigation a practical possibility, and then going to permit its future development to rest in the hands of our European competitors and thus let them secure the most efficient handmaid of future foreign trade?

We may confidently expect that the army of the future will spend much time and thought in developing Military Aeronautics, and the navy, similarly, in the growth of Naval Aeronautics. Then who is to look after Commercial Aeronautics? Who is to conduct the fundamental experiments in the use of the air? Who is to carry out the meteorological surveys to be made before aerial transportation can be fully developed? Who will establish the aids to aerial navigation, such as air ports, wind breaks, lighthouses, beacons, storm warnings, life saving stations, with aerial patrol ready to give assistance to wrecked airships? Whose business is it to do all these things? Until these are done; until proper wharves and suitable harbors are prepared for the reception of airships, where they will be as safe in time of storm as are those sailing vessels which plow the seven seas, the future of aviation, as far as we are concerned, will be relatively insignificant. We recognize the fact that a coast without ports and harbors does not attract commerce, does not develop sailors, and does not conduce to a prosperous merchant marine. We have hitherto failed to recognize the fact that a land without air ports and air harbors cannot expect to witness the rapid development of Commercial Aeronautics. The future of Aviation depends in large measure on the speed with which we provide aids for aerial navigation.

These are not needs which concern the army or the navy nearly as much as they concern the merchant and the manufacturer, who depend on them for their support. The commerce of the future demands special consideration from a governmental department of aeronautics. Such a department would give it the fostering care that has been shown by the Department of Agriculture in its bureaus of animal industry and plant importation. Just as the Department of Agriculture has helped to provide better horses for the cavalry and better seeds for the farmer; just as it has helped us to produce more healthy crops and to solve the complex problems of farming, so must the Department of Aeronautics provide winged steeds for the "mounted officers" of the field artillery, reconnaissance planes for the cavalry, and adequate aerial transportation for our merchants and manufacturers.

Finally, we must not allow aerial accidents to blind us to the importance of aerial navigation. Two thousand ocean vessels were wrecked on the shores of Cape Cod prior to 1915. Nevertheless, in the preceding centuries the progress of ocean navigation went steadily ahead on the New England coast in spite of loss of life and property. We may confidently expect that aerial navigation will slowly advance, in spite of fatal accidents and numerous crashes. Still, if we believe in aviation, it is our duty to strive by every means in our power to secure the construction of those aids to navigation that will reduce the risks and encourage the enterprise of the daring young pilots who are ready to do their part in making the Air Service of the future a glorious page in the history of America.

APPENDIX

APPENDIX

ADMINISTRATION ROSTER* OF OFFICERS ON DUTY AT THE THIRD AVIATION INSTRUCTION CENTRE, A. E. F.
November 24, 1918

STAFF

Lieutenant-Colonel Hiram Bingham, A. S., *Commanding*
Major Thomas G. Lanphier, Infantry, *Executive Officer*
Major Victor W. Pagé, A. S., *Aero Engineer Officer, O. I. C. Trans.*
Captain Lester E. Cummings, A. S., *Summary Court Officer*
Captain Leo R. Sack, A. S., *Liaison Officer, O. I. C. "Plane News"*
Captain Theodore C. Knight, A. S., *O. I. C. Fields* 1 *and* 2
Captain St. Clair Street, A. S., *O. I. C. Field* 5
Captain Richard S. Davis, A. S., *O. I. C. Field* 7
Captain George Bleistein, Jr., A. S., *Disbursing Officer*
Captain Henry C. Ferguson, A. S., *O. I. C. Flying*
Captain Harry L. Wingate, A. S., *O. I. C. Field* 8
Captain Henry H. Simons, A. S., *O. I. C. Field* 3
Captain Vernon H. Simmons, A. S., *O. I. C. Training*
First Lieutenant Richard H. Merkle, A. S., *O. I. C. Field* 10
First Lieutenant Frederick A. Vietor, 6th Cavalry, *Assistant Provost Marshal*
First Lieutenant Emil H. Molthan, A. S., *O. I. C. Field* 9
First Lieutenant George W. Eypper, A. S., *O. I. C. Aerial Gunnery*
First Lieutenant William V. Saxe, A. S., *Adjutant*
First Lieutenant Raymond A. Watkins, A. S., *O. I. C. Field* 12
First Lieutenant Selmer J. Tilleson, A. S., *O. I. C. Aero Supply*
Second Lieutenant Robert H. Clark, A. S., *Personnel Officer*

10th AERO SQUADRON

First Lieutenant Louis H. Kronig, A. S., *Commanding*
First Lieutenant George W. Fish, A. S., *Engineer Officer Field* 8
First Lieutenant Earl W. Sweeney, A. S., *Assistant O. I. C. Aerial Gunnery Field* 8

*This roster does not include the names of student officers, of whom there were at that time about one thousand.

248 APPENDIX

First Lieutenant John A. Taylor, A. S., *Squadron Supply Officer*
First Lieutenant Thomas Munroe, A. S., *Moniteur Field* 8
First Lieutenant Duerson Knight, A. S., *Moniteur Field* 8
Second Lieutenant Charles W. Seaton, A. S., *Unassigned*
Second Lieutenant Lewis A. Barcelo, A. S., *Maintenance Officer Field* 8
Second Lieutenant Henry A. Colver, A. S., *O. I. C. Aerial Gunnery Field* 8 •

21st AERO SQUADRON

First Lieutenant Frank L. Doty, A. S., *Commanding*
First Lieutenant Lee E. Ellis, A. S., *Squadron Supply Officer*
First Lieutenant Edgar Youngdahl, A. S., *Moniteur Field* 3
First Lieutenant George D. Floyd, A. S., *Moniteur Field* 3
First Lieutenant Hugh Lowery, A. S., *O. I. C. Cross-country Flights*
First Lieutenant Alfred J. Ralph, A. S., *Assistant O. I. C. Cross-country Flights*
First Lieutenant Arthur L. Lewis, A. S., *O. I. C. Flying Field* 3
First Lieutenant William R. Baxter, A. S., *Adjutant Field* 3
Second Lieutenant Bernard H. Baker, A. S., *Moniteur Field* 3
Second Lieutenant Robert S. Oliver, A. S., *Moniteur Field* 3
Second Lieutenant Stuart F. Auer, A. S., *Moniteur Field* 3
Second Lieutenant James H. O'Neil, A. S., *Chief Engineer Officer Field* 3
Second Lieutenant John T. Eagleton, A. S., *Duty with Aero Supply Department*
Second Lieutenant Kent H. Smith, A. S., *Police Officer Field* 3
Second Lieutenant John E. Gans, A. S., *Adjutant*

26th AERO SQUADRON

Captain James C. Calvert, S. C., *Commanding*
First Lieutenant George W. McNamara, A. S., *Claims Officer Third A. I. C.*
First Lieutenant Thomas W. Ward, A. S., *Information Officer and Duty with Training Department*
Second Lieutenant Massey S. McCullough, A. S., *Assistant Transportation Officer*
Second Lieutenant Karl H. Kloo, A. S., *Photographer Third A. I. C., Assistant O. I. C. "Plane News"*
Second Lieutenant R. W. Prestridge, A. S., *Squadron Supply Officer and Adjutant*

30th Aero Squadron

First Lieutenant Raymond M. Lewis, A. S., *Commanding, Assistant Adjutant Third A. I. C., O. I. C. Band, Judge Advocate Special Court-Martial*

Second Lieutenant Roy W. Gottschall, A. S., *Duty with Aerial Gunnery Department*

Second Lieutenant Arthur E. Stevens, A. S., *Assistant Supply Officer Third A. I. C.*

Second Lieutenant William G. Kieck, A. S., *Assistant Supply Officer Third A. I. C.*

Second Lieutenant Eugene W. Silver, A. S., *Duty with Engineering Department*

31st Aero Squadron

Captain Charles R. Melin, A. S., *O. I. C. Night Flying Field* 7

Second Lieutenant James B. Andrews, A. S., *Commanding*

First Lieutenant Robert N. Dippy, A. S., *Duty with Engineering Department*

First Lieutenant Schuyler L. Hoff, A. S., *Supply Officer Field* 5

First Lieutenant Walter C. Davis, A. S., *O. I. C. Training Field* 5

First Lieutenant Roy Robinson, A. S., *O. I. C. Training Field* 12

First Lieutenant Lloyd L. Harvey, A. S., *Moniteur Field* 5 ·

First Lieutenant Wesley J. Hunt, Jr., A. S., *Moniteur Field* 5

Second Lieutenant Parker Blair, A. S., *Assistant Adjutant Field* 5

Second Lieutenant Walter Sturrock, A. S., *Engineer Officer Field* 5

32^d Aero Squadron

Captain Duncan Dana, A. S., *Commanding, O. I. C. Aero Repair Shop*

First Lieutenant Roland E. Coates, A. S., *Assistant Engineer Officer Aero Repair Shop*

Second Lieutenant Arthur B. Coryell, A. S., *Assistant Engineer Officer Aero Repair Shop*

Second Lieutenant Eliot B. Foot, A. S., *Assistant Engineer Officer Aero Repair Shop*

33^d Aero Squadron

Captain Clarence Oliver, A. S., *Commanding, Adjutant Field* 9

First Lieutenant Roger E. Martz, A. S., *Chief Engineer Officer Field* 9

First Lieutenant Samuel W. Rynocker, A. S., *Squadron Supply Officer, Fire Marshal, and Police Officer Field* 9

First Lieutenant Robert Haverty, A. S., *Moniteur Field* 9
Second Lieutenant Clare E. Rollins, A. S., *Moniteur Field* 9
Second Lieutenant James O. Peck, A. S., *Moniteur Field* 9
Second Lieutenant Heber W. Peters, A. S., *O. I. C. Flying Field* 9
Second Lieutenant George S. Koyl, A. S., *Maintenance Officer Field* 9
Second Lieutenant Edward L. Gulick, Jr., A. S., *Supply Officer Field* 9
Second Lieutenant John L. Barnes, A. S., *Assistant Adjutant Field* 9

35th AERO SQUADRON

Second Lieutenant Preston M. Albro, A. S., *Commanding*
First Lieutenant Golden H. Benefiel, A. S., *Moniteur Field* 2
First Lieutenant James B. Kincaid, A. S., *O. I. C. Flying Field* 2
First Lieutenant Arthur T. Bissonette, A. S., *Assistant O. I. C. Flying Field* 2
First Lieutenant Thomas L. Dawson, A. S., *Moniteur Field* 2
First Lieutenant Herbert F. Duggan, A. S., *Moniteur Field* 2
First Lieutenant Irving D. Fish, A. S., *Moniteur Field* 2
First Lieutenant Dean Hole, A. S., *Moniteur Field* 2
First Lieutenant Barney M. Landry, A. S., *Moniteur Field* 2
First Lieutenant James P. Moonan, A. S., *Moniteur Field* 2
First Lieutenant William J. Ritchie, A. S., *Moniteur Field* 2
First Lieutenant William E. Rogers, A. S., *Moniteur Field* 2
First Lieutenant Horace W. Stunkard, A. S., *Moniteur Field* 2
First Lieutenant Bernard M. Wise, A. S., *Moniteur Field* 2
First Lieutenant Walter M. Wotipka, A. S., *Moniteur Field* 2
Second Lieutenant Russell M. Bandy, Jr., A. S., *Moniteur Field* 2
Second Lieutenant Erhardt G. Schmitt, A. S., *Moniteur Field* 2
Second Lieutenant Edgar A. Rogers, A. S., *Moniteur Field* 2
Second Lieutenant Joe W. Savage, A. S., *Moniteur Field* 2
Second Lieutenant Edwin C. Hurlburt, A. S., *Assistant Engineer Officer Field* 2
Second Lieutenant Charles H. W. Berry, A. S., *Assistant Engineer Officer Field* 2

37th AERO SQUADRON

First Lieutenant Malcolm C. Wall, A. S., *Commanding*
First Lieutenant Francis U. Wilcox, A. S., *Adjutant Field* 7

First Lieutenant Foster R. Rozar, A. S., *Engineer Officer Field* 7

First Lieutenant John N. Murray, A. S., *Assistant Adjutant and Mess Officer Field* 7

First Lieutenant Thomas L. Onativia, A. S., *Tester Field* 7

First Lieutenant Wilbur B. Stonex, *Moniteur Field* 7

First Lieutenant Harry F. Thomas, A. S., *Moniteur Field* 7

Second Lieutenant Dracos A. Dimitry, A. S., *Moniteur Field* 7

Second Lieutenant George W. Bogardus, A. S., *Supply Officer Field* 7

43ᵈ AERO SQUADRON

Second Lieutenant Thornton T. Perry, A. S., *Commanding*

Second Lieutenant Earl R. Crebbs, A. S., *Engineer Officer*

Second Lieutenant T. C. Thorp, Infantry, *Assistant Adjutant Field* 12

Second Lieutenant Edward E. Webster, A. S., *Supply Officer*

101ˢᵗ AERO SQUADRON

First Lieutenant George S. Walden, A. S., *Commanding*

Second Lieutenant Frederick W. Niedermeyer, A. S., *Moniteur Field* 5

Second Lieutenant Lloyd M. Dudley, A. S., *Moniteur Field* 5

Second Lieutenant Herbert L. Kindred, A. S., *Moniteur Field* 5

Second Lieutenant Howard E. Willlams, A. S., *Moniteur Field* 5

149ᵗʰ AERO SQUADRON

First Lieutenant John B. Hayes, A. S., *Commanding*

First Lieutenant John C. Wiler, A. S., *Engineer Officer*

Second Lieutenant Howard C. Riley, A. S., *Supply Officer*

158ᵗʰ AERO SQUADRON

First Lieutenant Phil E. Davant, A. S., *Commanding, Duty with Police and Prison Officer*

Second Lieutenant Kenneth S. Hall, A. S., *Supply Officer*

Second Lieutenant Freeman A. Ballard, A. S., *Duty with Engineering Department*

173ᵈ AERO SQUADRON

First Lieutenant Joseph B. Irving, A. S., *Commanding*

First Lieutenant Thomas P. Sultan, A. S., *O. I. C. Training Field* 7

Second Lieutenant Morgan J. Flaherty, A. S., *Adjutant*

Second Lieutenant Roscoe C. Griffin, A. S., *Assistant Engineer Officer Field* 7

Second Lieutenant William G. Barnes, A. S., *Assistant O. I. C. Training Field* 7

257th Aero Squadron

First Lieutenant Ray Traxler, A. S., *Commanding*

First Lieutenant George J. Layton, A. S., *Moniteur Field* 9

Second Lieutenant Strong B. McDan, A. S., *Moniteur Field* 9

Second Lieutenant Samuel C. Smart, A. S., *Moniteur Field* 9

Second Lieutenant Arthur L. Lott, A. S., *Supply Officer*

Second Lieutenant Richard P. Carlton, A. S., *Assistant Engineer Officer Field* 9

369th Aero Squadron

First Lieutenant Robert Edmisson, A. S., *Commanding*

First Lieutenant Walter J. Zapp, A. S., *Supply Officer*

Second Lieutenant Paul E. Smith, A. S., *Engineer Officer*

372d Aero Squadron

First Lieutenant Theodore W. Koch, A. S., *Commanding*

Second Lieutenant Victor G. Paradise, A. S., *Supply Officer Squadron, Entertainment and Athletic Officer Field* 10

Second Lieutenant S. G. Farris, A. S., *Duty with Engineering Department*

374th Aero Squadron

First Lieutenant Paul C. Bellow, A. S., *Commanding*

Second Lieutenant William J. Peddie, A. S., *Supply Officer*

Second Lieutenant Henry Frink, A. S., *Engineer Officer*

640th Aero Squadron

First Lieutenant William G. Rector, A. S., *Commanding*

Second Lieutenant Fred H. Belford, A. S., *Duty with Engineering Department Field* 3

Second Lieutenant John F. McCormick, A. S., *Supply Officer Field* 10

641ˢᵗ AERO SQUADRON

Captain Boyd F. Briggs, A. S., *Commanding*
First Lieutenant Lewis A. Smith, A. S., *Duty with Aero Supply*
Second Lieutenant George B. Keeler, A. S., *Supply Officer Field* 10
Second Lieutenant Stanley G. Wilson, A. S., *Duty with Aero Supply Department*
Second Lieutenant Wilbur B. Stonex, A. S., *Supply Officer Field* 8
Second Lieutenant Clay E. Smith, A. S., *Squadron Supply Officer*
Second Lieutenant Oliver T. Massey, A. S., *Adjutant*
Second Lieutenant Frederick B. Andrews, A. S., *Duty with Training Department*

642ᵈ AERO SQUADRON

First Lieutenant Robert G. Alexander, A. S., *Commanding*
First Lieutenant Donald F. Gilbert, A. S., *Duty with Construction Officer*
Second Lieutenant John H. Cozzens, A. S., *Duty with Engineering Department*
Second Lieutenant John J. Flaherty, A. S., *Duty with Aero Supply, O. I. C. Entertainment*
Second Lieutenant Giles J. Leath, A. S., *Company Duty*
Second Lieutenant Maurice J. Freeman, A. S., *Duty with Aerial Gunnery Department*
Second Lieutenant Bayliss W. Hunter, A.S., *Duty with Executive Officer.*
Second Lieutenant Lowell W. Bassett, A. S., *Adjutant*
Second Lieutenant William K. Donaldson, A. S., *O. I. C. Field Service*

644ᵗʰ AERO SQUADRON

First Lieutenant John H. Clayton, A. S., *Commanding*
First Lieutenant John G. Fleming, A. S., *Transportation Officer Field* 8
First Lieutenant George S. Vincent, A. S., *Moniteur Field* 8
Second Lieutenant Lewis H. Steward, A. S., *Moniteur Field* 8
Second Lieutenant Royce D. Hancock, A. S., *Moniteur Field* 8
Second Lieutenant Samuel E. Lawyer, A. S., *Moniteur Field* 8

801ˢᵗ AERO SQUADRON

First Lieutenant Edward Fenway, A. S., *Commanding, Adjutant Field* 2
First Lieutenant Jacob S. Yerger, A. S., *Adjutant*
First Lieutenant George W. Forrester, A. S., *O. I. C. Field* 1

First Lieutenant Henry L. Badham, A. S., *Moniteur Field* 2
First Lieutenant Gerald C. Bishop, A. S., *Moniteur Field* 2
First Lieutenant William E. Cameron, A. S., *Moniteur Field* 1
First Lieutenant Harry O. Fishel, A. S., *Moniteur Field* 2
First Lieutenant Irvin J. Higgins, A. S., *Moniteur Field* 1
First Lieutenant Frederick W. Horton, A. S., *Moniteur Field* 2
First Lieutenant Charles R. Mackan, A. S., *Moniteur Field* 2
First Lieutenant Walter W. Randolph, A. S., *Moniteur Field* 2
First Lieutenant George E. Smith, A. S., *Moniteur Field* 2
First Lieutenant Gerritt V. Weston, A. S., *Moniteur Field* 2
First Lieutenant James R. Worthington, A. S., *Moniteur Field* 2
First Lieutenant Charles P. Maloney, A. S., *Moniteur Field* 2
Second Lieutenant Russell C. Gates, A. S., *Moniteur Field* 2
Second Lieutenant Russell Gomes, A. S., *Moniteur Field* 2
Second Lieutenant Howard B. Hankey, A. S., *Moniteur Field* 2
Second Lieutenant John Q. Kiler, A. S., *Moniteur Field* 1
Second Lieutenant Rodman B. Montgomery, A. S., *Moniteur Field* 2
Second Lieutenant John H. Thompson, A. S., *Moniteur Field* 2
Second Lieutenant Franklin H. Devitt, A. S., *Moniteur Field* 1
Second Lieutenant John B. Swen, A. S., *Moniteur Field* 2
Second Lieutenant John P. Morris, A. S., *Moniteur Field* 2
Second Lieutenant Lyle C. Smith, A. S., *Moniteur Field* 2
Second Lieutenant Orah G. Douglas, A. S., *Supply Officer Field* 2

802ᵈ AERO SQUADRON

Captain Oliver B. Wyman, A. S., *Commanding, Adjutant Main Barracks Division, Trial Judge Advocate, General Court-Martial*
First Lieutenant Lee F. Lanham, A. S., *O. I. C. Telephone and Telegraph System*
Second Lieutenant James O. Craig, A. S., *Duty with Engineering Department*
Second Lieutenant Murchie R. Thomas, A. S., *Duty with Maintenance Department*

1104ᵗʰ REPLACEMENT SQUADRON

First Lieutenant Oris P. Embleton, A. S., *Commanding*
Second Lieutenant William M. Reck, A. S., *Duty with Maintenance Department*

Second Lieutenant Robert N. Landreth, A. S., *Duty with Aero Supply*
Second Lieutenant H. P. McLaughlin, A. S.
Second Lieutenant James B. Doles, *Engineers, O. I. C. Railroad System*

1st COMPANY, 2d REGIMENT, AIR SERVICE MECHANICS

Captain Charles W. Babcock, A. S., *Commanding, O. I. C. Machine Shops*

3d COMPANY, 2d REGIMENT, AIR SERVICE MECHANICS

Captain Oakley Bolton, S. C., *Commanding*
First Lieutenant Otto H. Lambrix, A. S., *Assistant O. I. C. Machine Shops*

12th COMPANY, 3d REGIMENT, AIR SERVICE MECHANICS

Captain Robert P. Oldham, A. S., *Commanding*
Second Lieutenant Frank R. Meyer, A. S., *Duty with Engineering Department*

13th COMPANY, 3d REGIMENT, AIR SERVICE MECHANICS

Captain Albert Roberts, S. C., *Commanding, Inspector Outlying Fields*
First Lieutenant Mathias P. Molburg, A. S., *Company Duty*

11th COMPANY, 4th REGIMENT, AIR SERVICE MECHANICS

Captain Frank Ondricek, S. C., *Commanding, Labor Officer Third A. I. C.*
Second Lieutenant Earnest Young, A. S., *On Detached Service*

12th COMPANY, 4th REGIMENT, AIR SERVICE MECHANICS

Captain Frank Connell, S. C., *Commanding*
First Lieutenant George O. Reynolds, A. S., *Duty with Engineering Department*
Second Lieutenant Elisha C. Howes, Jr., A. S., *Assistant Maintenance Officer*

13th COMPANY, 4th REGIMENT, AIR SERVICE MECHANICS

First Lieutenant John F. Bligh, F. A., *Commanding*
First Lieutenant Harley F. McCurdy, A. S., *Assistant Adjutant Main Barracks Division*
Second Lieutenant Henry F. Hauserman, A. S., *Athletic Officer, Third A. I. C.*

14th Company, 4th Regiment, Air Service Mechanics

Captain Robert A. Nelson, S. C., *Commanding*
Second Lieutenant Donald B. Regester, A. S., *Company Duty*

Headquarters Detachment

Major Howard S. Curry, A. S., *Commanding*

Captain Charles A. Hill, A. S., *Executive Officer*

Captain Arthur E. Simonin, A. S., *Duty with Training Department*

First Lieutenant Thomas A. Flaherty, A. S., *Duty with Engineering Department*

First Lieutenant Bradford B. Locke, A. S., *Adjutant*

First Lieutenant Raymond L. Suppes, A. S., *Garden Officer*

First Lieutenant Edwin T. Macbride, A. S., *Duty with Training Department*

First Lieutenant Merrill T. Miller, A. S., *Duty with Engineering Department*

First Lieutenant John J. Lyons, A. S., *Duty with Aerial Gunnery Department*

First Lieutenant Lyman G. Vollentine, A. S., *Duty with Maintenance Department*

First Lieutenant Charles E. Branshaw, A. S., *Duty with Q. M. C.*

First Lieutenant Robert L. Richardson, A. S., *Duty with Q. M. C.*

First Lieutenant Russell L. Duval, A. S., *Headquarters Detachment Personnel Officer*

First Lieutenant Frank G. Dennison, A. S., *Duty with Engineering Department*

First Lieutenant Frank E. Martin, A. S., *O. I. C. Assembly*

First Lieutenant Irving S. Morange, A. S., *Instructor at Field* 10

First Lieutenant Thomas O. Dye, A. S., *Duty with Training Department*

First Lieutenant Charles R. Knox, A. S., *Duty with Aerial Gunnery Department, Instructor*

First Lieutenant Rex F. Gilmartin, A. S., *Duty with Engineering Department*

First Lieutenant John Willard, A. S., *Unassigned*

First Lieutenant A. H. Young, A. S., *Unassigned*

Second Lieutenant Ben A. Calhoun, A. S., *Duty with Aero Supply*

Second Lieutenant George A. Dooley, A. S., *Duty with Maintenance Department*

Second Lieutenant S. V. Trent, A. S., *Duty with Engineering Department*

Second Lieutenant Marius Rocle, A. S., *Claims Officer, Third A. I. C.*

Second Lieutenant Edward M. Riggs, A. S., *Duty with Engineering Department*

Second Lieutenant Frederick H. Mead, A. S., *Duty at Field 12*

Second Lieutenant Gordon W. Clark, A. S., *Duty with Information Officer*

Second Lieutenant Harold F. Rouse, A. S., *Duty with Personnel Officer*

Second Lieutenant Samuel S. Stevens, A. S., *Intelligence Officer, Third A. I. C.*

Second Lieutenant Frank C. Brigham, A. S., *Headquarters Detachment Personnel Officer*

Second Lieutenant Adrian Cote, A. S., *Athletic Officer*

Second Lieutenant Theodore Jefferson, A. S., *Detachment Supply Officer*

Second Lieutenant George N. Lockridge, A. S., *Assistant Adjutant*

Second Lieutenant R. H. George, A. S., *Gosport Instructor*

Second Lieutenant A. N. Burkholder, A. S., *Gosport Instructor*

Second Lieutenant Davenport Pogue, A. S., *Gosport Instructor*

Second Lieutenant W. F. Rittman, A. S., *Avro Instructor*

70ᵗʰ Prisoner of War Escort Company

Captain Alonzo Pelham, C. A. C., *Commanding*

First Lieutenant L. W. Bowman, Infantry, *Supply Officer*

Company E, 26ᵗʰ Engineers

First Lieutenant D. W. Blakeslee, Engineers, *Commanding*

Headquarters Detachment, 128ᵗʰ Engineers

Major LeRoy H. Byam, Engineers, *Commanding, Maintenance Officer*

Captain Fred B. Dawes, Engineers, *Adjutant*

Company A, 128ᵗʰ Engineers

Second Lieutenant Clinton A. Bushong, Engineers, *Commanding*

Second Lieutenant R. W. Young, Engineers

Company B, 128ᵗʰ Engineers

Second Lieutenant Thaynes Williams, Engineers, *Commanding*

COMPANY B, 11th U. S. MARINES

Major Harry K. Pickett, Marines, *Commanding, Police and Prison Officer, Commanding Main Barracks Division, Member Board of Investigation*

Captain Joseph C. Bennett, Marines, *Company Duty*

First Lieutenant Merritt A. Edson, Marines, *Company Administration*

Second Lieutenant John M. McGregor, Marines, *Officer of the Day, Company Duty*

Second Lieutenant Miner P. Gross, Marines, *Officer of the Day, Company Duty*

Second Lieutenant Eldred I. Rawles, Marines, *Officer of the Day, Company Duty*

First Lieutenant Herbert L. Arnold, Medical Corps, *Duty with Camp Hospital*

Q. M. C. DETACHMENT

Major Charles W. Godfrey, Q. M. C., *Depot Quartermaster*

Captain Charles A. LaSalle, Q. M. C., *Disbursing Officer*

First Lieutenant Charles M. Stivers, Q. M. C., *O. I. C. Subsistence*

Second Lieutenant William J. Cotty, Q. M. C., *Commanding Bakery Detachment No. 334*

Second Lieutenant Milton Marks, Q. M. C., *Officer in Charge C. & E.*

Second Lieutenant George Beyer, Q. M. C., *Assistant to D. Q. M. (Finance)*

Second Lieutenant Oswald F. Stremmel, Jr., Q. M. C., *Assistant to D. Q. M.*

Second Lieutenant J. H. Neal, Q. M. C., *Assistant to D. Q. M.*

Second Lieutenant I. C. Rosenthal, Q. M. C., *Commanding Detachment Company B 345th Labor Bn.*

MEDICAL DETACHMENT, CAMP HOSPITAL No. 14

Major William G. Noe, M. C., *Commanding, Surgeon*

Major Everett G. Brownell, M. C., *G.-U. Specialist*

Major John J. McKenna, M. C., *X-Ray Specialist*

Captain Herbert N. Barnett, M. C., *Adjutant*

Captain Charles F. Clayton, M. C., *Surgeon*

Captain James R. Earle, M. C., *Surgical, Nose and Throat*

Captain Waldo C. Farnham, M. C., *Duty at Field 9*

Captain Alston Fitts, M. C., *Medical*

Captain Charles D. High, M. C., *Duty at Field* 5
Captain Harry V. Jackson, M. C., *Duty at Field* 8
Captain Joseph L. McLaughlin, M. C., *Medical*
Captain Percy D. Moulton, M. C., *Duty at Field* 7
Captain Eugene Palmore, M. C., *Medical*
Captain George A. Stevens, M. C., *Bacteriologist*
First Lieutenant James W. Allbritain, M. C., *Duty at Field* 14
First Lieutenant Morris Auslander, M. C., *Medical*
First Lieutenant Leon J. Barber, M. C., *Surgeon*
First Lieutenant Joseph A. Belott, M. C., *Duty at Field* 12
First Lieutenant Charles H. Brownlee, M. C., *Pathologist*
First Lieutenant James J. Dickinson, M. C., *Ear, Nose, and Throat*
First Lieutenant Sigurd H. Kraft, M. C., *Medical*
First Lieutenant Frank R. Nothnagle, M. C., *Surgical*
First Lieutenant Edgar E. Rice, M. C., *Surgeon*
First Lieutenant Clyde R. Van Gundy, M. C., *Duty at Field* 7
First Lieutenant Sidney J. Vann, M. C., *Duty at Field* 9
First Lieutenant LeRoy J. Wheeler, M. C., *Medical*
First Lieutenant Robert E. Wilson, M. C., *Sanitary Inspector*
First Lieutenant Ronald E. Esson, M. C., *Assistant Adjutant*
First Lieutenant William M. Barron, M. C., *X-Ray*
First Lieutenant Adolph Wood, M. C., *Duty at Field* 2
First Lieutenant Garland M. Herwood, M. C., *Duty with Medical Research Unit No.* 1
First Lieutenant Charles R. Farnham, M. C., *Surgeon*

DENTAL CORPS

Captain Austin R. Killian, D. C., *Dental*
First Lieutenant Joseph A. Schiller, D. C., *Dental*
First Lieutenant Elmer Steiner, D. C., *Dental*

MEDICAL RESEARCH BOARD

Colonel William H. Wilmer, M. C., *Commanding*
Lieutenant-Colonel Leonard G. Rowntree, M. C., *Executive Officer*
Lieutenant-Colonel Henry Horn, M. C.
Major James L. Whitney, M. C.
Major Edward C. Schneider, M. C.

Major Robert R. Hampton, M. C., *Flight Surgeon, Third A. I. C.*
Major William C. Meanor, M. C.
Major William F. Patton, M. C.
Major Robert S. McCombs, M. C.
Major Wilson M. Bassett, M. C.
Captain Eugene Cary, M. C.
Captain Claude T. Uren, M. C.
Captain Floyd C. Dockeray, Sn. C.
Captain Conrad Berens, M. C.
Captain Frank M. Hallock, M. C.
Captain Harold F. Pierce, Sn. C.
First Lieutenant Wilbur M. Blackshare, M. C.
First Lieutenant Harvey W. Kernan, Sn. C.
First Lieutenant Prentice Reeves, Sn. C.
Second Lieutenant Harold W. Gregg, Sn. C.

Made in the USA
Columbia, SC
15 March 2024

33087198R00226